Capital Walks

Walking Tours of Ottawa

Second Edition

Katharine Fletcher

Maps by Eric Fletcher

Fitzhenry & Whiteside

Capital Walks
Copyright © 2004 Fitzhenry & Whiteside

Fitzhenry & Whiteside Limited
195 Allstate Parkway
Markham, Ontario L3R 4T8

In the United States:
121 Harvard Avenue, Suite 2
Allston, Massachusetts 02134
www.fitzhenry.ca   godwit@fitzhenry.ca

Fitzhenry & Whiteside acknowledges with thanks the Canada Council for the Arts, the
Government of Canada through its Book Publishing Industry Development Program, and the
Ontario Arts Council for their support of our publishing program.

10 9 8 7 6 5 4 3 2 1

National Library of Canada Cataloguing in Publication

Fletcher, Katharine, 1952-
Capital walks : walking tours of Ottawa / Katharine Fletcher ; maps by Eric Fletcher. — 2nd ed.

First ed. published: Toronto : McClelland & Stewart, c1993.
Includes index.
ISBN 1-55041-763-0
1. Historic buildings—Ontario—Ottawa—Guidebooks.
2. Architecture—Ontario—Ottawa—Guidebooks. 3. Ottawa (Ont.)— Buildings, structures, etc.—
Guidebooks. 4. Walking—Ontario—Ottawa—Guidebooks. 5. Ottawa (Ont.)—Tours. I. Fletcher,
Eric, 1951- II. Title.

FC3096.18.F47 2003 917.13'84044   C2003-900906-8   F1059.5.O9F47 2003

U.S. Cataloging-in-Publication Data (Library of Congress Standards)

Fletcher, Katharine.
Capital walks : walking tours of Ottawa / Katharine Fletcher ; maps by Eric Fletcher. — 2nd ed.
[174] p. : ill. , maps ; cm.
Summary: Ten walking tours of Ottawa's magnificent heritage buildings and the natural green
space within the city.
ISBN 1-55041-763-0 (pbk.)
1. Ottawa (Ont.)—Buildings, structures, etc. 2. Historic buildings — National Capital Region
(Ont. and Québec) — Guidebooks.   3. National Capital Region (Ont. and Québec) —
Guidebooks. I. Title.
971.3/83 21   F1059.5.O9 .F61 2003

Interior book design by Karen Petherick

Printed and bound in Canada

Dedication

We learn much from those who go before us.
Capital Walks is dedicated to the memory of
former NCC historian, the late Michael Newton.

Contents

Preface to the Second Edition

Ten years have passed since I first wrote *Capital Walks*. A decade is a long time ... yet simultaneously it passes in what seems like the twinkling of an eye. The decade saw Ottawa follow Toronto's and Montreal's lead whereby "bigger" was deemed "better." Accordingly, on January 1, 2001 the original City of Ottawa officially absorbed ten other municipalities under the leadership of one mayor. The former cities of Ottawa, Vanier, Nepean, Kanata, Gloucester, the Village of Rockcliffe Park, townships of Cumberland, Osgoode, Rideau, West Carleton and Goulbourn now all comprise the megacapital. Of course, the land area ballooned, too: Ottawa is now a sprawling 275,776 hectares incorporating not just urban but also very rural realities.

How does heritage preservation fare in the context of a megacapital? How will satellite communities win an operational slice of the city's heritage budget, when their heritage homes, churches, farm complexes, or town halls must compete for funds with interests such as the preservation of Sparks Street? And, beyond saving architectural gems from demolition, what about the preservation of the vistas that define our sense of what our capital is?

These vistas are not just pretty views. They represent significant cultural landscapes and provide us with an unequivocal sense of place that resonates among residents and visitors alike. Think of the pastoral vision of hay bales or cows grazing in a meadow which recalls our agricultural roots. The Corel Centre, built upon what some called "waste land," destroyed this pastoral vista.

Or think of the view from Britannia Bay. Standing on the rocky breakwater projecting into Lac Deschênes we can look across the Ottawa River towards Aylmer and remember the rivalry between these two communities in days gone by, when steamers plied the "lake" upstream from Ottawa to Quyon and Fitzroy Harbour. We can imagine ourselves back in time, in 1613, when French explorer Samuel de Champlain's company of two canoes paddled to Allumette Island, seeking the passage to China ...

Such vistas are worth preserving because they define what we were ... and what we have become. This is what cultural landscapes do, and why they are worthy of our interest and preservation. To fully understand their merit, it is useful to consider what our capital region would be like without such vistas.

For instance, imagine what might happen if the National Capital Commission (NCC) or the City of Ottawa didn't maintain large sections of waterfront as public parkland. Imagine what the greenspace on both sides of the river would look like if it was sold and developed into privately owned high-rise condos. The present vistas would be forever lost, as would the cultural landscape that currently invites our reflection.

Can we count upon such vistas to be preserved? Can we count upon individual buildings to remain on our capital streetscape?

Sadly, no. As I write this, in January 2004, the Moffatt farm, a 34 ha wooded property on the Rideau River at Prince of Wales Drive is under threat of development. The sad demolition by neglect of the Daly building left what many considered to be a welcome open-air space in the heart of the city, adjacent to the Château Laurier. *The Ottawa Citizen* ran a survey, inviting readers to comment on what they wished the site to be used for; the public overwhelmingly cried, "Leave it alone! Create a park. Leave us some space so we can rest and appreciate the buildings around us."

But such is not to be, of course. Why? Because the space is too valuable and a park doesn't generate tax dollars. Accordingly, welcome open space where we can look about and appreciate the grand architecture here, will soon disappear. At time of writing a building designed by Montreal architect Dan Hanganu, containing a mix of condos and shops, is proposed for this space. The finished structure will be almost the same height as the Connaught Building, at its rear. A gap between the modern and old edifices would allow passersby on George Street in the Byward Market to glance westwards and still catch a view of the Château Laurier.

Other changes to the region in the interim since the first edition of this book in 1993 include political correctness interfering with art. After some intense lobbying, a kneeling First Nations' figure was removed from the foot of Hamilton MacCarthy's statue of Samuel de Champlain, the French explorer and father of Nouvelle France, on Nepean Point. The image of the native scout, crouching and looking intently upriver, offended some who considered the artist's depiction insulting. So today the sanitized and politically correct Champlain stands — with his astrolabe upside down — forlornly overlooking the Ottawa River. However, let's not forget that without his Algonquin and Huron guides, Champlain would have been hopelessly lost in the wilderness when he paddled up the Ottawa.

To me, his solitariness appears like an arrogant slap in the face of the First Nation's people. Europeans and subsequent immigrants to Canada forever owe a debt of gratitude to these people who guided our forebears through the *pays d'en bas*, the hinterland wilderness that was their home. We all know how Europeans rewarded that trust. But opinions clearly differ, and the crouching figure was removed with much public support. Such is the nature of revisionism, with its occasional disregard for history, and the concomitant disrespect for an artist's creative inspiration which, in sculptor Hamilton MacCarthy's case, was intended to praise and acknowledge, not offend.

More change is coming. The old Union Train Station opposite the Château Laurier was targeted to house the Canadian Sports Hall of Fame. But in October 2002 other plans were afoot. It now may become a Museum of Canadian Politics, part of former Prime Minister Jean Chrétien's "legacy project." At least the beautiful beaux arts building appears likely to be spared the wrecker's ball. And, the former American Embassy directly opposite Parliament Hill will open in 2004 as Canada's Portrait Museum.

Still another envisioned project involved the celebration of sixteen Canadian wartime heroes, including Laura Secord, Joseph Brant, Marquis de Montcalm, and General Wolfe. The plan was to erect a monument to them on either side of Elgin Street south of, and leading up to, the War Memorial. The budget (rumoured to be $4 million), would mostly be footed by the federal government, though a private organization hoped to raise a significant amount of funds. As of now, this project seems on hold; who knows where the statues will be placed?

Other projects — such as the building of the US Embassy on Sussex Street or the construction of the new War Museum on LeBreton Flats — arouse passionate debate among Ottawans. The former created considerable furor among citizens who adamantly opposed having the embassy symbolically dominate the downtown core. Now, after the terrorist attack upon the World Trade Centre on September 11, 2001, the embassy resembles a building under siege. Gigantic, ugly concrete traffic barriers protect the building from potential car bombs or other attacks, and as I write, Clarence Street has been blocked off. The shopkeepers and condo residents opposite this embassy might understandably resent or feel nervous about their proximity to this building.

Meanwhile, over at "the Flats," as LeBreton Flats is known, a massive project is underway which has finally given this "vacant space" in the city a new sense of purpose. Long an open area of parkland, the use of which had been debated for thirty years, it is now the home of the new Canadian War Museum whose sod roof will stretch close to the Ottawa River. From the surrounding park, visitors will be able to walk up a grassed "hill" and gaze out over the Ottawa River to the Spires of Parliament — from what is actually the grassed roof of the museum. Its completion date is 2005 — and I for one look forward to this new "capital walk."

So goes the city: change is inevitable.

Cultural landscapes. Heritage streetscapes. Historic buildings. Enjoy them and explore our city on foot, by bike, and by car. Look at the buildings from the outside, then enter and consider them again. Your opinion of them might alter, once you've explored "from the inside out."

And, as you go, cherish the greenspace of our capital. We take the Greenbelt (and Gatineau Park) for granted at our peril, and often don't notice when the NCC, the City of Ottawa, or private developers sell off a parcel here, trade a parcel there. Allow yourself the time to gaze upon our beautiful vistas and to imagine our colourful past and our promising, unknowable future.

Otherwise, before you know it, they just might have slipped away unnoticed, not with a bang but a whimper.

Nothing is as sure as change. *Capital Walks* celebrates our past and present, its architects and urban planners.

My book also acknowledges and applauds the dedicated work of archivists and heritage workers and city organizations such as Heritage Ottawa.

For instance, last May I was one of hundreds of Ottawans who thoroughly enjoyed "Doors Open Ottawa," a weekend where important Ottawa buildings were open to the public for appreciative inspection. Hopefully, this popular event will be an annual happening, whereby we can explore the permanent art of the city — our architectural landscape — again and again.

Katharine Fletcher
Quyon, Quebec, January 2004

A Question of Style

If asked to identify their city's most significant building, most Ottawans would point to the spires of Parliament Hill, the symbolic centre of the nation. But the restored façade of stone and brick buildings which crowd Sussex Drive and lead the eye down to Nôtre-Dame's twin steeples and the National Gallery equally well define the capital. And just as representative of the city as these public and commercial edifices are the houses in which Ottawans, past and present, live. A walk along the tree-lined avenues of Ottawa's first suburb, the Glebe, shows us the city's typical two- and three-storey red brick houses, many with gambrel roofs, others with front end-gables facing the street. Lowertown's busy streets lend the city a distinctly French-Canadian flavour. Here, dormers project from steeply pitched roofs, carriageways lead to rear courtyards, and "cliffhanger" second-storey porches distinguish its streetscape.

Structures have their own form, function and raison d'être. What influences the choice of style varies from building to building. Sometimes it is the whim of a politician, such as former Prime Minister Mackenzie King, who insisted upon copper roofs for buildings such as the Supreme Court of Canada and the Veterans buildings. His notion was to impose a pleasing continuity of design on the Wellington Street streetscape. The late Pierre Elliott Trudeau used his influence too: it was he who chose architect Moshe Safdie's "extrovert" — not "introvert" — design for the National Gallery on Sussex. Possibly Trudeau didn't realize what the significance of his choice would be upon the streetscape of the capital. In fact, his design selection would affect the style of the American Embassy. This domineering, battleship-like building sports a mock cupola whose shape and massing echo the crystal tower of Safdie's National Gallery as well as the Parliamentary Library.

Choice. For a multiplicity of reasons, the choices designers make have an overwhelming impact upon generations of architectural designs, all of which ultimately shape the appearance — and mood — of our capital. Often style is dictated by a detail as mundane as budget.

Sometimes nature deals the architect a wild card, like an unstable leda clay foundation. And sometimes a new technology allows stylistic experimentation or an owner insists on a period style. What is certain is that every building is the product of design constraints and the imaginations of the architect, builder and owner.

The style of individual neighbourhoods also varies, because of zoning restrictions, the wealth of residents, the era in which each was built. Ottawa neighbourhoods possess their unique atmosphere and charm. Rockcliffe's large lots and mansions are not comparable to the far more congested lots of New Edinburgh, originally designed by Thomas MacKay as a millworkers' village. Yet the two complement each other. Together, the neighbourhoods of Ottawa form a tapestry of textures, colour, and design — a livable city.

THE EARLY DAYS

The Kingston Chronicle of March 9, 1827, announced: "We rejoice to hear that it is resolved to build a town to be named after Lieutenant Colonel By of the Royal Engineers." It is fitting that Ottawa was first named for a man of military background, for Bytown's *raison d'être* was strategic defence after the War of 1812. What Britain wanted was an inland line of communications, so that militia supplies and men could be transported along a defensible corridor. As chief engineer, By was responsible for the construction of the 200 kilometre Rideau Canal that extends from Entrance Bay on the Ottawa River to Kingston. As soon as the canal project was discussed, Bytown experienced an infusion of capital and residents, as land speculators and labourers joined the already-booming lumber and service community.

Ottawa's first buildings were log shanties, constructed from immediately available local timber, which provided homesteaders with rudimentary shelter. As the walls went up, spaces between the logs were carefully chinked with clay or moss. Roofs of wooden shingles or strips of bark were common. Windows — if cut at all — were covered with oiled paper until glass panes could be afforded. When windows were cut, they were usually small, for the winters were long and bitterly cold. Floors were first of bare earth and, later, the dirt was covered with wooden planks. Limestone slabs packed with clay fashioned the fireplace, and a hole in the roof served as a chimney.

Earliest shelters were crude log structures.
W. H. Bartlett print, NCC, 172.

These first dwellings were replaced by houses of brick and stone as soon as the homesteaders could afford it. Thomas MacKay's Scottish stonemasons, who built the Rideau Canal, found ready employment building this "second wave" of dwellings and public edifices. Today, the capital still boasts several examples of their masonry skills. Classical features such as regularly spaced windows with a central doorway typify these early permanent structures. The Commissariat (1827), the Fraser Schoolhouse (1837) and the Donnelly House (1844) exhibit the solidity and simplicity of this design. Stone was readily availabe but its use required an infrastructure of transporation routes, therefore money and skilled craftsmen were needed. After the opening of the railways, such as the Bytown and Prescott in 1854, materials could be brought in from remote and even exotic locations. By Confederation in 1867, most ordinary people's houses were of frame construction, although most commercial buildings were brick or stone.

The *Ottawa City Directory* of 1866 details the wealth of material that was available to local builders: "Beside the Arnprior marble, the district of Ottawa furnishes all kinds of building stone. A black or grey limestone which gives a fine massive appearance to buildings, and which has been extensively used in this neighbourhood, is known as the Trenton limestone. A very beautiful white or light-yellow freestone is found at Nepean; and another, white as Carrara marble, is found at Perth."

By 1866, the spires of Parliament graced the Hill. The East and West blocks, designed by architects Stent and Laver, and Thomas Fuller's original Centre Block (which burned in 1916) and Parliamentary Library, were all built between 1859 and 1865. The architects incorporated local stone into their design as it made aesthetic and economic sense. Their picturesque Gothic Revival designs inspired contemporary architects and builders to use local materials with confidence and pride. Local industries reaped the benefit as quarries, sandpits, brickworks, foundries, lumber mills and skilled craftsmen met the requirements of the capital's swelling population and housing needs.

Thomas Coltrin Keefer's 1864 map of Rockcliffe clearly shows a deposit of white marl clay. Thomas Clark recognized an opportunity here, and by 1872 his brickworks were producing the red and white brick that was used extensively in the capital region. Entrepreneurial opportunity presents itself in different ways to different people: Thomas Woodburn, carpenter at MacKay's New Edinburgh mills, built his Victorian Gothic double (73–75 MacKay Street) in 1874. Its fanciful wishbone-shaped gingerbread trim, called bargeboard, and pretty wooden porches were an effective advertisement of his trade and skill. Woodburn's ornate carpentry work was possible because of the coincidence of several factors: the ready availability of wood, such comparatively new technical advances as the jigsaw, and his proximity to the New Edinburgh mills at the Rideau Falls.

By the late 1800s, the enduring Gothic Revival style, with its picturesque ornamentation of steeply gabled roofs, pointed arch windows, lacy bargeboard (gingerbread), bay and oriel windows became reinterpreted in a variety of ways. The Queen Anne style was the most whimsical extension of Gothic and was especially popular for houses. A major characteristic of this style was asymmetrical massing, which held special appeal in contrast to the more rigid lines of classical design. Houses now featured picturesque external silhouettes which, on the interior, translated into a flexible floor plan. Number 500 Wilbrod, the Fleck House, and, in a rarer example of commercial architecture, the Central Chambers on Elgin reflect the late Victorian love of colour, mixed texture, and form as interpreted in the Queen Anne style.

Other styles and influences competed in the neighbourhoods of Ottawa. In 1905, three hundred master stonemasons and stonecutters from Scotland built architect David Ewart's castle-like Victoria Memorial

Museum, today known as the Museum of Nature. Like the Scottish masons brought here in the 1820s by Thomas MacKay for the construction of the Rideau Canal, Ewart's stonemasons settled in the Ottawa area, and went on to build many private houses and public buildings. Ewart's triptych on Sussex Drive, the Connaught Building, the War Museum and the Mint, all are monumental edifices that further utilized the skills of these stonemasons.

Road gang, n.d. City of Ottawa Archives, CA 17000.

NEW TECHNOLOGIES

Construction of multiple-storied, multiple-windowed commercial office towers — which would become generally known as *skyscrapers* in the 1880s — had to wait for supporting metal technologies to be devised. The term "skyscraper" had been used to describe buildings of four stories — in addition to tall tales and tall people! Then, in 1848, New Yorker James Bogardus developed the steel frame.[1]

In the late 1890s a flurry of buildings was erected in North America, particularly in Chicago where the work of Louis Sullivan and others became recognized as the "Chicago School." He designed such commercial skyscrapers as the Schlesinger-Mayer Store (now Carson, Pirie and Scott's) in Chicago, built between 1899 and 1904, and the Guaranty (now Prudential) office building in Buffalo, built between 1894 and 1895.

Sullivan's influence was felt in Ottawa: Moses Edey built the Daly Building after the Chicago style in 1904 (demolished in 1992), and the Transportation Building, designed by Ottawa architect J. Albert

Ewart, was erected in 1916. The latter office building still stands at the corner of Rideau Street and Colonel By Drive, diagonally across the road from the Château Laurier. It still possesses its ornate copper cornice, a detail typical of Sullivan's Chicago style. (A piece of the Daly building's cornice fell off the building, killing a pedestrian, which prompted the removal of the ornamentation in the mid–1960s.)

The Chicago style pioneered metal-frame grid construction technologies: it did not take long for developers and investment property managers to figure out the multi-storied buildings made superb "flats," or apartments. So, thanks to steel frame construction, apartment towers joined commercial offices in "growing up," as opposed to horizontally configured row- or terrace-homes.

Skyscrapers became an almost-instinctive design methodology because, during the turn of that century, land (particularly in the downtown core of cities) was becoming increasingly valuable. Therefore, it was less expensive to build a vertically oriented high-rise structure with a relatively small "footprint." The metal "skeleton" support imposed a grid-like façade of windows ... something with which we are extremely familiar with today.

Incidentally, apartments were not universally embraced. Ottawa author and journalist Madge Macbeth relates:

> ... between the homes of Dr. Echlin and Dr. Church, another doctor proposed to build a flat. Dr. Echlin loudly and violently opposed the plan. We had only two or three apartment houses [in Ottawa], then, and they were not highly regarded: too strong a suggestion of slumminess, of the tenement clung to them. "Nice" people objected to sharing a common stairway with those of dubious social status. Said a judge to me, 'I don't want anyone using *my* front door.'
>
> And a lady speaking on the same theme declared, "I wouldn't live in a flat. I wouldn't know where to hang my turkeys!"
>
> Having an apartment house next door to you was only slightly less objectionable than a zoo would have been.[2]

However, although apartments may not have been appreciated by everyone, steel frame construction allowed many buildings to grow to multiple stories in the late 1800s. For example, the 1890 Central Chambers on Elgin Street is Ottawa's first experiment with vertical bay windows. This innovative fenestration, which today seems technically unremarkable, although beautiful, was possible only because architect John James Browne used steel girders to build a sturdy frame. However, the weight of his building is still supported on masonry load-bearing walls: its steel girders rest upon brick structural walls.

The Central Chambers was also one of the first buildings in Ottawa to incorporate electric elevators. Reliable elevators meant people could be transported up and down multi-floored buildings. The advent of technologies such as electricity and new systems for indoor plumbing and ventilation coincided with inventions such as the telephone, and modern skyscrapers were born.

As the 1900s advanced, steel cage construction with stone exterior sheathing was increasingly used for commercial buildings. Architect W. E. Noffke (1878–1964) designed the Blackburn Building at 85 Sparks Street with fire resistance clearly in mind: its steel frame is covered by a non-structural façade of concrete and brick. On the southeast corner of Rideau and Sussex stands the Transportation Building (1916), designed by architect N. Ogilvie. This building exhibits its steel skeleton-frame construction, with repetitive bands of windows topped by an exposed, elaborate copper cornice. It is a good example of how the change in technology liberated earlier height restrictions. Stone walls couldn't support multi-storeys simply because of their own weight, whereas steel frames truly birthed the skyscraper phenomenon.

In the late nineteenth and early twentieth centuries many architects reached back into historical memory, designing structures inspired by Second Empire, Italianate, Scottish Baronial and Romanesque Revival traditions. For example, the Second Empire Langevin Block on the corner of Elgin and Wellington sports a deep mansard roof. The mansard roofline (named after seventeenth century French architect François Mansart) permitted the use of the attic floor as functional, and well-insulated space. The incorporation of dormer or Palladian windows set into the mansard's lines allows light into the top floor. Although in the Langevin it is highly ornamented and grand, the mansard roof was an extremely popular roof design for many people's dwellings. In fact, you will discover it in every Ottawa neighbourhood and all construction periods. Many of today's postmodern buildings, such as the mall on Beechwood (see New Edinburgh walk) have mansard roofs.

W. E. Noffke was inspired with the sheer walls and clean lines of the Spanish Colonial Revival style. Perhaps his best building is at 85 Glebe Avenue, overlooking Central Park. Designed as part of a planned community development by the Clemow-Powell realty firm, this house is one of several that Noffke created bordering the park. Noffke was a prodigious producer of more than 200 Ottawa buildings which widely varied in style. His Spanish Colonial residences, although in a revivalist style, still impart freshness to the streetscape. Those such as 85 Glebe seem far closer in feeling to the modernist movement of pared-down and organic design than to the asymmetrical massing and picturesque silhouettes of Victorian Gothic and Queen Anne.

Architect Francis Sullivan (1882–1929) was inspired by Frank Lloyd Wright and his Prairie School philosophy. Wright, who spurned historical motifs and promoted the concept of organic, environmental design, became Sullivan's friend and mentor. Sullivan's 1914 Horticultural Building at Lansdowne Park displays the horizontal planes and wide overhanging eaves typical of Prairie School design. Noffke occasionally incorporates the *feeling* of Prairie Style into such homes as the Glebe's 517 O'Connor (1913). Here he uses the extension of a covered carriageway or porte-cochère on one side and a balancing covered sunroom on the other to achieve a sense of horizontality.

Canadian Pacific Railway steam train leaving Union Station in early 1940s. City of Ottawa Archives, CA 18210.

And then the First World War came, destroying a way of life and vision of the world. After the Depression years of the 1930s and World War II, architects wanted to move ahead, not to look backwards for inspiration. An enthusiasm to experiment with forms, coupled with the prohibitively expensive cost in materials and labour associated with the ornate revivalist styles, stimulated the new, minimalist designs of the modern movement.

Experimentation with space and form grew into the recognizable styles of modernism, also known as the International Style. The movement was born in Europe in the 1920s at the Bauhaus school in Germany. Architects such as Mies van der Rohe and Walter Gropius were leaders of the modern movement who were tremendously influential internationally after they fled Germany during Hitler's regime and landed in England or the United States. Internationalist buildings celebrate the technological advances of cantilevered construction, and concrete, glass, and steel replace wood, brick, and stone as the primary materials. External ornamentation is reviled, and repetition encouraged. The many storeys resemble one another: one band of horizontal ribbon windows is placed upon another, emphasizing rather than obscuring the steel skeleton-frame construction.

Modernism in Ottawa is represented in such buildings as the International Style former City Hall (1958) on Green Island and two residences in Sandy Hill (265 Goulbourn and 68 Range). In Rockcliffe, Hart Massey's International Style design for his own home at 400 Lansdowne Road won him a Massey Award in 1959. This residence is a "cubist" delight, a composition of exposed steel frames with a glassed front overlooking MacKay Lake and, on the street façade, inset wood panels for privacy. However, modernism, typified by its "factory-like" appearance of sheer, flat walls and rectilinear planes, was never popular with the public, especially not for private houses. Most people in the post-war years opted for comforting period revival styles or else the convenient new bungalow house, with its cozy spaces and broad, welcoming porches.

Ottawa's urban environment continues to reflect changing styles and new technologies. The Ottawa Courthouse on Elgin is a 1986 example of Brutalism, a style which evolved in the 1960s and 1970s and which became popular on university campuses such as the University of Ottawa. The Court's monumental, sheer walls are unrelieved save by narrow, almost inconsequential strips of windows. The humanizing touches in this imposing, depersonalized courthouse are achieved only in its interior spaces, which are flooded with natural light from a triangular-shaped atrium. On the street, the courthouse is delightfully offset by the heritage Teachers' College (now City Hall) of rough-faced limestone. Built very much on a human scale, this 1874 composition is as welcoming as its neighbour is deliberately intimidating. Looking at these two buildings, which design looks inviting? I bet most of us would pick the old Teachers' College ... What does that say for the design of a "people place" such as a courthouse of public appeal where, supposedly, we are considered innocent until proven guilty?

Postmodern office buildings now dot the Ottawa landscape. Postmodernist style is an intriguing "new look backwards" which features a conscious attempt by the architect to integrate historical ornamentation and idiosyncratic detail into concrete and glass structures. Such motifs as stylized mansard or steeply pitched roofs and dormer windows have been incorporated into new structures such as the little mall on Beechwood, directly opposite Alistair Ross's postmodern Royal Bank at 25 Beechwood. An excellent example of "rococo postmodern" is Barrister House on Elgin opposite the old Teachers' College. It is a high-rise postmodern tower with an interior of highly polished marble and art deco-like light sconces.

As styles change, it is always challenging to know what to call the new architectural flavour. What, for instance, is the style of the Canada and the World Pavilion (see New Edinburgh walk)? Even professors of architecture such as Ivan Cazaban at Carleton University ponder what to call it. "You might call it retro-, new-, or neo-modernist," he told me during an interview in the winter of 2003. "Postmodernism was almost a blip. Now we're looking back at the modernist aesthetic, so retro-modernism, that might be it. It's a very good question!"

Not only are buildings built and/or heritage façades renovated, interiors are also restored or otherwise "improved." Four million dollars was spent renovating the interior of the Nôtre Dame Basilica. Stepping inside its interior, reveals heritage sculpture, art, and artifice (the columns are faux, resembling stone but actually being wood) that urgently needed restoration.

Horse-drawn fire engines at corner of Albert and Kent streets, Upper Town, May 1899. City of Ottawa Archives, CA 15213.

FIRE

External influences directly affect the construction and style of a building. One such factor is fire, which has repeatedly ravaged the twin cities of Ottawa and Hull. Both lighting and heating were provided by open flame in the first wooden and stone buildings. Whale oil and then gas illuminated all buildings, from the lowliest cottages to the vice-regal residence, Rideau Hall. Open hearths, wood-burning stoves and the furnaces of the early forges, mills, and tanneries contributed to the threat of fire. Until the late 1800s the all-too-frequent fires were extremely difficult to extinguish because water had to be drawn laboriously by horse and cart to the site in large barrels called puncheons. Some puncheon drivers haggled with owners over the fee, while houses and businesses perished in flames. In the Great Fire of 1900, flames leapt across the river from Hull, turning the piled lumber stored on Victoria Island into an inferno. The fire almost destroyed Ottawa — only a shift in wind direction saved the capital.

Fire prevention was thus a major consideration for architects and builders throughout the early years. On February 3, 1916, fire swept through the Centre Block of Parliament. The only surviving part of Thomas Fuller's original design is the Library. Fuller had incorporated a steel fire door into his design that isolated the Library from the flames.

Fleeing the 1900 fire.
NCC, M. Newton Heritage file E12-0-11; Box 39.

THE SHAPE OF OTTAWA

Topography and layout also influence the design and shape of a city. The men who surveyed Ottawa were British, and they used a regular-spaced grid layout for property and street definition. Ottawa is further described by lot sizes that characterize individual neighbourhoods. For example, Lowertown's houses, built on tiny lots, bear little resemblance to those on nearby Metcalfe Street, where grand old mansions give a hint of that street's early ambitions to be a grand approach to Parliament Hill.

The 1919 community of Lindenlea represents a planned garden homes suburb. Based upon English architect Thomas Adams' popular concept for suburban living, Lindenlea is not laid out on a grid pattern: its streets curve and flow into one another, forming yet another shape inside the city.

The balance between lot and building size is a key design element, and the most attractive buildings are scaled to their environment. New Edinburgh's 34 Alexander is a whimsical Second Empire home that sports flamboyant wishbone gables. Once renowned for its splendid gardens, today it is a victim of additions, and it perches forlornly in its now tiny grounds. In contrast, the horizontal planes of the Danish Embassy in Rockcliffe nestle agreeably into the hillside in a truly organic design.

Far different are the tightly packed streetscapes of St. Patrick Street in Lowertown. The Irish and French workers who first lived here never enjoyed large, treed gardens. Instead, their backyards contained only cramped outhouse toilets and perhaps a stable. In the years 1850–70, Lowertown, and especially the Byward Market, was the commercial centre of Ottawa. Successive waves of immigrants chose it as their new home. On tiny lots they constructed small buildings that were both their business and residence. Those that could afford to build doubles did so, and rented them for income. The flavour of Lowertown's neighbourhood became peppered with European accents, with trades such as saddle, shoe, carriage, and candle makers beside colourful market stalls.

Today, space is increasingly at a premium throughout the city, in every neighbourhood. Lots are rezoned to permit the construction of infill houses or additions, and architects now win prizes for infill projects. As well, high-rise apartment buildings and condominiums have forever altered the profile of the streetscape. The character of a neighbourhood perceptibly changes when the density of families, pets, businesses, and traffic increases. Rockcliffe is no stranger to this. In 1992 Thomas MacKay's 1865 Victorian stone "cottage," Birkenfels, was razed. Today its spacious grounds are broken up into small estate lots and at least one house, 272 Soper Place, has been built in a scale too large for its gentle wooded setting.

The debate over the intrinsic value of open space at the address 700 Sussex is ongoing. In 1992, a wrecker's bulldozer demolished the last remains of Moses C. Edey's 1905 landmark, the Daly building. As soon as its walls came down, light and space illuminated the northwest corner of Rideau and Sussex. It exposed hitherto unseen views of David Ewart's massive, castle-like Connaught Building, the Château Laurier, and the restored façade of Sussex Drive. The National Capital Commission considers the space too valuable to be left as an open park. But the people of Ottawa still lobbied for the preservation of this liberating open area.

A typical Glebe street with red brick homes and enclosed porches. October 1991. K. Fletcher.

The people of Ottawa lost, and a new condominium will be erected here, with commercial space on the first two or possibly three levels. The architect is Montreal's Dan Hanganu. It will be interesting to see the new building completed, some time in 2004 — and to see how we like it.

View southeast from the Peace Tower, around 1890; foreground: East Block; left: canal with Major's Hill with Chapel of Ease (burned 1912) on east side of Sussex St. facing George Street; right rear: Canal Basin. NCC 172.

View north along the Rideau Canal in 1961. Note the railway tracks east of the canal. NCC 172-22.

A CAPITAL MOOD

Ottawa's style has been studied relentlessly since Queen Victoria decided, in 1857, to locate "the United Province of Canada's" capital here. At that time, city founders, architects and residents alike looked about them at the small town surrounding Colonel By's military barracks and wondered if their homes, businesses, and public buildings were fit to grace the new capital. They unanimously agreed that what they saw did not quite measure up. The congregation of the first Christ Church Cathedral built in 1832 decided their building was unsuited to Ottawa's new capital status. They hired architect King Arnoldi to design a new church and requested he keep the cost of the project below $25,000. (Arnoldi demurred: he submitted a bill of just less than $50,000.)

The intervening years have seen much torn down, much changed in order to satisfy what succeeding generations of architects, consultants, prime ministers and developers have deemed to be structures befitting the capital of an emerging nation.

What we've lost: now demolished and developed, this photo depicts barns, outbuildings and farm life at "Wildwood," Mr. Lee's farm located at Lees and Main Streets. Mr. Lee was a lawyer who had a large farmhouse and estate in the south part of the city.
City of Ottawa Archives, CA 7904.

Sir Wilfrid Laurier's Liberal government created the capital's first planning body — the Ottawa Improvement Commission (OIC) — in 1899. This was the first of four commissions mandated with the task of beautifying Ottawa.

Operating on an annual budget of $60,000, the four commissioners of the OIC made sweeping recommendations that resulted in large-scale improvements to Ottawa. To their credit goes the clean-up of the industrial sprawl of warehouses and construction materials along the canal, where the former Union Station now stands opposite the Château Laurier. Under the leadership of Montreal landscape architect Frederick G. Todd, the OIC was especially successful in the construction of parkways, drives, and public squares. Patterson Creek was defined, the Queen Elizabeth Driveway was started, and responsibility for the maintenance of Rockcliffe Park was transferred to the federal government.

The Château
Laurier Hotel
from the roof
terrace of the
Rideau Centre,
1991.
K. Fletcher.

In 1913, Sir Robert Borden appointed the Sir Henry Holt Commission which two years later released a report, the first to identify the need for a national capital region beyond the borders of the city. It also recommended the relocation of railway lines away from the downtown core. But World War I and the devastating loss of the Centre Block to fire drained the coffers of government. Holt's recommendations were shelved.

The Federal District Commission (FDC) was appointed in 1927. It was given an annual budget of $250,000, and under its control Ottawa was transformed. Prime Minister Mackenzie King took personal interest in the FDC and championed land acquisition for the creation of a ceremonial grand boulevard to Parliament Hill. His proposal was accepted and a special budget of $3 million was passed. Confederation Square is part of King's, and the FDC's, legacy to Ottawa.

King met Parisian urban planner Jacques Gréber in Paris in 1937 and invited him to Ottawa. They spent long hours discussing the ceremonial approach to Parliament. Although basically of like minds, they did not agree on the placement of the War Memorial. Gréber lost. In 1939 King George VI unveiled the War Memorial at the top of Elgin. King later said that Gréber had probably been right, for the memorial disturbs smooth traffic circulation. Later that year the FDC's plans were put on hold when war was declared.

On August 22, 1945, only eight days after armistice, King sent Gréber a letter inviting him back to Ottawa to define a Capital Master Plan under the FDC. Gréber accepted and the Gréber Report was tabled in the House of Commons in the 1951 government of Louis St. Laurent. Gréber was listed as its Consultant, while Canadians John M. Kitchen and Edouard Fiset were recognized as Associates. In 1958 the National Capital Commission (NCC) replaced the FDC. This is Ottawa's present commission.

Ross and MacFarlane's adaptation of original architect Bradford Lee Gilbert's "Roman bath" classical design for the Grand Trunk Railway's Union Station (1912). PAC-PA-10579.

Eventually the railway was relocated to the southeast of the city and in 1966 the present Ottawa train station was erected. Its architect, John B. Parkin, won a Massey Award a year later for its state-of-the-art design. The removal of the railway tracks alongside the Rideau Canal permitted the creation and landscaping of Colonel By Drive, the building of the National Arts Centre and the conversion of Union Station into the Government Conference Centre. As of late 2003, the future of the old Union Station is undetermined: it may become a Museum for Canadian Politics.

In the late 1950s, the NCC purchased many properties, and transformed them into public parks. These include Rideau Falls Park, Vincent Massey Park, the Greenbelt, and Gatineau Park. Later, in 1972, the NCC bought the former E. B. Eddy industrial property opposite Parliament Hill on the Hull side of the Ottawa River. There have been several proposals for its development, but none has yet been approved.

Part of the NCC's mandate is heritage preservation. Although it has been sharply criticized for not doing enough to ensure that historic properties are not lost, the NCC can still be credited with preserving the Sussex Drive façade. Their means, however, are not always appreciated. In 1961 the NCC commenced expropriating property bordering Sussex. Today, many merchants claim the NCC's rents are exorbitant. In 1993 the old block of buildings formerly known as the Institut Jeanne d'Arc was vacant; however, during the past ten years it has been transformed into condominiums. The advent of condos has had a humanizing influence, since apartments keep people in the city core after business hours. This keeps merchants happy, and comforts those residents who like to live in a safe city, where people can feel free to stroll the streets after nightfall.

Ottawa's face is ever-changing. The parking lot on Sussex immediately north of David Ewart's Connaught Building is now the site of the United States Embassy (completed 1999). Even before the destruction of New York City's World Trade Centre on September 11, 2001, many residents opposed the downtown location for this embassy because of fears of terrorist threats. Even more than the bombing in Oklahoma City, 9/11 has drastically affected public use of space in cities throughout the world. Ottawa is no exception: the public can no longer drive through Parliament Hill as we could before the 9/11 attack.

The question that occupies the minds of city planners (to say nothing of the general public) is: where can we locate buildings which represent prime symbolic targets? On one hand it is easy to succumb to fear and build them far away from the city core. Some of us, however, perhaps the majority of us, are reluctant to bend to potential terrorist threats. Whatever you think, I'm confident you would agree that such issues prompt lively debate. Certainly the United States Embassy continues to create much controversy, particularly since in the wake of the 9/11 attacks the surrounding streets of Sussex, Mackenzie, and Clarence have been narrowed by giant ugly cement traffic barriers which serve to deter potential car bombers. Their presence — an undeniable consequence of building the embassy here — alters the core of our capital city by creating an atmosphere of dehumanizing austerity if not outright fear. Plans are afoot to soften this look — but as of yet the barricades persist.

But not all new structures are quite as controversial as the United States Embassy. In 1993, when the first edition of *Capital Walks* was published, the heritage triptych created by the Central Chambers, the Scottish Ontario Chambers, and the Bell Canada Block overlooking Confederation Square was being incorporated into a new office complex. Today, the headquarters of the National Capital Commission at 40 Elgin towers over the Chambers building. Thankfully, designers salvaged the façades of the three heritage structures so that the streetscape retains its old-time feel.

Meanwhile, Confederation Square has altered substantially. The Tomb of the Unknown Soldier won its symbolic home beneath the War Memorial, and the Plaza Bridge was completely reborn after having been opened up with new staircases leading to the Rideau Canal below. And, come nightfall, this is one of the most theatrically illuminated places in the city.

Only change is certain. As I was preparing this edition, work started on the new Canadian War Museum. Ironically, at the same time as that new sod-roofed building goes up, soil on The Flats is being decontaminated because of industrial waste from its earlier uses. (As a matter of record, being environmentally responsible has a hefty price tag, as the NCC well knows: its budget of $99 million to fix up The Flats included relocating the Ottawa River Parkway and bringing services to the LeBreton area, not to mention an estimated $30 to $50 million for the clean-up itself.)

On The Flats opposite the Fleet Street Pumping Station, former homes whose foundations were briefly exposed while earth cleaning was conducted are being bulldozed and re-covered. As a result of all this activity and expense, the LeBreton Flats will be reborn, taking on new life as a museum site and future residential community. Even the Ottawa River Parkway is being rerouted so that it will curve south of the new war museum and north of Pooley's Bridge. Thomas Keefer's aqueduct and the tailrace of the pumping station that is so beloved by kayakers will, however, be retained.

What will the capital look like in fifty years? Who knows. The NCC is merely one actor in the drama that defines its face. Change is both inevitable and needed, however, for as a city expands and grows functions shift, densities alter, and urban planners — everyone's easiest scapegoat — remain busily occupied.

What we've lost: stacking hay on a horse-drawn wagon at "Wildwood" Mr. Lee's farm located at Lees and Main Streets. City of Ottawa Archives, CA 7923.

The Walks

The purpose of this book is to introduce you to Ottawa through the exploration of ten neighbourhoods: Parliament Hill, Sussex Drive, Lowertown, New Edinburgh, the Canal, the Glebe, Sandy Hill, Rockcliffe, the Ottawa River Parkway, and Central Experimental Farm. Each walk includes the approximate length in kilometres and an indication of timing.

Here are a few things to consider before setting out.

- Respect private property — lawns, gardens, and front walks.
- Wear comfortable shoes and layered clothes.
- Take along a backpack so you can keep your arms free. The pack can hold your camera, a picnic lunch, binoculars, extra film, or a collapsible umbrella.
- Take your dog as long as it is restrained on a leash. (Don't forget to stoop and scoop and also to ensure parks are dog friendly, because the National Capital Commission has restricted canine access on some walks.)
- Public washrooms can be found in buildings such as the City Hall, the museums, and restaurants.
- There are guided tours of the interiors of many public buildings and in some cases (like the water filtration plants) this is the only way to view them. Most are free, and all tours give you further information on the architect's design and the history of the capital. Watch for special interest tours such as those given by Heritage Ottawa.
- Consider exploring in different seasons and at different times of the day to enjoy the capital's varied moods.
- Some walks incorporate opportunities for swimming (see Rockcliffe and Ottawa River Parkway walks). However: obey the no swimming signs. In the summer of 2002 a youth drowned just east of Lemieux Island where the Ottawa River appears shallow and calm. A treacherous and invisible undercurrent took his life. Be smart; be safe.

The Walks

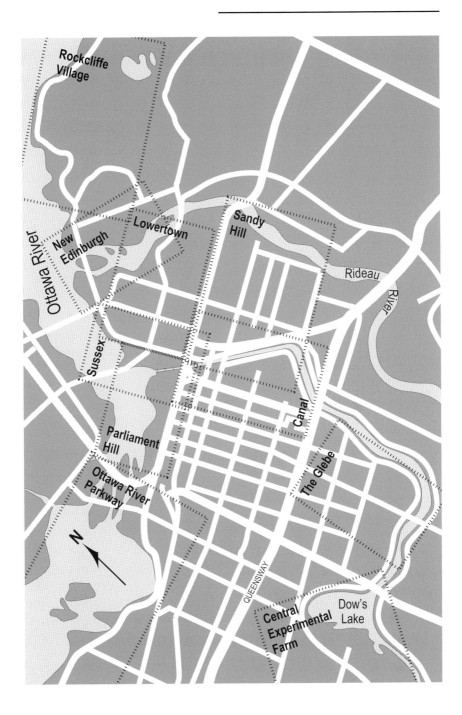

Parliament Hill

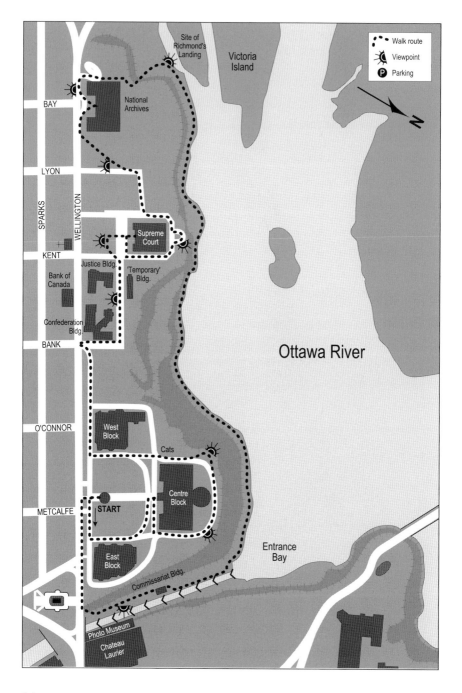

Site of Richmond's Landing

Victoria Island

Walk route

Viewpoint

P Parking

N

BAY

National Archives

LYON

SPARKS

WELLINGTON

KENT

Supreme Court

Justice Bldg.

'Temporary' Bldg.

Bank of Canada

Confederation Bldg.

BANK

Ottawa River

O'CONNOR

West Block

Cats

METCALFE

START

Centre Block

East Block

Entrance Bay

Commissariat Bldg.

Photo Museum

Chateau Laurier

The lofty outcrop of rock overlooking the Ottawa River first determined the city's development. When Lieutenant-Colonel John By, Royal Engineer, arrived in 1826, he agreed with Lord Dalhousie about the site's strategic significance. In 1823 Dalhousie had purchased approximately 400 acres, including what is today's Parliament Hill, for the sum of £750 from settler Hugh Fraser. In 1826 he wrote a letter to By, underscoring the site's suitability for a canal and transferring ownership to By's care. Colonel By then reserved the Hill as a government reserve under Ordnance control and erected a barracks and army hospital. By's principal task was to select a site for the start of the Rideau Canal, which would serve as a military link between the Ottawa River and Kingston. After considering several locations, (including Richmond Landing, adjacent to LeBreton Flats), By chose the gorge just to the east of the Hill, Entrance Bay, then known as Sleigh Bay. Construction on the canal began in 1826, and in 1832 the 200 kilometre waterway was completed.

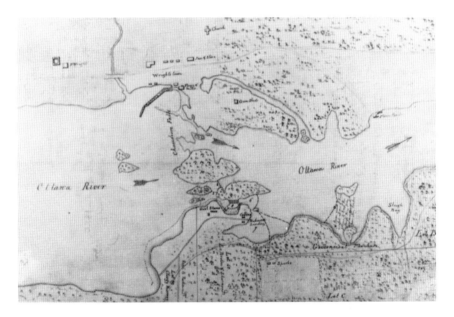

1825 map of the Ottawa River at Bytown by Major George Eliot.
The upper section shows Wrightsville (formerly Hull,
now Gatineau). PAC-C-16156.

Wellington Street near Bank, 1853, looking east;
watercolour by Lt. C. Sedley. The fence defines government land
west of the canal. The rise of land at the rear is Barracks
[now Parliament] Hill and the Hospital; homes, businesses and
hotels throng either side of Wellington. PAC-C-1548.

When Queen Victoria chose Ottawa as the United Province of Canada's capital on December 31, 1857, Barracks Hill was deemed the most desirable site for the Parliament Buildings. *The Ottawa Tribune* of May 21, 1859, posted a "Notice to Architects" specifying the budget for the buildings: "For Parliament House, $300,000; for Departmental Bldg. $240,000."

The first sod was turned on December 20, 1859. However, the Centre Block was not completed until six years later. Delays followed one another, and the original budget was quickly exceeded. Problems included instability in the underlying rock bed, the need to install water tanks in case of fire, and the transportation of the stone from the Nepean quarry twelve miles away. In 1862, a Royal Commission was assigned to study the costly delays that caused layoffs of up to 1,700 skilled tradespeople. The buildings were deemed ready on September 8, 1865, although not all doors and windows had been installed. Still, the exterior appearance of Parliament Hill was acclaimed, its Gothic Revival spires described variously as "imposing," "picturesque," and "inspirational."

Fuller's winning design for Parliament Buildings, Centre Block; lithograph by Burland Lasricain, Montreal. The fountains and stairs represent artistic license. NCC 172-116.

The foreground depicts the East Block under construction in 1860. Beyond are heaps of debris and the head of the Rideau Canal locks, with Sapper's Bridge and the Canal Basin to the right. The future Château Laurier site is in the centre left.
City of Ottawa Archives, CA 0223.

Unfortunately, fire precautions were insufficient to prevent flames destroying the Centre Block on February 3, 1916. Only the Library survived the conflagration. Stent and Laver's designs for both the East and West blocks were untouched. Canadian poet Duncan Campbell Scott witnessed the spectacle: "The fire was terrible and tragic; it was the most terrifying and beautiful sight I have ever seen. ... I hope that the building may be restored without the practice of any vandalism, but I have my doubts. I hear talk of 'a larger, more imposing, up-to-date building'. The very phrases make one shudder. We had a building that was beautiful and harmonized with the site, and there will be some people who will want to destroy it because they can put up something more beautiful. If they can put up a more beautiful building, let them put it somewhere else. Let us preserve the beauty that we have."[3]

But the structural damage was such that the Centre Block had to be demolished. Architect John A. Pearson's Neo-Gothic design won the ensuing competition and the present Centre Block was erected between 1916 and 1920. During these years the seat of government was located in the Victoria Memorial Museum (now the Museum of Nature; see Canal walk) at the foot of Metcalfe Street.

The original workshop that once graced the Hill was demolished to make way for a parking lot in September 1956. This building was located at Bank and Wellington and extended to the entry to the Lover's Walk, which descended the cliffs to the river. In its lifetime, the workshop also served as the Justice Building and the National Gallery. Near the public washrooms behind the West Block once stood a greenhouse, built in 1879.

The civil service soon outgrew its departmental buildings on the Hill proper. Extensions were made to the East and West blocks, but more office space was still needed. Thomas Fuller, architect of the Centre Block, was retained to design the Langevin Block (1883–89) on Wellington. Made of olive-green sandstone from New Brunswick, the block houses the Prime Minister's Office. It was named for Sir Hector Louis Langevin, Father of Confederation and Secretary of State between 1867 and 1869. The Confederation Building on Wellington at Bank was erected between 1927 and 1931. Increased numbers of staff is not the only reason the Civil Service relocated away from the Hill: in the 1950s many departments moved about five kilometres west to Tunney's Pasture because of the fear of nuclear attack during the Cold War.

Construction of Parliament Centre Block (John Pearson, architect) Nov. 2, 1916. The original Thomas Fuller Library (rear) escaped the fire. PAC-C-19216.

Successive governments expropriated the entire north side of Wellington Street, razing private properties to build a variety of government buildings. The promontory of cliffs overlooking the Ottawa River is currently dominated by the Supreme Court, Justice, and Confederation buildings and by the National Archives of Canada.

Because they house the federal government of Canada, the Parliament Buildings — especially the Centre Block — are used as a symbol for the nation. In 1901 the Centre Block's Gothic spires were draped in black to symbolize a Dominion grieving over the death of Queen Victoria. Today the Hill is the site of public demonstrations and celebrations, and there are sound and light shows during the tourist season. The Changing of the Guard ceremony is reminiscent of the Hill's original use as a military barracks.

Visitors to Parliament Hill particularly enjoy hearing the bells, or carillon, which were inaugurated by Prime Minister Mackenzie King in 1927. The carillon is a percussion instrument comprised of fifty-

1880s view of rear of original Parliament Buildings.
The old pump house is at the base of the cliffs; on the left are the
first canal locks at Entrance Bay and the stone Commissariat
building. NCC, M. Newton heritage file E12-024, Box 51.

three bronze bells that cover four and one half octaves. Installed in
the Peace Tower, they weigh sixty-six tonnes. The carillonneur renders
the beautiful cascading sounds by using his fists to pound a keyboard
whose keys are connected by steel wires to clappers on the bells. A
concert is played from 2:00 to 3:00 every afternoon on the Hill, and
the bourdon, the largest bell of the carillon, automatically strikes the
hour.

STYLE

The Neo-Gothic spires of John A. Pearson's Centre Block, and the
Gothic Revival buildings of Fuller and Jones's original Library and
Stent and Laver's East and West blocks are stylistically sympathetic.
The Gothic style, popular in its revivalist form in the mid to late
1800s, represented "the highest expression of man's aspiration" according
to Canadian poet William Wilfred Campbell.

Stylistic grandeur after the fashion of a great boulevard is maintained
along Wellington Street. The copper châteauesque roofs of the

Confederation Building, the Justice Building, and the Supreme Court integrate successfully with the deep mansard roof of the Langevin Block. But although the copper roofs provide an illusion of stylistic continuity, the buildings exhibit widely diverging styles. The Supreme Court is essentially a severe interpretation of the châteauesque style with an Art Deco interior, and the Langevin Block sports ornamental Second Empire features. And, across the canal from the promontory of the Hill, the Canadian Museum of Contemporary Photography, the Château Laurier, the twin spires of Nôtre-Dame Basilica, and Safdie's National Gallery complete the image of monumental grandeur befitting a capital city.

WALK TIPS

🚶 4 km; 1.5 hours

This walk encompasses splendid vistas of the historic Ottawa River and leads you along a pathway hugging the waterfront. The circuit route includes the Parliament Buildings, the Supreme Court of Canada and the oldest standing stone building in Ottawa, the Commissariat Building, now the Bytown Museum. Most buildings are open to the public. Tours of the Centre and East Block and Supreme Court are available year round. The Bytown Museum is open May to October.

As you walk you will "meet" prominent political leaders of our past. Statues proliferate upon the Hill; most recently, in 1992, Queen Elizabeth II unveiled an unusual statue of herself astride a horse. Other statues include the likenesses of Thomas D'Arcy McGee, who was murdered on nearby Sparks Street, and Prime Ministers Sir John A. Macdonald and William Lyon Mackenzie King.

A regrettable result of the terrorist attack on New York's World Trade Towers on September 11, 2001 is that the Hill is now closed to vehicular traffic.

THE WALK

Start at the Centennial Flame in the middle of the lawn directly in front of the Centre Block. It was installed and then lit in 1967 by Prime Minister Lester B. Pearson in celebration of Canada's 100th birthday.

Look north. Facing you is the ninety-metre-high Peace Tower, the symbolic centre of Parliament Hill, Ottawa and the nation. On your left is the West Block, on your right the East Block. The architects of these flanking buildings, Stent and Laver, did not create identical structures, yet the two lend the Hill a symmetrical composition.

East Block; note the variegated slate roof now replaced by copper. NCC 172.

First visit the **East Block**, built 1859–66 in the highly ornate Gothic Revival style. Some original features have been altered: in 1870 dormer windows were added to the roof, wings were added 1910–13, copper replaced the variegated slate roofs of all three government buildings in the 1940s, and in 1976–80 the Department of Public Works renovated the interior space. We can be thankful a proposal to paint the exterior stone yellow was not adopted.

Note the delicate wrought iron cresting running on top of the roof. Although the spires appear to be composed entirely of copper, it is actually this fanciful ironwork that catches your attention creating the effect of Gothic spires. This ironwork **trompe-l'oeil** lends a picturesque airiness to the overall design.

Typical of the Gothic Revival style, the exterior of the building is extremely fanciful. There are gargoyles in the East Block's southwest corner tower, both at the entrance door and the second-storey. Note the dramatic keyhole effect above this tower's doorways, accentuated by the uncoursed red and yellow sandstone — a random patterning which is echoed in the East Block's window bays. Hourly tours in the summer (and on weekends in the winter) allow you to explore the interior.

The Prime Minister's and Privy Council's offices were in the East Block until 1976, when they were moved across the street into the Langevin Block. As you turn left to pass in front of the East Block, notice the carriage-porch, called the Governor General's entrance. It once led to the vice-regal offices, but they were relocated to Rideau Hall in 1942. From the time of the first governor general, Lord Monck, capital planners have wrestled with defining a ceremonial route between this office and Rideau Hall. Part of the NCC's Confederation Boulevard represents the latest attempt to provide a picturesque approach from the Hill to Rideau Hall.

Follow the curving drive to Pearson's **Centre Block** (1916–27). Pearson's Neo-Gothic design provides a fascinating contrast to Stent and Laver's East and West blocks. Pearson's rendering of the Gothic style is far more restrained, and despite exterior ornamentation in the form of gargoyles and grotesques, the Centre Block conveys a more solid, imposing presence.

Yet Pearson's ninety-two metre high **Peace Tower** is inspired by Victorian Gothic fancy. It is here that the architect allowed his design to echo the flanking blocks. Elaborate tracery surrounds the imposing front doorway which is dramatically guarded by a rampart lion and unicorn. The tower was renovated in 1981, and the once airy lookout was enclosed by curved clear plastic. It is well worth ascending the tower via the first inclined elevator installed in Canada (1919–1927) to experience the most remarkable panorama views of the city. The viewing gallery is located just beneath the base of the flagpole. Once inside the Peace Tower's oak and brass doors, you enter a world of lush Gothic detailing. Ribbed vaults, compound pointed arches, elaborately carved capitals and intricate bosses lift your eye upwards. Interior Gothic detailing continues in the foyers and chambers of the Senate and Commons. The Senate, which is carpeted in crimson and panelled in dark-stained oak is especially rich looking and features massive murals depicting scenes of World War I. But the eye is allowed repose in the Memorial Chamber, where sheer cut stone gives sudden rest and inspires thoughtful reflection.

The carvings here are part of an interior and exterior project commenced in 1921 and still ongoing. Chief Parliamentary Sculptor Eleanor Milne worked on the "History of Canada" relief in the Commons foyer. This project alone took eight years and was executed at night, with Milne working atop metal scaffolding.

Public tours of the Centre Block introduce you to many of its interior delights. Security is tight on the Hill, and you are now required to pass through security checks. Tours are the best way of experiencing the majesty of Parliament's interior Gothic spaces and the intricacy of the Centre Block's elaborate stone carvings. After the tour, you can watch Parliament in session from the public galleries.

Joining a tour is the only way you can step inside the **Parliamentary Library** which is otherwise closed to the public. It is the only surviving element of Fuller and Jones's original design. Buttresses — integral structural supports — divide its ornate interior into sixteen bays, each three storeys high. Originally, the arcade galleries had glass floors. These were replaced with wood after women joined the Library staff. Ornate wrought iron balustrading coloured in matte black with gold highlights contrasts effectively with the honey-coloured maple and white pine of the walls, floor, and shelves. As you step out of the Library, note the steel doors painted to resemble wood. These doors saved the Library from the 1916 fire.

Return outside and turn left (east) to circle around to the back of the Centre Block. Go to the iron fence overlooking Entrance (Sleigh) Bay and the first eight locks of the Rideau Canal. Now continue walking behind the Centre Block. You pass the original bell of Thomas Fuller and Chilion Jones's first Parliament Building, now located at the rear of the Parliamentary Library. The library's iron dome, one of the first of its kind in North America, is supported by projecting flying buttresses of Gloucester limestone. The dome was custom made in England, but had to be returned by ship several times for small adjustments, so that it would fit its space. This is no doubt one of the reasons that preliminary budgets and time estimates for the Parliament Buildings were exceeded. The architects' concept for the Library incorporated the medieval Gothic tradition of a polygonal-shaped Chapter House attached to English cathedrals such as Salisbury and Westminster.

Continue walking around the exterior of the Library beside the railing overlooking the Ottawa River. Look for the staircase descending the cliff face, part of the **Lovers' Walk**, closed in the Depression years due to public concern about the danger of attack from "undesirables." Farther on, you'll find the carpeted, box homes of the parliamentary cats. René Chartrand is their constant, self-appointed keeper.

Next you'll see the statue of **Queen Victoria** flanked by a lion. This statue was unveiled in 1901 during the Royal Visit of the Duke and Duchess of Cornwall and York. During the ceremony one hundred men from the Governor General's Foot Guards served as a guard of honour on the Hill. From here there is a spectacular view along the Ottawa

Construction of Thomas Fuller's Parliamentary Library, c 1860.
PAC-C-7374.

River. Beyond the statue, roughly where the statue of Lester B. Pearson now stands, is the site of the original military barracks hospital.

Now walk on to the **West Block**. In 1884, Ottawa's City Clerk William P. Lett described the two blocks: "The principal material used in their construction is a hard, cream-coloured sandstone, from the adjacent Township of Nepean. The dressings, stairs, gablets, pinnacles, etc. are of Ohio free-stone, whilst a pleasing variety is given to the whole by the relieving arches of red Potsdam sandstone, over the window and door openings. The roofs are of Vermont slate, of a dark colour, variegated by light green bands. The marble was obtained at Arnprior, and the timber used, excepting the oak, at various localities in the Ottawa valley."[4]

The West Block was the site of the first telephone conversation in Ottawa. Prime Minister Alexander Mackenzie's private secretary, William Buckingham, recited the Lord's Prayer to him by phone in September 1877. Their success prompted immediate results: Governor General Lord Dufferin and Mackenzie authorized a two-mile telephone line from Rideau Hall, the Governor General's residence, to Mackenzie's office in the West Block.

Roof of the West Block on fire, 1897. NCC 172-105.

Before leaving the Hill, pause to appreciate how the Gothic design emphasizes the elevation of this lofty site. John Pearson intended his Centre Block to lead observer's eyes heavenwards. He designed the windows on each storey to be smaller than those on the storey below. The layers of gabled dormer windows are similarly designed. Finally, the narrow, pointed lancet windows in the Peace Tower pull one's gaze up to the Canadian Flag flying at its crest.

At the far corner of the West Block, turn right along its southern face and continue through the stone pillars until you emerge onto Wellington Street. Ahead is the 1927–31 **Confederation Building**, featuring a dramatically angled, massively arched main entry complete with croisette windows. It was the first government building erected to the west of the Hill. Although it shares similar construction materials (such as sandstone and copper) with the Parliament Buildings, the Confederation Building's towers, turrets, steeply pitched roof with multiple layers of dormer windows, and its vertical massing are typical châteauesque features. Note the corbelled projection just beneath the attic (top) floor windows. This decorative motif resembles a castle, a feature you will observe later this walk in the Château Laurier Hotel.

Confederation Building under construction, looking northwest on
Wellington from the corner of Bank, May 4, 1929.
NCC, M. Newton file H12-288, Box 42.

Confederation Building under construction, showing the framing of dormers in its châteauesque style roof, 1929. NCC 172.

Turn right (north) on the extension of Bank Street and left (west) at the next corner. You now start to walk behind the Confederation Building. Observe its interesting three-wing ground plan, and note the amount of open space used for parked cars. Periodically, there are proposals for underground parking on the Hill, but none has thus far been adopted.

Pause in the space between the Confederation and the next large building, the Justice Building. Look left (due south) to view the beaux arts style Modern Classical **Bank of Canada Building** made of granite from the Eastern Townships. The original 1937 structure, designed by Marani, Lawson and Morris, is dominated by its 1975–78 addition, the silvered glass towers of Arthur Erickson and Marani, Rounthwaite & Dick which house the bank's Central Garden Court and the Currency Museum. The 1937 structure features seven spandrels, or vertical "bands," of windows punctuated by fluted pilasters that mimic columns.

Their subdued capitals are barely visible where they meet the horizontal band of the stringcourse. In between the spandrels you can find relief sculptures carved by Jacobine Jones. Note how the Bank's copper roof is reproduced in the 1975–78 addition: the copper was chemically aged so that it would immediately integrate with the Wellington streetscape.

To the rear of the Confederation Building there is a low white clapboard "temporary building," known as the **Justice Annex**. Designed by architect Thomas Dunlop Rankin and built during World War II (c. 1940) to provide temporary wartime offices, this is the sole survivor of three structures that once sprawled between the Supreme Court and the National Archives, ahead of you. The annex has simple colonial Georgian touches: the stylized entryway, with its columns and pediment, the wooden sash windows, and the ventilator cupolas on top of the roof. Rumour has it that it will be demolished, but at time of writing it still stands.

The **Justice Building** (1935) is now on your left. Architects Burritt and Horwood continued the Château style for this edifice, whose exterior is decorated by Gothic-inspired stone carvings. Note the life-size First Nations' scout, crouched over the western entryway.

Look left (due south) to view **St. Andrew's Presbyterian Church**, designed by architect W. T. Thomas of Montreal. The original church on this site was built by Thomas MacKay's Scottish stonemasons. This 1874 replacement features a steeple offset to the left, rather than centred above, the doorway. This reflects the Victorians' love of asymmetry. The main entryway is dramatically arched. Note how the old church is encircled by the glass curtain walls of 275–283 Sparks Street. This building, owned by the Temporal Committee of St. Andrews, houses more offices of the Bank of Canada. Its clever design emphasizes the limestone heritage church by contrasting it against the stepped, non-reflective dark brown panels inset directly behind the church. The patterns created in the modern glass towers lend an attractive "modern art" texture to Wellington Street.

Now resume your walk. Ahead is the beaux arts style **Supreme Court of Canada** (1937), Montreal architect Ernest Cormier's only Ottawa commission. Its construction replaced a fine old Ottawa home: the Devlin residence. The highest court of appeal possesses an austere, distinguished presence. Cormier emphasized this in the balanced massing of the projecting east and west towers and the massive scale of the central entry with its imposing stairs. Six column-like piers support the châteauesque copper roof and its stepped dormers. The dormers interrupt the steeply pitched roof and provide light to the interior space. Note how the sheer, unadorned cut stone walls also emphasize the building's imposing nature. Cormier was forced to change his original plans to accommodate Prime Minister King's insistence upon the châteauesque roof.

Note the two bronze statues of Justice and Truth sculpted by Walter S. Allward on either side of the sweeping entry stairs. Ironically, the statues were misplaced when Allward was invited to design Canada's Vimy Memorial in France in the 1920s. In 1969, Truth and Justice were rediscovered in crates in a parking lot and only installed in their rightful places in the early 1970s. Enter the Court to examine its magnificent interior space; you'll find the Supreme Court in session when both Canadian flags are flying above the building.

Cormier's interior is art deco. The central raised classical stairway with its flanking stairs provides a suitably imposing yet balanced entry to the courtrooms. The overall effect of the interior design is of hard, shiny surfaces which demand respect: this is no unassuming or welcoming space. Only the hushed tones of lawyers (in woollen wigs) and the rich scarlet robes of the judges add a human touch.

Return outdoors and walk to the rear of the building, through the parking spaces, to discover a secluded lookout over the river from which you can look east to Parliament Hill.

Return to the front of the Supreme Court and continue walking west. At the intersection with Lyon pause yet again to look across Wellington at the **East and West Memorial Buildings**, 284 and 384 Wellington Street built in 1949–56 and 1954–56 respectively. Architects Allward and Gouinlock created a neo-classical façade with a suggestion of châteauesque detailing through the imposition (due to Prime Minister Mackenzie King's insistence) of shallow copper roofs. Lyon Street is wide where it intersects with Wellington: it used to be Uppertown's West Ward Market. Connecting the East and West buildings is a stylized Art Deco sculpture, "The Canadian Phalanx" by Ivan Mestrovic, honouring Canadian WW I veterans.

Now walk through the next park (site of the proposed Federal Court Building, to be completed c. 2005) to the **National Archives and Library of Canada** (1963–67), designed in the International Style by Mathers and Haldenby. The building is a departure from the Château and Gothic styles, being a series of severe monolithic blocks relieved by relentlessly marching rows of tiny windows.

National Archives of Canada. October 1991. K. Fletcher.

Go inside, since the interior space reveals the structure of this building. In the foyer you can discern the layout of its steel posts and girders beneath their finish of white marble and gilt mosaic tiles. Art and artifacts add to the archives: inside the main door is a bronze sculpture by Henry Moore, and murals on the second-floor reading room are by Charles Fraser Comfort, friend of the Group of Seven and the only artist to be appointed director of the National Gallery of Canada. Among many other treasures here, you'll find Glenn Gould's piano on the ground floor where the marble staircase winds its way upwards.

Return outside. Walk straight ahead to Wellington Street and pause one last time to look across the street. Look above the cascading fountain in the Garden of the Provinces to observe the stone wall delineating the western end of Sparks Street and the tall spire of **Christ Church Cathedral**. Landowner Nicholas Sparks donated land for this church, first built in 1833 but completely rebuilt in 1872–73 to the design of architect King Arnoldi. Rough Nepean sandstone animates its exterior, as do the stepped gables which also accentuate the verticality of its position atop the hill. Its steeple stands in counterpoise to the spires of Parliament Hill.

Now turn right on Wellington and find the path leading down to the parking lot directly west of the archives. Find the steps leading around the "porch" of the archives' rear wing, where you will find a statue of Arthur G. Doughty, Dominion Archivist 1904–35. Descend the stairs to the parking lot, and join the waterfront paved walking/bicycle path running east towards Entrance Bay and the Rideau Canal locks. To your left (west) is the Portage Bridge to Gatineau, Quebec, and farther west is the Chaudière Falls. Pause here.

Chaudière Falls and the construction of the Portage Bridge spanning the twin cities of Ottawa–Gatineau (formerly Hull), 1972. Note the piers of the Portage Bridge.
City of Ottawa Archives, CA 11656.

Juxtaposed to the modern Portage Bridge and the four grey staggered complexes of **Place du Portage** (1969–79) in Gatineau is Victoria Island's four-storey Ottawa Carbide Company Mill, built in the 1890s by Canadian inventor Thomas Leopold Willson. Between the pathway and Victoria Island is a small spit of land once known as Bellow's Landing. This was the earliest settlement of Bytown, where travellers and voyageurs caught a breath of hospitality and a bite of warm food at Mother Firth's Tavern. In September 1818 this was where four hundred disbanded soldiers from the 99th and 100th Regiments alighted. They renamed it **Richmond Landing**, after the Duke of Richmond, the Governor General who later died from the bite of a rabid fox. The men quickly built log cabins or sheltered in tents. Their goal was to build a road to the Jock River and settle there on the free land the Crown had given them as soldiers. Afraid of a repeat of the War of 1812 with the States, the British government gave grants of free land to trained army personnel and their families. The Richmond Road, as it became known, was one of the earliest roads built in Upper Canada, and the first in Carleton County.

Now walk east along the river with the cliffs of Parliament Hill on your right. Throughout the years there have been a variety of proposals for their development, including designer-built condominiums. The path meets the start of the Rideau Canal at Entrance Bay, first christened Sleigh Bay, by the founder of Hull, (now Gatineau) Philemon Wright, in 1818. The name commemorated his son's mid-winter wedding. Being from Perth, the Justice of the Peace had no licence to wed the couple in Wrightsville (today's Gatineau), in Lower Canada. Undaunted, the wedding party bundled up in furs and dashed over the ice in their smart horse-drawn sleighs. The couple were married in the shelter of this bay — in Upper Canada.

On the near side of the locks is the **Commissariat** building built in 1827 of limestone quarried from the adjacent cliffs. Its front gable and low pitched roof are a characteristic design of its Scottish stonemasons.

The building has a rich past, being variously a military supply warehouse, military museum, and, during the late 1800s, an apartment. Tenants Auclair and Seed were a nuisance; complaints were lodged about the former because he allowed his fifty free-range chickens to eat lawn seed, and against Seed because he encouraged his children to throw stones and tamper with the building's lock mechanisms. Since 1951 the **Bytown Museum** has operated from the Commissariat, the oldest stone building in Ottawa. It's well worthwhile to venture inside

1913 view of the entry locks, Alexandra Bridge, Canadian Pacific
and Hull Electric Railway Entrance to Union Station.
A steamer is docked at the wharf below Major's Hill Park.
NCC, 172-376.

and to pay the small entry fee so you can see the video of the Canal
and the interior exhibits.

Once back outside, look to the east side of the Entrance Locks to
find the foundations of another building, once the Royal Engineer's
office, located at the second lock. It served as Lt.-Col. By's headquarters
until the completion of the canal in 1832. From 1859–1878 it was the
home of William Foster Coffin, Commissioner of Ordinance Lands. It
was demolished at the turn of the last century to make way for the
railway embankment for the Alexandra Bridge, which still spans the
Ottawa River, on your left.

Now turn right to proceed up the hill, observing the operations of
the locks in summer. At the eighth lock, you pass by the 1888
lockmaster's house, also constructed of rough-hewn limestone. The
digging of the canal posed continual problems to Pennyfather, the
contractor in charge of excavation, because the walls repeatedly
collapsed. Two workers died during blasting, a fate all too common for
itinerant workers, many of whom had no proper instruction in the use
and science of explosives. Thomas MacKay was the masonry contractor;
his team of stonemasons completed the channel for the entry locks in

1832. The massive limestone blocks were quarried by MacKay's labourers from the cliffs you see surrounding Entrance Bay. In 1993, the exterior limestone slabs were removed and cracks in the canal's walls cemented. The excavation was then stabilized with brick and the exterior facing of limestone replaced.

Before climbing the stairs ahead of you to rejoin Wellington Street, stop to look left. Crowning the opposite cliff is the long, tunnel-like western façade of the **Canadian Museum of Contemporary Photography**. It opened on May 6, 1992, and was designed by the architectural firm of Rysavy & Rysavy. Indiana sandstone was imported for its exterior to match the sheer cut-stone walls of the 1908–12 Château Laurier Hotel directly above it. Look up the façade of the hotel to note the corbelling below its attic (top) storey. This echoes the projecting corbel of the Confederation Building you viewed earlier on this tour.

If you wish, you could now continue to walk alongside the canal, beneath the much-renovated "Sapper's Bridge" now renamed the **Plaza Bridge**. Lighting designer Martin Conboy created a theatrical effect of soft lighting during nighttime which lends this space a very people-friendly aspect. If you walk beneath the bridge, you can turn right and walk up broad steps to view the War Memorial and Confederation Square, or continue south to find yourself beside the National Arts Centre (see Canal walk).

Now climb the stairs to **Wellington Street** and look over the bridge for an aerial view of the locks. A short walk right (west) from the top of the stairs returns you to the Parliamentary precinct and the Centennial Flame, the start of this tour.

Mouth of the Rideau Canal, from Parliament Hill. Engraving,
1882, from Picturesque Canada, by Schell and Hogan.
NCC 172

Horse-drawn cab on Sapper's Bridge between War Memorial and
East Block, n.d. but pre-1912 since Union Station is not visible at
rear. City of Ottawa Archives, CA 1764.

Sussex

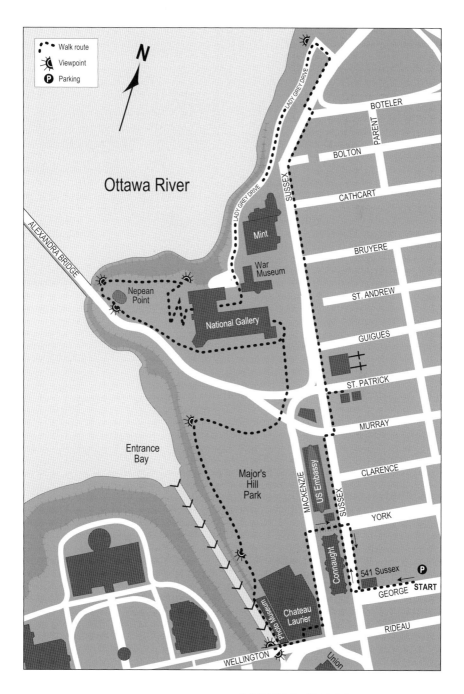

Legend:
- Walk route
- Viewpoint
- P Parking

Ottawa River

ALEXANDRA BRIDGE

LADY GREY DRIVE

SUSSEX

Mint

War Museum

Nepean Point

National Gallery

BOTELER

PARENT

BOLTON

CATHCART

BRUYERE

ST. ANDREW

GUIGUES

ST. PATRICK

MURRAY

CLARENCE

YORK

Entrance Bay

Major's Hill Park

MACKENZIE

US Embassy

SUSSEX

Connaught

541 Sussex

P

START

GEORGE

Photo Museum

Chateau Laurier

RIDEAU

WELLINGTON

Union

c. 1855 drawing of Lowertown showing McArthur's British Hotel,
front centre with widow's walk on top.
NCC, M. Newton file H12-28, Box 43.

In Ottawa's early days, Major's Hill Park and Nepean Point represented
two valuable pieces of land that shared the clifftop with Barracks Hill
(Parliament Hill). If military action was necessary, the canal below
would serve to transport troops or goods. And so the strategic cliffs
overlooking the Ottawa River were reserved for the Crown under
Ordnance control.

Not coincidentally, Colonel By built his residence on Colonel's
Hill (now Major's Hill), beside Entrance Bay. In June 1827, Lieutenant
Pooley and Colonel By were living in homes overlooking the
Commissariat. A footpath linked the Colonel's house to the Engineers'
Yard at the corner of Rideau and Sussex Streets. The little path became
first a well-travelled lane and then Mackenzie Street, along which
tradesmen in their horse-drawn wagons made pickups and deliveries at
the back entries of the growing businesses along Sussex. As Sussex
Street and Lowertown grew into the commercial hub of Ottawa, the

Construction of the first Canal Lock, the Steamer Wharf and the
Alexandra (Interprovincial) Bridge. Harmer photograph, 1899.
NCC, M. Newton file E12-003, Box 40.

west side of Sussex was built up. Prior to 1843 most buildings on
Sussex Street were wooden.

Farther east on the north side of Rideau at William stood the
wooden civilian barracks housing MacKay's Scottish stonemasons and
their families. The barracks were luxurious in comparison to the squalid
homes of the "dispensable" itinerant labourers in Lowertown, who
were predominantly Irish or French Roman Catholics. The contractors
had the Clerk of the Works, John MacTaggart, to speak for them:
"Every care should be taken with respect to the comfort of the
contractors and their people; they will have places near the works ...
whereon the temporary buildings may be erected ... so that every
person will be safely sheltered, and no time lost in coming and going
to the works."[5]

Colonel By tried to assist the labourers "who had been wounded
by the accidental explosion of mines, and the caving in of earth, [and
who] were suffering dreadfully from being frost bitten owing to the

utter impossibility of keeping them warm in the miserable log huts in which they were laying."[6] Human misery abounded in those early years. Despite Colonel By's personal intervention, the squatters and labourers did not enjoy consideration from the Ordnance Board.

Ordnance leasing of land prevented freehold ownership, and landlords who rented premises to tenants were loathe to erect permanent buildings of brick or stone lest the government confiscate the properties. As well, wood was readily available for the frame or log buildings, which were easily built, unlike stone or brick buildings, which required skilled tradespeople, building contractors, and sometimes the design of an architect.

As Ordnance control diminished after the Vesting Act was passed in 1844, stone and brick buildings were erected on either side of the street, reflecting the confidence of freehold ownership.

The 1854 MacTaggart Street Station of the Bytown and Prescott Rail received freight just north of Cathcart Street. Later, the railway became the St. Lawrence and Ottawa prior to being absorbed by the

Sussex at Rideau, c. 1865. Note horse cab stand at corner, the Chapel of Ease on west side Sussex fronting George St., the British Hotel with three-tiered verandah, and streetcar tracks. PAC-12527.

Canadian Pacific Railway. Steamboats transported goods from Montreal to the wharves at the foot of the cliffs. By the 1850s Sussex Street was thriving as a commercial centre and merchants sold a gamut of goods from local products to imported luxuries from Europe and Asia.

British Hotel after 1880, showing Thomas Askwith's addition fronting Sussex and James Skead's rear extension of 1865 along George Street. NCC, NCP 9747.

When work started on the Parliament Buildings in 1859, Ottawa's military encampment on Barracks Hill had to be moved. James Skead, owner of the British Hotel at the corner of Sussex and George offered his premises to the army. Skead and his partner had completed a major three-storey extension 132 feet along George Street to the rear of the original hotel which fronted onto Sussex. On March 1, 1866, the British Hotel was officially accepted as the new barracks' location. It remained a barracks for four years.

In November 1866, the Champagne Hotel — later the LaSalle Academy and now Canada Mortgage and Housing Corporation offices — also became a barracks. And, on September 9, 1867, the Nuns' General Hospital, at the corner of Sussex and Bruyère, became another. Until the permanent removal of Imperial troops from Ottawa in August 1870, Sussex was a military enclave. This was the period of the threatened Fenian invasions.

In the decade between 1857 and 1867, Ottawa's population more than doubled, from 7,760 to 18,700, due to the growth of the civil service and the accompanying infrastructure of business services. This influx of people started a boom of building and renovation, and affected such seemingly mundane details as the building of sewers and drains.

Poor drains and a basement full of smelly water perennially plagued the British Hotel, and the location of the latrines at the General Hospital caused considerable ill feeling among the residents of Cathcart Street, the nuns, the city's Board of Health, and the troops. The concern was the siting of the latrines: they were located first adjacent to the wall surrounding the nuns' enclosed gardens, and then near the residents' wells. After the departure of the troops in 1870, the temporary barracks reverted to their owners. Number 541 Sussex Street, the British Hotel, continued to be the cornerstone of the street. It briefly served as the Clarendon Hotel, then in 1880 the federal government purchased it. The cover of *The Canadian Illustrated News*, March 20, 1880, depicts the Marquis of Lorne opening an art exhibition in the building — a collection that, under his patronage, became the forerunner of today's National Gallery.

In September 1880, Thomas Askwith, a local contractor, demolished the original 1838–51 section of the hotel and rebuilt it using limestone from the east side of Entrance Bay. It became the Geological Museum. The museum remained until 1912, when a succession of government departments took over. It is now maintained — as is the bulk of the Sussex façade — by the National Capital Commission.

In 1874, Major's Hill was already established as a popular public park. That year it was declared the first park in Ottawa and renamed the Dominion Park by the Ottawa's City Council. In 1875 a flurry of improvements were made, including the infill of sunken areas and the building of a stone wall to prevent strollers from falling down the cliff. A glass pavilion was built, and many fountains, ornamental pools and pathways attracted visitors. In 1885 control of the park reverted to the federal government and the old name of Major's Hill was re-adopted.

The erection of the Parliament Buildings in 1865 led many to call for a ceremonial route to link Parliament with Rideau Hall. Lord and Lady Aberdeen raised the idea. In her diary, Lady Aberdeen's entry of November 19, 1898, reveals how the Vice Regal couple encouraged

View of Parliament Buildings from Major's Hill,
drawn by F. B. Schell, showing noonday gun.
From *Picturesque Canada* by G. M. Grant, 1882. NCC 172.

Prime Minister Sir Wilfred Laurier to develop a far-reaching 50-year vision for the city's future development. It was in this spirit that their successors, the Mintos, encouraged the construction of the iron and steel Minto Bridges across the Rideau River, in the hope that King Edward Avenue would become a grand boulevard. But King Edward abutted Rideau Street, and even in the late 1800s, this was a congested traffic area. The proposal was turned down. However, Laurier's Liberal government did establish the Ottawa Improvement Commission (OIC), the first of several commissions to grapple with the planning of the capital.

By 1867, Confederation year, the city was booming. Colonel By's grid layout of lots and his survey of arterial routes had made provision for grand boulevards, but these were out of step with the reality of the city's growth. Even then, expropriation, demolition, and other costly nightmares prevented By's grand scheme from being realized.

J.G. Ferland Grocery on Sussex Street, n.d.
City of Ottawa Archives, CA 0013.

Although many politicians and citizens since the Aberdeens have shared their dream of a ceremonial route to link Rideau Hall to Parliament, the road was never built. The issue continues to dog successive governments and city planners. Jacques Gréber's 1951 Master Plan recognized the need for such a route, as do current plans of the NCC. In 1992, the NCC developed Confederation Boulevard, a ceremonial route marked by special street signs featuring a red maple leaf. The boulevard forms a superb driving, biking, or walking circuit spanning the Ottawa River, joining Ottawa to Gatineau. Visitors pass the Peacekeeping Monument and the National Gallery on Sussex, the Parliament Buildings on Wellington and the Canadian Museum of Civilization in Gatineau. An offshoot of the ceremonial route links Rideau Hall to Parliament Hill via Sussex Street.

Since 1912 the federal government has increased its presence along Sussex Drive. The lovely old stone Chapel of Ease (St. John the Evangelist Church) opposite the Geological Museum burned in 1912. The government took over the site and started expropriation of all properties to the west on Sussex. A long wooden workshop extending from the Connaught Building to St. Patrick Street was erected for stonemasons employed on the rebuilding of Parliament after the 1916 fire on the Hill. It was soon demolished and the site is now occupied by the Embassy of the United States of America. During World War II, another series of "temporary buildings" were erected and thronged Sussex until 1979.

Between January 1961 and March 1962 the NCC expropriated most properties on the east side of Sussex from George Street north to St. Patrick — except those owned by religious institutions. This acquisition precipitated years of restoration and preservation, which have transformed Sussex into its present grand streetscape.

NEIGHBOURHOOD STYLES

The restoration of Sussex's façade resulted in its designation as a historic preservation district. High-rise development is controlled by strict zoning to conserve the heritage quality of Sussex Drive, since it is the façades that usually possess most heritage features. A striking example of these efforts in the 1960s and 1970s was the preservation of the free space surrounding the tall twin Gothic spires of Nôtre-Dame Basilica. Its silhouette dominates not only the Sussex skyline but also all of Lowertown West, reflecting the crucial importance of the Roman Catholic Church in the development of the city. Unfortunately, the corresponding silhouette of Christ Church Cathedral on Sparks Street is muted by the high-rise development behind it. It is all too rare for a city to preserve such open space as is enjoyed by the Basilica: too often other buildings encroach, and the original beauty of a structure is lost. Space itself is often not considered to be a "heritage element" ... but it is.

Sussex façade at corner of George prior to the NCC's 1960s heritage conservation and urban renewal project. (Note third storey on 541 Sussex is now gone, restoring Askwith's 1880 façade.) NCC, M. Newton file, H12-350.

The architectural styles visible on this walk vary dramatically, and many buildings along the Sussex and Mackenzie loop are noteworthy, especially Skead's British Hotel, the Gothic Revival spires of the Basilica and David Ewart's fortress-like triptych, the Connaught Building, the War Museum, and the Mint. The Italianate style features in many shop fronts along Sussex, whose arched arcades and horizontal stringcourses serve to decorate the streetscape. Balancing these heritage sites is the modern architectural vision of Moshe Safdie's National Gallery of Canada and the fortress of the US Embassy. Anchoring Sussex at Rideau is the châteauesque Château Laurier Hotel and the classical form of Union Station. This walk presents you with the capital's most richly varied built environment — as well, perhaps, as the most hotly debated streetscape, for the location of the US Embassy continues to rankle with many residents concerned about security issues.

WALK TIPS

🚶 5 km; 2 hours

The Sussex–Mackenzie loop is a grand introduction to the capital, for its many lookouts reveal other neighbourhoods you can explore later on. There are many public buildings to see and some, such as the National Gallery, deserve repeated visits. The gallery is of particular note because it houses the carefully reconstructed interior of the Rideau Street Convent Chapel.

THE WALK

Find George Street and walk due west to Sussex. Cross at the lights so you are on the west side of Sussex. This will allow you to look down Sussex's east façade.

Stop and turn around to face **541 Sussex**, Skead's old **British Hotel**, once the Geological Museum and today home to shops, galleries, and offices. Regularly spaced windows are framed by mouldings with a prominent central keystone. Sturdy wooden brackets support the cornice. A prominent horizontal stringcourse separating the first and second floors provides a continuum around the entire structure. The doorway has a large overhead fanlight (transom) with sidelights on either side. Corner quoins in raised cut stone further enhance this grand old building. At the rear are courtyards where guests' horses, wagons, and carriages were once stabled. Today, restaurant patios occupy this sheltered, pretty space.

George Street is wide at its junction with Sussex. In the middle of George Street there used to be a popular public well, which was first opened in 1840; a pump and cover were installed three years later. In 1893 the Aberdeens donated a watering trough, visible in many old photographs of this corner.

Looking north along Sussex from George. Note the horse trough donated by the Aberdeens in 1893. NCC 172-175.

Turn around on Sussex and head north, staying on the west side of the street so that you can view the restored brick and limestone buildings extending as far as the twin spires of Nôtre-Dame Basilica, at St. Patrick Street. At York, pause to note the broad sweep of the York Street Stairs, inaugurated in 1999. Look right, due east, down this market street designed by Colonel By. A fountain was placed here on Canada Day July 1, 2000 and in the summertime, children splash about in its cool waters.

Find **489 Sussex**, the former **Institut Jeanne d'Arc**, at the corner of Sussex and York streets. The nuns vacated the premises in 1990 ending a century's tenure. The sisters were well known for their needlework and lace weaving in addition to their good works of charity and teaching. They once owned the block between York and Clarence. The oldest building is at the northern end of this block (now 481–471 Sussex), was built for Colonel Joseph Aumond in 1849 as the **Revere Hotel**. Starting in 1919, over a few years the nuns purchased all five buildings in this entire block for a women's residence. The three to the south are of limestone; the two to the north are yellow brick. Look for the joinery distinguished by stone quoins, projecting firewalls and changes in roof level. The NCC restored the façades of these buildings in the mid 1990s and today all serve as shops with apartments overhead.

Now you are standing beside the **United States Embassy** (1999). Despite the architect's incorporation of a central "cupola-like" tower that mimics the glass tower of the National Gallery (seen later on this walk) and the Parliamentary Library (see Parliament walk), this battleship-like building unapologetically attempts to dominates the streetscape. Many residents and businesspeople opposed the erection of this building here, so close to other national buildings and the popular Byward Market, because of concerns over terrorist attack. Such objections proved reasonable: following the destruction of the World Trade Center in New York City, the Americans have insisted on blockading the foot of Clarence Street, and concrete traffic controls jut out into Sussex, impeding traffic flow.

Between Clarence and Murray is **449 Sussex**, formerly the **Castor Hotel**. In days gone by, when illiteracy was far more prevalent, businesses depended upon visual aids as references. A carved wooden beaver ("castor" is French for "beaver") was once displayed here. Originally built around 1865 for François-Xavier Lapierre, the hotel became the property of Edmond Chevrier in 1877. For years it was Monette's barbershop, sporting the gay red, white and blue striped column announcing his trade. The NCC rebuilt the present brick building in 1978 after the original design featuring a steeply pitched roof with dormer windows. Iron guardrails march around the edge of the roofs to thwart cascades of snow from falling on passersby. Sometimes, in winter, you can see cleaners dressed like mountaineers, connected by ropes to the roof while they free the rails of dangerous accumulations of snow and ice. They add an odd type of above-sidewalk "street theatre" to a Canadian winter's day.

As you approach the corner of Murray and Sussex, look for the Italianate form of **419 Sussex**. Pause to note its polychromatic façade.

Slightly projecting verticals of yellow brick pilasters, which resemble stylized columns, contrast prettily with red brick walls. The ground floor arched arcade is echoed on the second and third floors by prominent window mouldings. The second-storey windows are framed by stone mouldings, while those on the third storey are brick. Tying the composition together are strong horizontal bands of stringcourses. The result lends a playful look to the streetscape. At the southeast corner, partially hidden by trees, you can find a statue of a bronze angel playing a trumpet. Behind it is Beaux-arts Court.

View from Peace Tower of National Gallery, with Major's Hill Park,
Nôtre-Dame Basilica and old City Hall in distance. 2002.
E. Fletcher.

Now look directly ahead to the Peacekeeping Monument. Built in 1992, the design allows you to enter its wide V to experience this celebration of Canada's internationally renowned peacekeeping efforts.

Cross St. Patrick Street, staying on the left (west) side of Sussex so you can look at the Basilica from a distance.

The towering twin spires of **Nôtre-Dame Basilica** balance Safdie's modern gem the National Gallery. Look carefully at its spires, the narrow lancet windows below them and the tracery detail in the central pointed-arched and decorated window. Surprisingly, this French Gothic Revival style is not evident on the ground floor, which sports a solid, classical, round-headed central doorway flanked by two smaller ones. The prominent entablature over the main entrance is also a distinctive classical feature. There is a reason for this juxtaposition of styles. A small wooden church was built on Nôtre-Dame's site in 1832 to serve the Catholic community of Bytown. As the town prospered, so did the parish, and the modest structure became insufficient for its needs. In 1839, Father Cannon designed a new church in the solid classical design. Antoine Robillard, a local contractor, started building in 1841. Work proceeded slowly, and in 1844 Father Pierre-Adrien Telmon replaced Father Cannon. Nôtre-Dame not only received a new architect, but also a new style, as Telmon was enthusiastic about the Gothic Revival style sweeping France at that time. The classical and Gothic styles are completely different, yet have been successfully combined such that the sturdy classical base effectively supports the Basilica's triumphant spires.

Detail in stone façade of Archbishop's palace depicts
Virgin and infant Jesus. 2002. K. Fletcher.

Now cross Sussex Street at the traffic lights at St. Patrick to see the Basilica close up. Unlike the other buildings on Sussex, Nôtre-Dame is set well back from the sidewalk, providing a grand recessed approach for its many ceremonial functions. Construction progressed for years: the twin spires were built in 1858; in 1862 the polygonal apse and the choir were added; in 1866 a wooden statue of the Virgin and baby Jesus was positioned atop the central peaked gable fronting Sussex, between the spires. Carved by an unknown European sculptor, he apparently received enough money from the commission to purchase his ticket home.

Enter the Basilica to discover serenity from the bustle of Sussex traffic and to view the highly decorative wooden interior which workers commenced carving in 1878. Here you'll find master sculptor Louis-Phillipe Hébert's thirty life-size images of the saints, including those of the Virgin and St. Joseph at the main altar. In the sanctuary are sixty mahogany stalls. Local gilder and woodcarver Flavien Rochon worked alongside Hébert and the woodworker Philippe Pariseau, executing the exquisite interior. Now return outside.

It's worth the short walk down St. Patrick to look at the southern face of Nôtre-Dame. The first projecting extension is a side porch entryway. Its twin is on the north face of the church. Both were built in 1897.

Further down the north side of the street is **143 St. Patrick**, the **Archbishop's Palace**, linked to the Basilica by a wall enclosing a private rear garden, a later addition. Built 1849–50 the Palace is attributed to architect Father Dandurand. It contained dormitories, church offices, and reception rooms. The Palace was originally the private residence for Bishop Guigues, who had been consecrated as bishop earlier that year. He moved here from the Donnelly House on Sussex in May 1850.

The Palace features a grand doorway embellished by finely detailed ironwork. Heavy iron chains suspend an overhanging canopy. The mansard roof — one of the first of its kind in Canada — features evenly spaced dormers. The eye is drawn upward by two "false-front" parapet gables projecting from the roofline. These are balanced by oriel windows on either side of the doorway. The NCC purchased and restored the Palace in the early 1970s, after it had fallen into disrepair.

Before returning to Sussex, view the two lovingly restored Lowertown houses directly opposite the Palace.

142 St. Patrick, Valade House. 2002. K. Fletcher.

Number **142 St. Patrick**, **Valade House**, sports an outstanding example of Lowertown's "cliffhanger," or second-storey cantilevered porches, supported by sturdy wooden brackets. It replaces the original balcony, which featured the initials of its owner, Dr. François-Xavier Valade, over its central peak. The fine stone house with its offset front door was built around 1865, and the doctor used it as both home and office until his death in 1916. The home is connected to its eastern neighbour by a carriageway that once led to a rear stable.

Number **138 St. Patrick**, **Rochon House**, built in 1832, is the former home of Flavien Rochon, master carver of the interior sanctuary stalls of Nôtre-Dame. He lived here from 1853–97. The house is typical of 1840s workers' houses once common in Lowertown. Although many have suffered the horrors of modern "improvements" such as angelstone cladding and aluminum siding, you can still find examples of well-restored wooden homes if you explore Lowertown proper.

Rochon House was originally a simple rectilinear design with a central living room and kitchen and sleeping quarters upstairs. The back addition was put on between 1851 and 1878, causing the removal of rear dormers. The addition contained a new kitchen, giving extra living space at the front.

Leave St. Patrick's Street for later exploration (see Lowertown walk) and rejoin Sussex. Turn right (north) and proceed past the Basilica to **373 Sussex** on the corner of Guigues. Once the **Champagne Hotel**, then the **LaSalle Academy**, the building now houses the offices of the Canadian Centre for Management Development. Built in 1852 as the Collège de Bytown, founded by the Oblate Fathers, this is the cradle of today's University of Ottawa. By 1856 these premises were bursting at the seams, and the school moved to land donated by Sandy Hill's landowner, Louis Théodore Besserer, at the corner of Wilbrod and Cumberland. The building here on Sussex became the Champagne Hotel, later used as military barracks for the 100th Regiment at the time of the Fenian threats in the mid 1860s. The hotel was well situated, being the closest to the MacTaggart Street Railway station.

Originally the building had a deeply recessed central doorway with two balconies. This feature was filled in by the Christian brothers, who purchased the hotel in the 1870s for a parish school, which they named the LaSalle Academy in 1888. Today's prominent cupola perched upon the mansard roof was erected in 1974, replacing a series of such adornments whose last version had been removed in 1913.

Next door is **365 Sussex**, the **Donnelly House**. Built in 1844 by Irishman Thomas Donnelly as his private residence, it is a classically inspired limestone townhouse. Notice the raised end gables, a feature intended to retard the spread of fire from one wood frame roofline to another. Bishop Guigues rented the home from Donnelly while his palace at Nôtre-Dame was being built.

Over the years the house suffered many alterations which ended up nearly destroying it. In 1974 architect John Leaning was hired to restore this picturesque residence. Note the pretty transom window above the door, an elliptical Adamesque fanlight that allows light into the interior hall.

On the opposite side of Sussex find **300–350 Sussex**, the **Canadian War Museum**, designed by David Ewart. Built 1904–07 to house the Dominion Archives of Canada, the function of the building possibly dictated Ewart's choice of the sturdy Elizabethan style. Here the style is characterized by a horizontal massing, accentuated by dominant stringcourses (longitudinal bands) between storeys, projecting symmetrical bays and evenly spaced windows. These windows are croisette, having stone mullions (vertical) and transoms (horizontal) —

both typical Elizabethan features. The main entry is set in a projecting
bay tower. The building's design speaks of solid grandeur, befitting its
incarnations as national archives and war museum. The wing on the
left by Band, Burritt, Meredith, and Ewart was added in 1924. It
integrates fairly well, but lacks the detail of Ewart's original design.

365 Sussex, Donnelly House. 2002. K. Fletcher.

Continue north on Sussex. At the southeast corner of Sussex and
Bruyère is the **Embassy of the State of Kuwait** (new in 2003). Its
grey stone façade allows its complex massing of forms to somewhat
integrate into the streetscape of heritage buildings such as the Bruyère
complex next door.

On the northeast corner, across from this embassy, find the **Mother
House of the Grey Nuns (the Sisters of Charity)**, founded in 1845
by Mère Elisabeth Bruyère. The south wing of the convent was built
in 1849 by the same Antoine Robillard who built the classical base of
Nôtre-Dame. The northern wing, on the corner of Sussex and Cathcart,
came later, built as St. Joseph's Orphanage in 1866. A recessed addition,
built in 1885, connects the first two buildings. The 1930s witnessed
the unfortunate removal of the original hipped, tin-plate roof. A fourth

storey was added at this time. A low wall fronts the convent on Bruyère and is continued north along Sussex to screen the gardens from public view. This section of the wall was repointed and stabilized in 1992.

See whether you can enter the Mother House (corner Bruyère and Sussex streets) to visit a small museum located in the basement showcasing Mère Elisabeth Bruyère's substantial contributions to Bytown. Also, ask if you can visit the small chapel dedicated to her memory: an urn here is said to contain her heart. Further down the quiet corridor you also may be able to visit the chapel architect W. E. Noffke designed for the sisters.

On the southwest corner of the Mother House (at Bruyère and Sussex streets) look up to find the **sundial**. Built in 1851, it is the City of Ottawa's oldest timepiece.

Across from the Mother House is **320 Sussex**, the **Royal Canadian Mint**, architect David Ewart's 1905–08 castellated masterpiece. Resembling a fortress, it assures onlookers that the nation's currency is well protected. In the 1980s it was dismantled, its stones numbered, and was carefully rebuilt to accommodate a major interior refurbishing. The Mint's buttressed walls look like battlements and sport turrets

David Ewart's Royal Canadian Mint, 1905.
NCC, M. Newton file, H12-138.

complete with slits for imaginary archers. Its Elizabethan styling includes box-shaped label mouldings surrounding the windows in a completely different fashion than the curved Italianate mouldings that framed the windows of 419 Sussex.

Continue on Sussex as it curves to the east, passing Cathcart Street. At the corner is a large brick residence, followed by a small apartment building and single house. They are of note as the only remaining residences along this entire stretch of Sussex Drive. Proceed to Boteler Street, following the curve of Sussex, and cross over to what is now the north, or Ottawa River side, of the street. Turn left (west) to follow the curve back to **Lady Grey Drive**.

This drive descends to the river. An early Bytown road, it was extended by the OIC as a possible link between Parliament and Rideau Hall — the extension was an unpopular failure. Steamship wharves once lined this stretch of the waterfront. First built by Colonel By in 1827 to receive supplies needed by his Royal Engineers to build the Rideau Canal, the docks were closed in 1901 when the Alexandra Bridge (also known as the Interprovincial Bridge) was built. At the end of Lady Grey Drive, climb the staircase on your left, which leads to the Curatorial Wing of the National Gallery. At the top you can see the rear of Ewart's Canadian War Museum with its English Tudor rose and French fleur-de-lis motifs carved in the stone.

Turn to your right and follow the passageway between the wings of the National Gallery to **Nepean Point**. Up the grassy slope find the rather obscure lookout point directly to your right, at the end of the gallery, which overlooks Lady Grey Drive and the Ottawa River. From here there is a superb eastern view of the large span of the **Macdonald-Cartier Bridge**, named after the two politicians most dedicated to Confederation. It is the largest box girder bridge in Canada, built 1963–65.

Just beyond it lies **Earnscliffe**, which you can identify by its white bargeboard (gingerbread) trim beneath a steeply pitched, gabled roof. Today its Union Jack flag claims it as the residence of the United Kingdom's High Commissioner. The 1857 English Gothic cottage, built for canal contractor Thomas MacKay's daughter Annie and his son-in-law, John MacKinnon, was Sir John A. Macdonald's last home. He died here in 1891. Sarah Grimason, one of the prime minister's Kingston constituents, was a visitor to Earnscliffe in 1889. Her letter describes the Macdonald residence: "They do have a lovely place all their own, down by the Rye-do. The house has a lovely slate roof like they have in England, and beautiful grounds and a man to wait on the dure [sic: door]. Lady Macdonald keeps her own cow and hins [sic: hens] and they make their own butter. ... They have two fine cows and six servants."[7]

Beyond Earnscliffe lie the National Research Council and the French Embassy, bordering Rideau Falls. You can also see the horizontal layers of red precast concrete and smoked glass of the **Lester B. Pearson Building (External Affairs)** on the south side of Sussex.

Now turn left and, keeping the cliff edge with its iron fence on your right, climb the hill to the promontory overlooking the western section of the Ottawa River. From here you can see the **Portage Bridge** in the distance, linking Ottawa to the **Place du Portage** complex in Gatineau, named for the old portage around the Chaudière Falls used by the Algonquin, Huron, and Iroquois peoples. Beyond it are the falls, bridge, and mills of the Chaudière. Once the falls were harnessed for their generating power, Lowertown's markets and the New Edinburgh mills gave way to an emerging, increasingly prominent Centretown development. By the 1880s and into the early 1900s, the Chaudière was producing millions of board feet of sawn lumber and employing about 300 men. Lumber was stacked in huge piles that became the tinder for the fire of 1900.

View of Nepean Point from Peace Tower, 1948.
NCC, M. Newton file L-12-001, Box 54.

On the Gatineau side of the river are the dramatically sinuous curves of Douglas Cardinal's **Canadian Museum of Civilization** (1989). Cardinal's building is, as he has said, "of nature." Its flowing lines not only echo the rolling Gatineau Hills in the background, but also the swirling eddies and currents of the Ottawa River. Similarly, its multi-layered storeys effectively mimic the cliffs of the Hill and Nepean Point on the Ontario side. Its design is reminiscent of Frank Lloyd Wright's organic style of architecture. However, Cardinal's aboriginal heritage is also at work here. Despite its striking contrast in style, Cardinal's museum is a fitting companion to its architectural mates, the National Gallery and the Parliament Buildings. It is the crowning jewel of the Gatineau side of the NCC's Confederation Boulevard.

Below you are the cantilevered spans of the **Alexandra Bridge** built in 1900 by the Dominion Bridge Company of Montreal, which also built the Chaudière Bridge in 1914. The Alexandra was built to accommodate two railways: the Pontiac and Pacific Junction (affectionately known as the "Push, Pull, and Jerk") and the Gatineau Railway. The former linked the capital with Pontiac County, west of Gatineau; the latter ran from Ottawa to Wakefield and Maniwaki. The left side of the bridge is a generous boardwalk of wooden planks, and in the early 1990s the NCC constructed a lookout with interpretive signs that's worth a visit. The railway tracks were removed in 1967.

Now descend the hill towards the National Gallery. You pass by a statue of Champlain by Canadian sculptor Hamilton MacCarthy. The sculpture originally included a crouching Anishanabe scout, but complaints by First Nations people caused its removal in the mid 1990s. Champlain is depicted holding (upside down!) an astrolabe, which he later lost about sixty kilometres west of here during his 1613 expedition. The original astrolabe is presently located in the Canadian Museum of Civilization, which you just spied, in Gatineau.

Proceed past architect John Leaning's **Astrolabe Theatre** built in Canada's Centennial year, 1967. Popular open-air concerts still entertain visitors. On your right is one of the most beautiful panorama vistas of the Parliament Buildings the city has to offer. Continue walking east towards the National Gallery, keeping to the immediate right of its main building.

The **National Gallery of Canada**, which opened in 1988, is a must-see. Its foyer is a glass-topped tower, featuring triangular "sails" of cloth which assist in temperature control of the building and reflect natural light. The foyer leads to the ramped colonnade, whose magnificent glass windows overlook Parliament Hill. Architect Moshe Safdie has designed the building so that the public spaces wrap around the galleries.

In true postmodernist style, Safdie reinterprets traditional design elements to create a structure that attempts to integrate itself into the historical streetscape of Sussex Drive. The polygonal "crystal" tower over the main foyer, for example, is a modern rendering of the Gothic Chapter House of Thomas Fuller and Chilion Jones's Parliamentary Library. Stylized flying buttresses along the Gallery's southern façade continue this motif.

Rideau Street Convent c. 1888, now rebuilt inside Moshe Safdie's National Gallery. NCC 172.

The Gallery is of special heritage interest because it is home to the interior of the **Chapel of the Rideau Street Convent of Our Lady of the Sacred Heart**, commissioned by the Sisters of Charity and built 1887–88. Its incorporation into the gallery is appropriate, for originally it was built inside a popular pre-Confederation hotel on the corner of Waller and Rideau. Public opposition to its demolition was among the most heated ever in Ottawa. The convent's defenders lost their battle, but compromise was reached by carefully reassembling the chapel in the gallery. Of particular importance are its cast iron pillars, which support the painted wood fan-vaulted ceiling. The pillars represent state-of-the-art European technology of the day. The delicate surface paintwork on these pillars is a wonderful *trompe-l'oeil* for they integrate perfectly with the painted wood.

Outside the gallery, turn right (south) on Sussex, as it curves right onto Mackenzie, and enter the shaded, grassy pathways of **Major's Hill Park**. The first public park in Ottawa, created in 1875, it has been continually altered, and today its pathways are well lit urban spaces after nightfall. It's the popular location for many Ottawa festivals, and a good spot from which to view the Canada Day fireworks. These days, it is a repository of many historical artifacts and interpretive signs.

Continue walking west until you arrive at the cliffs overlooking Entrance Bay, the eight locks, the former Commissariat (Bytown Museum) and Parliament Buildings.

Included among the several historic features in Major's Hill Park is the ruin of a house foundation that has been extremely well interpreted by the NCC. First Colonel By and then Major Bolton — after whom the park is named — lived here. The home, described as a rubble stone dwelling, featured a wraparound verandah from which to enjoy the spectacular view. To its south also find a statue of Lieutenant-Colonel By, forever surveying his Entrance Bay locks. Behind him, note the monument to the canal-building era.

You are now viewing the rear of the **Château Laurier Hotel**, best viewed from its front elevation at Rideau Street. The original section was built from 1908–12 by architects Ross and MacFarlane, in the châteauesque (Château) style which had become extremely popular specifically for railway hotels across Canada.

As you approach the hotel, imagine the mile-long toboggan slide that was erected here in 1922, then one of Ottawa's most popular winter tourist attractions. Old photographs located inside the hotel, near the gift shop, depict not only toboggans full of people hurtling

Château Laurier Hotel from Commissariat Building
at full moon, n.d. NCC 172-598.

down the slide's surface, but also a skier or two. Also in this gallery of
old photographs, you'll find Charles Melville Hays, the General Manager
of the Grand Trunk Railway, who was one of the promoters of this
hotel. Hays perished on the Titanic.

Follow the paved path south from Major's Hill Park onto Château
property, where an enormous "balustrading" of cut, shaped stone permits
you to view the Entrance Bay locks below. As you proceed south, you
pass alongside the Canadian Museum of Contemporary Photography,
then ascend a flight of steep steps to Wellington Street.

For the moment, turn right on Wellington and walk just a few paces onto the bridge to gaze back at the **Canadian Museum of Contemporary Photography**, which opened in 1992. The limestone used in its sheer walls was specially ordered from Indiana to match the Château Laurier. The design integrates with the sidewalk level of the street and closely resembles an underground subway, providing a historical link to the old railway hotel and Union Station. From the bridge, note the rhythmic pattern of arches on the museum's western face above the canal entry locks. These successfully echo the hotel's parking lot entryways. The balustraded railing along the top of the museum and the globe lights further lighten its façade.

Now face southeast, to look opposite the Château, towards **Union Station**, built in 1912 for the Grand Trunk Railway. For years it has served as the **Government Conference Centre**. Bradford Lee Gilbert was the original architect of Union Station, although the firm of Ross and MacFarlane took over when Gilbert was dismissed, making many changes to his original design.

The classical proportions and stately columns of the former station are an inspiring finale to the southern foot of Sussex Drive — yet it barely survived demolition in 1965. In 1966 the rail tracks were torn up, the terminus and rails removed to their current Alta Vista location, and in 1967 the once-proud station started a new life as the Centennial Centre and subsequently the Government Conference Centre. Today its future is undecided: it may become a Museum of Canadian Politics but apparently will not be a Canadian Sports Hall of Fame ... Whatever its ultimate function is to be, this is a beaux arts gem in the capital. (Go inside and explore it if at all possible.)

Monumental Doric columns and a prominent triangular pediment are characteristic of the classical style. Look up to the top attic windows above the heavy cornice: their understated placement successfully lightens the massive presence of Union Station. The incongruous canopy suspended by huge chains over the main doorway on Rideau Street compromises the classical strength of the building.

Now turn right and walk to the Château Laurier and take a close look at the hotel towering above you like a fairy tale castle.

The selection of an architect for the Château Laurier is shrouded in intrigue. Sensibly, Boston-born Bradford Lee Gilbert got the job of designing both the railway station and railway hotel. However, he was dismissed in 1908 despite Cabinet approval of his design a year earlier. The Montreal firm of Ross and MacFarlane adapted his plan to the châteauesque design before you.

The strong vertical massing, typical of châteauesque buildings, is accentuated here by its sheer sandstone walls, which are relatively unadorned until the top (attic) floors. The steeply pitched copper roofline lends the hotel its most dramatic châteauesque feature. But two other motifs emphasize the castle imagery. Note the projecting corbel beneath the attic (top) storey, which suddenly breaks the otherwise sheer walls of the hotel. Let your eye rise up the walls to note the crenellation atop the towers and parapets. On a real castle, it is this battlement feature that allowed archers to aim their bows and shoot arrows at their enemies.

Look for the projecting wall dormers that rise above the top floor and which punctuate the copper roofline. These projections are decorated by crockets that march down either side of their steep sides, and their peaks are topped with finials that carry your eye "into the sky." The castle-like atmosphere is enhanced by the corner tourelles, small towers that sport narrow slit windows as if for medieval archers.

Included in the design for the Château was an underground tunnel linking the railway hotel to its *raison d'être*, Union Station. Despite a

Union Station, the present Government Conference Centre, under construction, 1912. NCC, 172-149.

storm of controversy, created by those who thought a tunnel would attract vagrants and pickpockets the underground link was built — a tremendous convenience for disembarking passengers and, today, for beleaguered politicians. Interestingly, a network of underground tunnels reportedly links the hotel with Parliament Hill.

On 20 May 1920 the first radio broadcast to transmit the human voice over one hundred miles was sent from the Château, an event that apparently attracted immense crowds here. A private radio station was set up inside the hotel; it later incorporated into the Canadian Broadcasting Corporation in 1936. Since that time, CBC Radio and Radio Canada have operated from here. However, these "historic" offices will move to a brand new facility by 2005.

Enter this charming old hotel to view its ornately carved wooden panelling in the front foyer, which also is home to a marble bust of the hotel's namesake, Sir Wilfrid Laurier. Ask directions to the basement swimming pool — an art deco delight. A 1911 tourist guide proclaimed the hotel's advantages: "The corridors are divided into sections by means of fire doors to separate them in an emergency, although the hotel is absolutely fireproof, no wood, except frames for doors and baseboards, being used in its construction. The main corridors lead directly to fire escapes, iron balconies and stairways inside the building. All the windows and service floors will be screened with the best Canadian-made fly screens, and a special refrigerating room will be provided to freeze the garbage until it is removed from the building."[8]

From the lobby, turn right and down the stairs to exit via the east doors onto Mackenzie. Note the new building directly opposite across the street, on the corner of Mackenzie and Wellington (its street address will be 700 Sussex). At time of writing this combination condo and commercial property was merely a hole in the ground, however it promises to be a nine-storey edifice whose height will approximate that of the Connaught, next door.

Now turn north on Mackenzie towards the Department of Revenue's **Connaught Building,** David Ewart's third proud, fortress-like government edifice on Sussex. Built 1913–14 while Ewart was chief architect of the Department of Public Works, it is a successful complement to his Mint and War Museum. (See Sandy Hill walk to view Ewart's completely different design for his own home.) Of all his Ottawa designs, Ewart thought this to be the best.

The massing of the Connaught Building is in the fortress style of a Scottish baronial castle. Ewart softens the overall effect by such touches

Connaught Building, named after the Duke of Connaught,
Governor General from 1911–16. PAC-PA-43766.

as Tudor arched windows with Gothic tracery over the entrances.
These, in combination with other features such as multi-storey bay
windows with balconies and narrow, pointed lancet windows in the
turrets of the centre tower, lighten the façade.

Walk past the Connaught Building to descend the York Street
Staircase, a grand series of steps leading down to York Street. The
Embassy of the United States of America is to your left; Major's Hill
Park behind you. At Sussex, turn right and voilà, you're back at the
start of your tour.

Lowertown

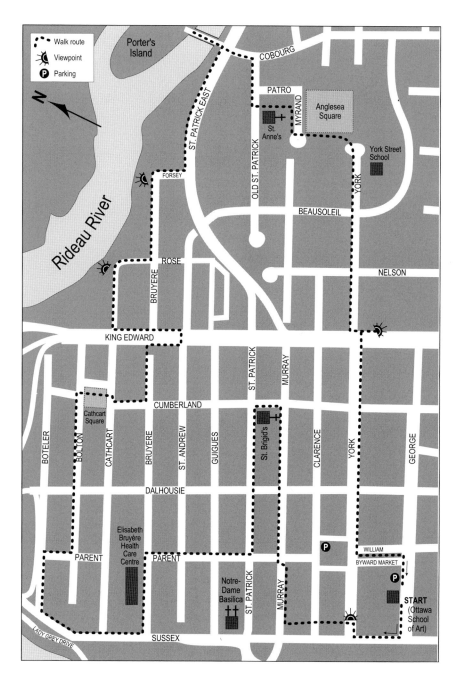

Legend:
- Walk route
- Viewpoint
- P Parking

Porter's Island

N

Rideau River

ST. PATRICK EAST

FORSEY

BRUYERE

ROSE

KING EDWARD

BOTELER

BOLTON

CATHCART

Cathcart Square

CUMBERLAND

BRUYERE

ST. ANDREW

GUIGUES

DALHOUSIE

PARENT

Elisabeth Bruyère Health Care Centre

PARENT

LADY GREY DRIVE

SUSSEX

Notre-Dame Basilica

ST. PATRICK

MURRAY

ST. PATRICK

St. Brigid's

CLARENCE

YORK

GEORGE

WILLIAM

BYWARD MARKET

P

P

START (Ottawa School of Art)

COBOURG

PATRO

MYRAND

Anglesea Square

St. Anne's

OLD ST. PATRICK

York Street School

BEAUSOLEIL

YORK

NELSON

Lowertown was originally an almost impenetrable cedar swamp. By 1827 Colonel By had had the area surveyed and had handed out the first lots to civil servants. At the same time he reserved land for a wide street (George Street) under which the Bywash — an outflow of the Rideau Canal — would pass. Once drained, these lands were quickly settled and log cabins and other wooden buildings were erected. Until the Vesting Act of 1844 was passed, land speculation was rife in Lowertown, rents to the Crown varied unfairly, and there was little incentive to build more permanent dwellings. Its earliest inhabitants were labourers on the Rideau Canal, shantymen and rivermen — and their families.

The bustle of York Street, c. 1902. On the left side is the Grant Building, 1901, with "Joseph Grant, Grocer" painted on its brick wall. Also, with its dormers piercing the third storey is 41 York, the St. Louis Hotel. The first building on the right is 18 York, then the Institut canadien-français, and farther along, the Lafayette House built 1849–50. NCC, M. Newton file H12-716, Box 43

A look at the reality of life for these workers perhaps explains Lowertown's rowdy reputation. Canal workers were unemployed during the winter months, and shantymen were idle in summer. Without welfare or other means of support they eked out a living in Lowertown. The fate of a widowed woman with children was appalling: if her husband died — or was maimed on the job — she had little choice but to turn to prostitution as a means of support. And so the rhythm of Lowertown established itself in its formative years.

In its earliest years, Lowertown was a boisterous, unlawful part of Bytown, bounded by Besserer's Sandy Hill estate to the south; the Ordnance Lands (reserve "O") extending to Rideau Falls to the northeast; Major's Hill, Barracks Hill and the Canal Reserve to the west, and Nicholas Sparks' land (Uppertown) south of Wellington. Unease in the settlement festered in 1832, 1834, and again in 1847 with the influx of desperately ill Irish immigrants. These were the years of typhus and cholera, sicknesses that ravaged Bytown's populations.

Workers at 13–15 Clarence St., A. Thibert, Carriage Builder, 1914.
NCC, M. Newton file, H12–184.

The Grey Nuns came to Lowertown from Montreal in 1845 to minister to its poor and sick residents. The pitiful state of the Irish immigrants, who arrived early in 1847 famine-weary and full of typhus, generated an outpouring of concern and care. The nuns organized doctors and ministers of all denominations and arranged for the building of shelters for the sick and dying. The Immigrant Hospital was located near the Grey Nuns' residence on Bruyère at Sussex. After the epidemic, no one wanted to buy or to reside in it, so great was the fear of contagion.

Just as the Irish vied with the French-Canadians for employment, so did educated and moneyed residents of Uppertown vie with the rapidly expanding population of Lowertown. Arguments raged over the location of the city hall, post office, and market. The 1836 brawls between Irish Shiners and their French counterparts, such as legendary hero Joseph Montferrand, were echoed by the struggles for power of the upper and middle class politicians and businessmen.

For economic reasons, situating the market between George and York streets was critical. First water transportation routes, then rail (thanks to the Bytown and Prescott Railway Station on McTaggart Street (1854)), gave Lowertown an edge.

Uppertown residents looked askance at booming Lowertown and fretted that this upstart group would dominate their traditional power base. Politically the two groups were adversaries: Uppertown was a Tory Protestant stronghold, Lowertown was the dominion of the Reformers. In September 1849, Bytown was rocked by civil insurgence pitting Tory against Reformer in the September 1849 insurrection called Stoney Monday. A stone-throwing mêlée, complete with gunshots, in Market Square left twenty-nine men injured and one man dead. The next Wednesday saw further insurrection. A thousand Reformers armed with canon and firearms from Philemon Wright's Hull armoury faced 1,700 Tories similarly fortified. Between them, on the Sappers Bridge, stood a military attachment from Barracks Hill. Reason prevailed, no battle ensued, and the day ended peacefully.

After the incorporation of Bytown in 1850, Lowertown was dealt several blows that shifted most of the activity and commerce of its bustling market and attractive Sussex promenade of shops to Uppertown. The harnessing of the Chaudière Falls was one factor. The second was Queen Victoria's choice of Ottawa as capital, and the subsequent decision to locate the Parliament Buildings on Barracks Hill. Uppertown gained prominence as businesses vied for addresses adjacent to the seat of power.

Lowertown peddler with horse-drawn cart and children,
corner of Water (Bruyère) and Dalhousie, n.d.
City of Ottawa Archives, CA 1320.

But Lowertown did continue to grow and prosper. Today its colourful farmer's market, and its varied streetscape of shops, public buildings, and residences give Lowertown a vibrant life all its own.

"Sir, — If we want to have a nice town we must pass a by-law to prevent people building those one and two storey shanties as on Rideau Street, near Dalhousie. I think it a disgrace to have such buildings in our town. In future let them do better and go out to the bush and build their shanties for the owls to see."[9]

So wrote "lover of architecture" John Pink in 1888. He would be surprised to learn his concerns are echoed in the Lowertown of the 2000s. Ottawa's oldest section of town still arouses hearty debate as property owners, developers and politicians struggle with issues such as density, height restrictions and heritage conservation.

York St. looking east from Sussex, October 1991. Compare with the c. 1902 photo of York St. on p. 104: all buildings remain.
K. Fletcher.

Until the Vesting Act of 1844, which released Ordnance land to private ownership, buildings of any permanence were rare. Stone represented wealth and permanence — both features being strangers to many Lowertown residents. Only on Sussex Drive, Lowertown's western boundary, were the buildings quite grand from an early date: the Basilica was started in 1841, the Bruyère Hospital in 1849. (See Sussex walk).

Then, on May 10, 1860, a new city by-law prohibited the building of wooden structures in designated parts of Ottawa, notably opposite the Parliament Buildings and also in Lowertown, along Sussex, York, and George Streets. The old log and frame homes were eventually replaced or were clad with brick, pressed tin, angelstone, and, eventually, aluminum siding as technology and residents' means improved.

WALK TIPS

🚶 **6 km; 4 hours**

This is a long walk introducing you to both Lowertown East and West. Many public buildings can be explored both inside and out — a great benefit on cold or wet days. The market is fun to explore: there's a lot to see and do and many a street corner offers much for the eyes, ears, and stomach to feast upon. (Detailed descriptions of the Sussex façade, Nôtre-Dame Basilica, the Donnelly House, and LaSalle Academy are given in the Sussex walk. However, because their influence dominates Lowertown, they are briefly mentioned here.)

THE WALK

Start your walk in the Byward Market, on George Street. There is ample parking in the area.

Number **35 George Street**, the **Ottawa School of Art**, directly across from The Bay, is our first building of note. Built in 1907, this rough-cut limestone Romanesque Revival building originally housed the Ottawa Wine Vault Company. Its rounded arched windows set between pilasters form a sturdy ground floor arcade. (Next door immediately to the west lay underground wine vaults — I'm told all the bottles and vats have been long since removed!) Although this space was a parking lot for years, in 2002 a heritage wall complete with arches was removed and a new building (Librarie du Soleil) erected.

Stand back to appreciate how the School of Art's façade is lightened at each storey. This is achieved by a vertical progression from three

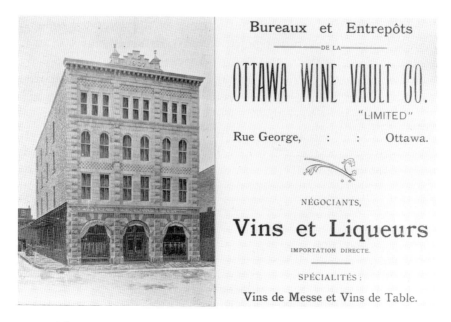

Advertisement with date 1907 visible on the parapet front gable.
Note wooden wine casks on the left. NCC 172-375.

large, arched storefront windows to paired windows on the second and third floors, to groups of three on the fourth. The column-like pilasters emphasize the building's verticality even more, while stone horizontal stringcourses bind the composition together. In 1983 it became the Ottawa School of Art's new home. The school is often open, so you may be able to view its much-altered interior and its original stone walls, still exposed in the stairwell.

Outside, proceed west on George Street a few steps. Find the walkway and steps descending to a cobblestone courtyard, built around 1865. This is **Clarendon Court**, which takes its name from the early hotel (whose precursor was the British Hotel, see Sussex walk). The courtyards are an important heritage feature of Lowertown, relics of the day when horses and wagons needed both stabling and rear access to businesses fronting the street. Today the tidy courtyard is peppered with art, benches, and cafés, a reprieve from the hustle-bustle of the street.

Retrace your steps onto George, then turn right (north) onto Sussex Drive. Walk up to York Street and view the York Street Millennium Fountain, installed on this broad market street on August 11, 2000.

Before leaving Sussex, note the Embassy of the United States of America immediately to the north of the York Street Stairs, located on the west side of York.

Now, locate **12 York**. Its red brick façade forms an arcade sheltering a glass-enclosed office with rounded corners on the ground floor.

Next door is **18 York** (1876), once the **Institut canadien-français**, then the **Château Cheese Factory**. It suffered devastating fires in 1880, 1887, and most recently in 1970, when only the exterior limestone façade was saved. Today the property is owned by the NCC. *The Ottawa Citizen* of October 6, 1876, reported that it had six lofty meeting rooms in its basement, one of which held 400 people. Above it was a hall, which had seating for 1,000. The Institut leased rooms to theatre companies, and even circuses performed inside its walls. In 1889, after the second fire, George Matthews bought the building for $2,850 and rebuilt the interior to accommodate a pork packing plant.

George Matthew's Pork Packing Establishment at 18 York in 1892; next door is a blacksmith, J. Mahoney, and to the right is the Central Fire Station (since demolished). PAC-PA-27270.

Directly across the road, on the north side of the street, is **17A York**, once "Grant's Grocery," built in 1901. Cross to the centre island of the road and look up the building's western façade. You can see the remnants of a painted sign, a reminder of how merchants advertised their wares in years predating neon signs, television and radio ads. Notice the alleyway entrance to the left of 17A with its blue gateway, marking the entry to Cour Jeanne d'Arc Court (gates open from 7:30 a.m. to 11:00 p.m.).

Before proceeding there, pause to glance right (east) on York Street. It was here that Reformers ran from pursuing Tories in the Stoney Monday riot of September 1849. Some dashed into **42 York**, the **Château Lafayette**, a four-storey stone and brick hotel and watering hole operated by Francis Grant in the early 1840s. Others ran across the street to **41 York**, then the **St. Louis Hotel**, and now a restaurant, built 1874–75. Shots rang out and a grand mêlée ensued. This is the heart of the Stoney Monday riot.

View of the Parliamentary Library from a congested York Street, n.d. NCC 172-213.

Now cross the road and slip into the alleyway beside 17A York Street, passing through **Cour Jeanne d'Arc Court**. The entire block on Sussex from York to Clarence was part of the Institut Jeanne d'Arc (see Sussex walk), but is now a mix of stores on the street floor with condominiums above. The corner building on Clarence was Colonel Joseph Aumond's 1849 brick Revere Hotel — the oldest building on the block.

The courtyard is charming. Explore it fully, noting the whimsical dancing bear sculpture carved by Inuit sculptor Pauta Saila, in Nunavut (1999). Also find British Columbian sculptor John Ivor Smith's dancing woman, just before you exit the courtyard. Commissioned specifically for this site, it harkens back to the time (1917) when the Institut Jeanne d'Arc was a young women's residence.

Exit to Clarence Street. Pause to view **13–15 Clarence**, built in 1892 as an apartment above, and carriage-maker's business on the ground floor. Today the apartment above is graced by a highly detailed cantilevered wooden balcony, while the business below has evolved into a restaurant.

Inside 13–15 Clarence; A. Thibert, Carriage Builder, 1914. NCC, M. Newton file, H12–184.

Cross Clarence and enter the beautifully restored **Tin House Court**, immediately to the left of 13–15 Clarence. You are walking through the original tradesmen's entrances and stables of such mid to late nineteenth century Sussex businesses as the Castor Hotel (see Sussex walk). Take special note of the preserved façade of roofer, contractor and tinsmith Honoré Foisy's 1905 home, now mounted on a limestone wall. It has all the appearance of a fantastical metal sculpture, but it is the actual façade of Foisy's house, which once stood at 136 Guigues Street. Tin was once a commonly used construction material as it was inexpensive and shielded the building from rain, sleet and snow. As with many artisans, Foisy used his own home to advertise his considerable talents.

Continue through this enchanting courtyard. A cascading fountain enlivens the quiet mood, and park benches are conveniently placed, inviting you to stop awhile, to imagine the days of horse-drawn wagons and bustling activity that once was the life of Lowertown.

You emerge onto Murray Street. Turn right (east) at the corner of Parent Street find **55 Murray**, once the **Martineau Hotel**. Named after its first owner, Eugene Martineau, the original hotel was built in 1872. The building was purchased in 1977 by the Heritage Canada Foundation. The Martineau possesses a simple Georgian classical design, with regular windows accentuating a horizontal composition. Slightly raised end gables were built to retard fire. Made of limestone, 55 Murray is a good example of the handiwork of the Rideau Canal masons who passed their knowledge on to their sons. Kitchens were located in four stone wings at the back. In its heyday, the Martineau, which boasted seventy rooms, was one of the most popular taverns for Ottawa River raftsmen. Inside its arched doorways, which have replaced the old carriageway entries to the rear yard, you can see how the hotel has been adapted to shops and offices. The windowsills reveal the depth of the walls.

Now walk right (east) on Murray Street. Cross Dalhousie and continue to **159 Murray**, the (1904–5) **École Guigues School**. The school was almost demolished, but was purchased in 1993 to be renovated and transformed into the **Centre de jour Guigues**, a community centre occupying the basement, ground and first floors of the old school. The remaining floors were converted into fourteen condominiums. (**Note:** The entry to the old school is from St. Patrick.) Its symmetrical classical façade features regularly spaced rectangular windows with stone lintels and sills, a raised portico with flanking stairs, and wooden columns.

École Guigues School is a famous Ottawa landmark. In 1915 the Province of Ontario forbade the instruction of students in French. Rule 17 provoked a public outcry, and this school was the site of a large demonstration against the ruling. The historical plaque explains the struggle of French Canadians to ensure the survival of their language and culture. Rights were reinstated. The school continued to teach in French and reconfirmed the Franco-Ontarien presence in Lowertown.

A few steps along is **179 Murray, St. Brigid's Presbytery**. Its wishbone central gable and mansard roof lends drama to the streetscape. The pillared verandah is set wide upon the front of the brick home. The 1892 home is one of Ottawa's best examples of residential Second Empire style so popular in Victorian times. The Goad insurance map of Ottawa dated 1878 shows several small wooden frame buildings on this site predating this brick home.

Continue along Murray and turn left (north) onto Cumberland, walking beside **St. Brigid's Church**, built 1889–90 as the first Roman Catholic Church in Lowertown to serve the English-speaking members of the parish. St. Anne's (in Lowertown East) and the Basilica served French Catholics. The best view of the church is from St. Patrick at the intersection ahead.

Turn left (west) on St. Patrick. As you do, note the luxury condominiums (erected 2002) at the northeast corner of St. Patrick at Cumberland. Architect Kimon Caragian's block of twenty-four units is another example of infill, which will bring more people and vehicles to this increasingly popular and upscale neighbourhood.

Continue walking west on St. Patrick. Look up to examine the two spires of St. Brigid's: they are of unequal height and completely different shape. Such disparity appealed to the Victorians' delight in asymmetrical composition, which represented an exciting departure from the regular features of classicism. Together with the Basilica, these two spires are signature landmarks of Lowertown.

Although it possesses a Gothic interior, St. Brigid's exterior exhibits Romanesque Revival detailing, notably in its three heavy, rounded arched portals fronting onto St. Patrick Street, and its paired, round-headed windows. The colonnettes — narrow non-supporting columns on the front façade — are adorned with foliated capitals, a typical Romanesque detail.

Continue up St. Patrick, walking on the south side of the street. Watch for the entryway to Centre de jour Guigues and the old École Guigues School. Enter and proceed to the second floor which has been preserved as a heritage interior, complete with blackboards that have been retained in some old classrooms, plus an old photo gallery (ask for instructions at the reception centre). There are also washrooms here. The original entry to the school from St. Patrick Street is a designated heritage property. Wainscoting has been maintained, and heritage paints used to enhance the restoration. Look inside the classrooms: one has been converted to a billiard room, and here you'll discover several blackboards on the wall.

Return outside, turn left (west) to find **288–290 St. Patrick, Brulé House**, built around 1842. It is a well-preserved French-Canadian style wooden clapboard double with a steeply pitched, gable roof with dormers. It is one of the few remaining workman's doubles once common in Lowertown.

Cross Dalhousie, continuing along St. Patrick. On the south side, note **230 St. Patrick**, Johnson's, with its large tempered glass front. Its showcase window provides effective advertising to passersby.

Number **224–226 St. Patrick** is a four-storey flattop apartment block featuring an overhanging porch of finely detailed wood. Note the cornice with its wooden bracket supports. Farther along, **215 St. Patrick, Barrett Lane**, is a 1991 infill project by Ottawa architect Barry Hobin and Charlesfort Development Corporation. Two bays feature wooden porches that integrate into the Lowertown streetscape.

Number **204–210 St. Patrick, Brousseau Terrace**, is decorated with dramatic cliffhanger porches. There is also the characteristic Lowertown carriageway to the rear of the lot. The flat-roofed terrace was built in 1898 by Evangeliste Brousseau as a Victorian two-storey investment property. The fancy brickwork patterning on the front somewhat alleviates its plain façade.

Continue west on St. Patrick. As you walk towards Parent you will see Nôtre-Dame's two spires. The rear view of the apse shows its splendid Gothic curves and buttresses. Turn right (north) down Parent Street and continue until you reach Bruyère Street. Turn left (west) at the corner of Parent and Bruyère. Built in 1916, **62 Bruyère** is a painted brick fourplex, with a central gabled parapet breaking its flat-top roof.

This large city block bounded by Bruyère (south), Dalhousie (east), Sussex (west), and Cathcart (north) shows the tremendous impact of the Grey Nuns upon Ottawa. The Nuns arrived in Bytown on February 20, 1845, and built their first hospital at 167 St. Patrick — a wooden frame building with dormers. Although it soon proved inadequate, the Order was thwarted for many years in its attempts to purchase more land and build a larger hospital. The typhus epidemic of 1847 helped convince reluctant politicians that the nun's petition was justified.

On the north side of Bruyère is the **Elisabeth Bruyère Health Care Centre**. It is a composite of buildings erected after Confederation — 1898, 1909, 1929, 1936, 1949, and 1953 — that reflects the forever-expanding needs of the capital's population. The east wing addition was designed by the firm of Noffke, Morin and Sylvester, erected upon the original site of the wooden typhus hospital. Noffke's plans can be viewed in the National Archives. They describe the layout for operating rooms, birthing rooms, private, semi-private, and common wards.

Number **40 Bruyère**, opposite the hospital, is an early wooden clapboard Quebec-style house. Two dormer windows punctuate the roof. Note the offset doorway. A common later addition to these early dwellings was the rear kitchen extension built to alleviate the cramped living quarters. The original rear dormer windows were lost in the construction of these additions.

Continue along Bruyère to Sussex Drive. At the corner, look up to see the **sundial** designed in 1851 by the nuns' geometry teacher, Father Jean-François Allard. It graces the 1849 Mother House of the Grey Nuns. A limestone wall, stabilized and repointed in 1992, encloses the front garden on Sussex. It is possible, with permission, to enter the Mother House where Noffke's exquisite chapel can sometimes be viewed. Opposite is the new Embassy of the State of Kuwait (2002–03). (See Sussex walk.)

Turn right (north) on Sussex Drive. On the southeast corner of Sussex and Cathcart is the old (1866) St. Joseph's Orphanage. The two old stone buildings were connected by an addition in 1885. Cross Cathcart, and pass the now blocked-off end of Bolton Street, effectively barred to traffic. While walking, look northwest to the Ottawa River, Jacques Cartier Park in Gatineau, and the Gatineau Hills, beyond: it's a spectacular view in all seasons. Proceed to Boteler Street and turn right (east).

You are now beside **255 Sussex**, the **Japanese Embassy**. Built in 1977, it was the first embassy in what the NCC calls Embassy Row. The wall was an integral part of the design by architect Takeshi Sakamaki with Murray & Murray, associate architects. The driveway leading through its walled confines is adorned with elegant sculpture, a tasteful touch repeated by ironwork at the entrance and on the ground floor windows. From its northeast (Boteler Street) side, look up to examine the embassy's layered planes, reflecting a design of simple massing.

Want to go inside? Check the times (it's open from 10 a.m. to noon, 2:00 p.m. to 4:00 p.m.), ring the bell at the embassy gate, and ask if you can step inside to view the small rock garden so popular in Japanese culture.

After the older buildings of Lowertown, this embassy seems to be an incongruous modern border to the parkland forming the northern limits of the old neighbourhood. In the spirit of urban renewal and in an effort to create a ceremonial route from Parliament to Government House, the old streets and once bustling northern limits of Lowertown were razed. Landscaped lawns obliterate the memory of Redpath, Baird, MacKay, and Carleton Streets. North of Cathcart were the tracks of the Bytown and Prescott Railway culminating in the MacTaggart Street station. In 1847–49 Irish squatters populated this area; imagine their rough-hewn houses dotted amongst the muddy, pot-holed roads and footpaths.

Today, new additions to the streetscape lessen the incongruity of the Japanese Embassy. Across from it is the $25 million Embassy of Saudi Arabia (Domus Architects, after a 1989 design of Arthur Erickson's), completed in 2001. With absolutely no lettering on its exterior to inform passersby of its identity, and despite its two entrances, the building seems unnecessarily brutalistic and forbidding. Although the ornate octagonal limestone building has been ready for occupancy since the autumn of 2001, as of late 2003, the embassy was operating from a Bank Street address. The delay is due to Canadian William Sampson who was sentenced to death in Saudi Arabia for two bombings. Although Sampson returned to Canada late in 2003, politics surrounding his case remain sensitive.

Interestingly, the site has been controversial for years. The Saudi's purchased the property in 1978 for $900,000 but by 1989 the land was still undeveloped. By that time, the NCC decided it did not want any more embassies constructed along Sussex. However, the Saudi government pressed ahead; nine years later construction commenced. The Boteler Street neighbourhood community stepped in, protesting the removal of land from greenspace. The City of Ottawa waded in, first of all approving the plan — though they determined the guardhouse and entry from Boteler Street shouldn't be built. Their fence-sitting compromise — probably designed to curry favour with the community protestors — caved in. They rescinded their rejection of the guardhouse and Boteler Street driveway and the entire design was approved. Construction began in 1999. When will the embassy be occupied? Perhaps by the time you walk past.

Now turn right on Boteler to another modernistic structure at **40 Boteler, Le Sussex,** a tall brick apartment building. Turn right (south) on Parent and walk to Bolton, then turn left, passing **163–165 Bolton,** labourer **Thomas O'Brien's House,** an 1897 example of Lowertown's once common double cottage-style residences. The four dormer windows in the bell-cast, mansard roof add extra light and space in the second floor. Many of the windows in these early structures were a combination of solid wooden shutters over oiled paper. Considering the rowdy reputation of Lowertown, they possibly served as useful protection from hurled objects, too. Another interesting old home is found at 184–186 Bolton: it possesses a setback porch.

Continue to **Cathcart Park,** which was originally surveyed in 1846. It became an auxiliary market to Byward in 1877 on the recommendation of the city insurance inspector. Its proximity to the MacTaggart Street rail station allowed cattle to be brought to market, butchered and sold for retail to Bytown residents and for shipment to the lumber camps. Today there is nothing to remind us of the butcher's shops and meat stalls once crowding Cathcart Park. Instead, the quiet park is rimmed by tidy looking end-gabled residences.

Turn right to cross the square, then continue south on Cumberland to Bruyère. On Cumberland notice the modern modular stone complex called **Oldentowne, 183–189 Cumberland**. Architect Barry Hobin's 1986 postmodern design imitates its historical Lowertown antecedents. Of special interest is its front façade with arched openings. It functions as a screen for roof terraces, affording residents privacy from the street. Look up behind this "false-front" screen to find the bracketed, pedimented parapet breaking the otherwise flat roofline. Dark, tunnel-like private entryways give residents privacy. Adjacent to number 189, note the remains of an old roofline's "shadow" on the exposed wall of the adjacent house, the limestone heritage building at **193 Cumberland, Rathier House**.

Constructed circa 1862, this rough-cut stone building is a charming feature of the street. Built by carpenter Abraham Rathier as a combination residence and grocery shop, the classically inspired house features a welcoming angled doorway. Notice the regularly spaced windows and the contrasting corner quoining.

Now walk left (east) on Bruyère to King Edward Avenue. The **Armand Pagé Community Centre** is on the corner, built in 1887 as Fire Station Number 5. This closed in 1952. The tower, which once served as a conveniently tall place to dry hoses (a characteristic feature of early fire stations), has long gone.

(**Note:** This is a logical spot to cut short this long walk, if you wish. You could walk north on King Edward, turn right on George, and return to your car. If you do this, or, if you simply want to venture a few steps north, visit **174–176 King Edward**, a stone cottage that is the last remaining stone duplex in Lowertown. In urgent need of restoration, this symmetrical residence with its stone lintel and porches is similar to the William Garvock house in New Edinburgh [see New Edinburgh walk]).

Cross King Edward at the St. Andrew Street traffic lights and return to Cathcart by walking left (north) past the east extension of Bruyère, then turn right (east). The 1981 **Cathcart Mews** complex of townhouses is on your right as you walk towards the Rideau River. Like the Oldentowne complex on Cumberland, the Mews was built during the recent influx of middle class residents in to what was once the boisterous domain of squatters and raftsmen.

At the corner of Cathcart and Rose there is a park from which you can see the Rideau River. Just north of Cathcart, find the remnants of the old Bytown and Prescott Railway Bridge, its stone supports still rising out of the river. It's a favourite summertime spot for young boys, who enjoy fishing from its rough cut limestone piers. Still farther north spy the fanciful looking **Minto Bridges** spanning the river between Green and Maple Islands and New Edinburgh, to the east. Even in 1871, this area represented an isolated part of the city, the main reason for it being chosen for a hospital for infectious diseases.

Walk south along Rose, then turn left (east) on Bruyère. You pass **N. A. Bordeleau Park** and, on the south side, **324–334 Bruyère**, a set of flat-topped row houses that were investment properties in the early 1900s.

At the corner of Bruyère and Forsey streets, observe the old brick duplex embraced by a contemporary condominium complex that wraps itself around its host. Interestingly, the architect made no effort to integrate the old with the new: there is no common building material, no mirroring of red brick in the condominium. Instead, the California-style beige stucco walls boldly assert their newness. The stepped-back floor plan cleverly affords privacy not only to ground floor entryways, but also to the roof terraces. These are further defined by stuccoed frames that add depth and the appearance of movement to the streetscape. Now turn right on Forsey to view the less dramatic eastern façade of these row houses.

Minto Bridges and Green Island from Cathcart Park. 2002.
K. Fletcher.

Turn left on St. Patrick. Behind a stone wall on your left are the gardens of what was originally the **Good Shepherd Convent**, built in 1875. In 1961 *The Ottawa Citizen* called it "a convent for young ladies — formerly a home for wayward girls." Today it is the **Embassy of the People's Republic of China**, its front entry guarded by two carved stone Foo dogs. These so-called dogs are really stylized lions, an ancient Buddhist symbol of wisdom strategically placed to guard the entryway to residences, businesses, and important edifices.

Continue along the north side of St. Patrick until you reach traffic lights at Cobourg. On your left is the bridge leading to Island Lodge on Porter's Island. Cross it for a glimpse of the grounds. The tall curved residence on the east side of the island, **Allan House**, was built in 1964 by McLean and MacPhadyen. From the north side of the island you can catch a glimpse of New Edinburgh.

Backtrack across the bridge and cross St. Patrick at the lights to Cobourg Street. Turn right onto Old St. Patrick Street and walk the few steps west to **St. Anne's Church.**

This 1873 church, designed by architect J. P. LeCourt, is perhaps the only true example of the Quebec tradition of religious architecture in the city. It is characterized by a severely plain stone façade, alleviated by a medieval-inspired circular rose window, classical round-arched

Foo dog guards entry to Chinese Embassy. 2002. K. Fletcher.

St. Anne's Church, an old Quebec-tradition church. NCC, M. Newton file H12-59, Box 54.

doors, and statuary niches. The statues, side turrets, and three entry doors balance each other both simply and beautifully. The effect is complimented by St. Anne's plain, three-tiered belfry.

Bishop Guigues was pivotal in the creation of St. Anne's parish. By the 1870s, Nôtre-Dame could not accommodate the booming French Catholic population. Pierre Rocque, the contractor who had built the Grey Nuns' St. Joseph's Orphanage and General Hospital on Sussex, teamed with James O'Connor to assist LeCourt in building St. Anne's. Guigues laid the cornerstone to the church on May 4, 1873.

Take the footpath on the left (east) side of St. Anne's south to Myrand Street. Here you will find **17 Myrand**, formerly **St. Anne's Rectory** and now destined to become another condominium. This is a 1921 W. E. Noffke design — in fact, it was the first of his many Catholic commissions. Built in Noffke's much-loved Spanish Revival style, this massive structure sports his favourite feature: a tiled roof. But this building is by no means typical of Spanish Revival: its heavy-looking form is peculiarly emphasized by large, smooth cut stone blocks. Its classical two-storey portico with Corinthian capitals and a pedimented door make this building an odd architectural hybrid.

St. Anne's Rectory, November 1991. K. Fletcher.

The rectory overlooks **Anglesea Square**, the second of the two markets (the other being Cathcart) created in 1877 as additions to Byward. Turn around, and with your back to Noffke's rectory look at the Square: today's grassy playground echoes the bustling clamour of bygone market days. Anglesea, however, had an even earlier use as a rifle range. As a rifle range it fostered a bad memory for the community of Lowertown East: an unfortunate man was shot dead while setting up targets one day.

Playgrounds became necessities as the urban population of Ottawa grew. In his August 1903 report, Frederick Todd, OIC landscape architect, recommended recommended a park be developed here, and on May 5, 1913, the newly formed Playgrounds Association of Ottawa was granted permission to develop Anglesea Square as a children's playground.

Now look right (west) on Myrand towards the apartment on the western end of Anglesea Square. In the 1970s more than 300 houses in Lowertown West and East were demolished and 1,400 families were displaced. The multi-level and multi-coloured rows of townhouses and apartment buildings peppering the landscape represent the urban renewal projects undertaken jointly by the city, province, and Canada Mortgage and Housing Corporation. It is to the credit of the people of Lowertown East that they have managed to maintain their largely French-speaking community centres in the face of the near annihilation of their neighbourhood.

Turn left on the walkway beside the apartment building at the foot of the playing field and walk south to York Street.

Number **340 York**, formerly **École Ste. Anne's School** and presently the **Centre prescolaire et parascolaire**, defines the end of York Street and serves the Catholic community of Lowertown East. Now turn right and walk west, returning towards the Byward Market area. On your immediate left is the "collegiate Gothic" **310 York Street School**, designed in 1921 by architect William C. Beattie. Typical of this castle-like style are the stone-capped corner piers, complete with their slits for imaginary archers. Crenellated parapets and imposing Tudor-arched doorways are additional collegiate Gothic touches. Note the elaborately carved sign "GIRLS" over the east entry; its mate, "BOYS," is above the west portal, surrounded in carvings of oak leaves, symbols of steady growth and wisdom.

Continue west on York, noting the relatively unobstructed view of the Hill and the Parliamentary Library. Pass Nelson Street and note

247 York, a brick home whose east façade is faced with original pressed tin, once a common building material. Continue to King Edward.

On the corner is **321 King Edward**, the **Champagne Baths**. By the 1920s, city councillors were grappling with the concept of providing public recreational facilities for young and old alike. Many city dwellers could not afford the luxury of heading to the Gatineau Hills cottage country to escape summer's heat and dust. In a combined effort to promote health, recreation, and "cleanliness among the poor," the Champagne Baths was built (1921–1922). The tiled roof is the signature of its architect, W. E. Noffke. (Its counterpart in the city is the Plant Bath in Plouffe Park, which opened at the same time at Gladstone and Preston. Although not designed by Noffke, this bath was also created by the city in a neighbourhood that, like Lowertown, lacked sufficient plumbing facilities.)

The front of the Champagne Baths is decorated, while the rear extension housing the pool is plain brick. On either side of the main entry are two smaller porch entries, accented by tiled caps. The main doorway is framed by double pilasters. Above it is an ornately curved broken pediment and window that carries the eye up to the wooden brackets supporting the overhanging eaves. The low-pitched roof was

Champagne Baths. 2002. E. Fletcher.

originally tiled with Noffke's favourites, which today have been replaced by asphalt shingles. (Unfortunately, clay tile cannot easily withstand the extremes of Ottawa's weather.) By all means go inside and, if you've telephoned ahead to find out swim times, you might be able to take a break and enjoy a swim in this heritage pool.

Cross King Edward at the lights and stop on the grassy median. It is here that the Bywash, the outflow of the Rideau Canal, curved from York Street to head north before connecting with the Rideau River at the Rideau Falls. The boulevard was planned as a grand avenue to Rideau Hall, but the idea never caught on, despite the erection of the Minto Bridges connecting Lowertown to New Edinburgh via Green Island.

Looking left (south) from the median, you can see two other heritage structures. Number **351 King Edward** is **Ottawa Hydro Electric Commission Substation #4**, designed in 1931 by the same William C. Beattie who designed the York Street School. This is an art deco building featuring a huge metal doorway that rises vertically to accommodate the transformer equipment. Note the copper canopy over the double front doorway attached by sturdy chains to copper rosettes. Copper panels and coping (flashing), sandstone, and multi-paned windows animate this building's dark brick façade.

Farther south is the Moorish-looking **375 King Edward**, the **Jewish Memorial Funeral Chapel**, designed by J. W. H. Watts in 1904. A Star of David is prominently featured in the central window over the door and in the ironwork. Its front façade is extended by a curvilinear and stepped front gable, balanced on either side by onion-domed corner turrets.

At the turn of the twentieth century, Lowertown was an eminently desirable neighbourhood for many immigrants who wanted to establish businesses in the market area. Most built dwellings that had apartments above ground floor shops. Jewish immigrants started arriving in 1900 and started to build homes along Clarence Street. By 1930 they were the dominant ethnic group of the market business community and, to accommodate their special needs, kosher facilities were set up within the market building.

Now cross at the lights to the west side of King Edward. In early years, it looked quite different: once the Bywash coursed down here, flowing north from York Street up King Edward to the Rideau River. And, years ago, the boulevard was lined with gracious elms. Their loss from the Dutch elm disease in the 1950s and early 1960s devastated many streetscapes — this is no exception.

Continue walking west on York Street. At the southeast corner at Cumberland find **350–352 Cumberland**, a pink brick double with gabled roof. At first glance it appears to possess symmetrically classical proportions. But its doors are off-centre, as are its two chimneys. One door is set at the extreme left end, diagonally balanced by the chimney at the far right; the second entry is centrally situated just to the bottom right of the second central chimney. The six regularly spaced second-storey windows contribute to the illusion of symmetry. The brick veneer covers an earlier wood frame exterior.

On the right (north) find **153–161 York**, formerly the **Brown Tenements**. This is the only surviving example of a four-unit row in the area, and as such is a significant heritage building to remind us of what once were common, vernacular residences. Stand back to examine the façade and you will see the carriageway, now spoiled by a modern garage door. Because the tenements extend the length of the lot allowance, a passageway was necessary to allow horse and wagon entry to the rear.

Continue to **126 York Street**, the **S. J. Major Building**. Sylvini Major and his wife, Marie Corinne Lebel, founded a grocery in the Byward Market. After his death in 1903, Mrs. Major and her son, Asconi Joseph, developed the business into the largest in Eastern Canada. In 1913, the family had a residence built in Rockcliffe at 541 Acacia, now known as Stornoway — home to the leader of the Opposition (see Rockcliffe walk). Their market business was merged in 1923 to form National Grocers. The S. J. Major building was a warehouse, but it is an attractive building nonetheless. Carved above the pedimented doorway are the words "S. J. Major Ltd." framed by two copper lions' heads. Extra interest is found in the rhythmic repetition of arches in the cornice and in the terra cotta tiles decorating the brick façade.

Across the street is **113–115 York**, home to John Cundell, the last horse trader to keep a business in downtown Ottawa. His spotless stable at the rear of the dwelling is home to the horses you still see hauling gaily painted wagons through Lowertown, New Edinburgh, and Rockcliffe. His wagon tours are another "heritage" way to view the capital, incidentally.

Continue west along York and cross Dalhousie at the lights. Number **325 Dalhousie**, on your left, is the **Union du Canada** building. Strong verticals and a bold capped roof are dramatically enlivened by slightly angled windows. Such uncommon window treatment creates intriguing reflection patterns — a feature that adds both texture and liveliness to the streetscape.

Number **62 York**, is the old **Richelieu Hotel**, now a bar and restaurant. Jean-Baptiste LaCroix leased the land from Colonel By in 1827. Ten years later, baker George Shouldice rented it as both a home and bakery until he purchased it in 1844. Shouldice built the present stone two-and-a-half storey building that became known as the Richelieu Hotel.

Continue west on York, and enter the **Byward Market** area. You see the **Byward Market Building** sandwiched between two one-way streets: William and Byward Market. Explore the lively market buildings and, in season, the open-air flower, vegetable, maple syrup and craft stalls. This Byward Market building is the fourth built in this Lowertown vicinity. All previous buildings were destroyed by fire.

The present building, built 1926–27 and altered in 1977 by the City of Ottawa Property Branch, has a functional design. It is essentially a long warehouse with a shed-like roof attached below the protruding top storey, rather like a huge wraparound verandah. It is well suited to shelter the outdoor stalls, which enjoy its shade and shelter. Four cross-gables with their rounded-arched windows break the length of the structure, which extends the length of an entire city block. The end gables also feature a round-arched window, and are further decorated by a contrasting flashing to the red brick and the black asphalt roof. Beneath the end gables find the seven square steel plates, which anchor the steel cables exposed in the interior of the roof.

Go inside the Market Building and walk upstairs to look down upon the craft stalls from the second-floor balcony. McClintock's Dream is the name of the 1978 papier-mâché sculpture by Victor Tolgesy, which is suspended from the ceiling. The **Artists at Work Gallery** is also on the second floor, where you can spend time watching and speaking with artists who are working at their creations.

The market's William Street façade is full of trendy restaurants, "country" shops, and clothing stores. It is the Byward Market street façade that best approximates the ambiance of bygone market days. Sensitive heritage restoration has restored many of the functional yet colourful buildings, which feature rounded-arch windows and polychromatic brickwork. Among these crowded cheese, meat, fish, and poultry shops you can recapture the colourful Market days of old.

During summer, street buskers such as jugglers, street theatre groups, and musicians compete with the bilingual calls of fruit and vegetable vendors. Bushel baskets overflowing with brilliant red and green peppers and long plaits of garlic compete for your interest.

To return to the start of the tour, head south on Byward or William to George. Turn right to the Ottawa School of Art.

McClintock's Dream, a papier-mâché sculpture by Victor Tolgesy, suspended from the ceiling in the Byward Market Building, 2002. K. Fletcher.

Byward Market looking north to York Street c. 1902. Note the wooden porches and frame buildings. Compare this bustling horse and carriage scene to the next photo. Both are taken from the same spot. NCC, 172-4.

Byward Market c. 1920: there is only one horse and wagon now, the mode of transportation has changed to the car. Frame buildings are now replaced with brick. NCC, 172-94.

New Edinburgh

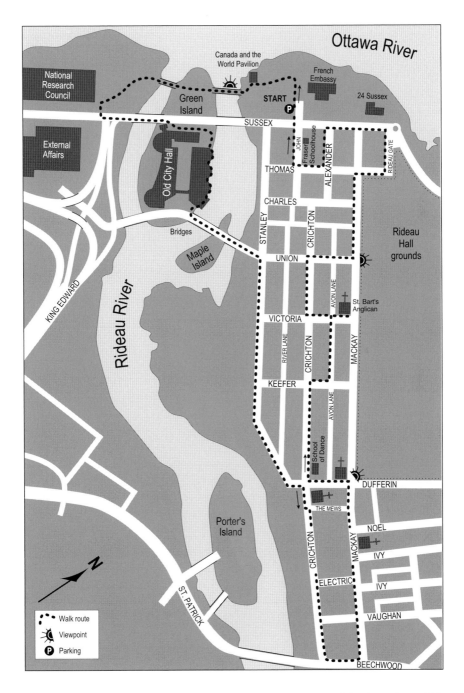

In 1613 French explorer Samuel de Champlain paddled past the curtain of the Rideau Falls and described its beauty in his journal. More than two hundred years later it was considered by Lord Dalhousie and Colonel John By as a site for the start of the Rideau Canal. It was bypassed in favour of Entrance Bay (see Parliament Hill walk). But Thomas MacKay, the main contractor for the canal, recognized the opportunity the falls represented. He purchased more than 1,100 acres of surrounding land. In 1825 he founded the village of New Edinburgh and encouraged his Scottish stonemasons and labourers to settle here. MacKay appears to have been generous, building homes for his labourers, donating land and labour for churches and schools.

Today the parkland and municipal government buildings on Green Island belie the industry that once hugged the confluence of Rideau and Ottawa Rivers. The rattle of the horse-drawn street railway extending from New Edinburgh to the Chaudière and the whistle of the Bytown and Prescott train are both long gone. The "Mile of

Mill on the Rideau River, near Bytown, the present site of the National Research Council. Jean-Baptiste St-Louis' 1831 mill. W. H. Bartlett print. PAC-C-2368.

History," that once-dusty road connecting New Edinburgh's Rideau Hall to Ottawa is now busy Sussex Drive. Pigs and cattle no longer roam the streets to feed on the waste mash from Isaac McTaggart's 1840 distillery. His operation was located at the foot of Alexander Street which, in those early days, extended to the waterfront.

McTaggart's ale and whiskey was shipped by barge along the Ottawa River and Rideau Canal to its various destinations. The whiskey was piped downhill from the distillery into barrels. The distillery itself was driven by a thirty-five foot water wheel powered by water transported from the Rideau River via a three-foot wooden pipe.

The falls inspired Jean-Baptiste St-Louis to leave his mill at the Bywash on York Street, in Lowertown, and build the first mill at Rideau Falls in 1831. MacKay purchased it in 1837 and entered into partnership with several other businessmen including his son-in-law, John MacKinnon, resident of Earnscliffe. By 1847 their joint operation of a flourmill, cloth factory, distillery, and sawmill was prospering on the west side of the falls. In one season, the sawmill turned 20,000 Ottawa Valley logs into 2,400,000 board feet, most of it destined for the American market.

Mills at Rideau Falls with gentleman in top hat and friends admiring the view. Note the mills at rear, where the Canada and the World Pavilion is now located, n.d.
City of Ottawa Archives, CA 2688.

MacKay also built a cloth factory of stone, with "six looms, four double, two single, 150 yards of cloth per day and 25 employees."[10] By 1852 he owned and operated an extremely prosperous industrial complex at the Rideau Falls. The buildings were variously built of wood or stone. They included a large wool factory where raw wool was carded and woven into fine tweeds, blankets, and flannels; other mills produced shingles and doors, Venetian blinds, and assorted farm equipment. As many as a hundred horse-drawn wagons could be seen along this part of Sussex, as farmers waited to stock up with much-needed provisions.

In 1851 MacKay received the gold prize from the London Exhibition for his New Edinburgh blankets. By the 1870s imported bales of wool from South America, Australia, England, and the United States shared warehouse space with domestic raw wool.

After MacKay's death in 1855 the mills continued operation, eventually being purchased in 1866 by the Maclaren brothers of Wakefield and subsequently, in 1894, by the W. C. Edwards Lumber Company. In 1907 fire destroyed much of the original complex. Although the mills were rebuilt, they did not regain their dominance of the market. By this time the easily accessible Ottawa Valley pine and hardwood stands had been logged.

The MacKay Mills on east side of Rideau Falls, c. 1900 photo by Samuel J. Jarvis. NCC, M. Newton files M12-004A&B, Box 41.

In 1928 the Dominion Bureau of Statistics purchased the mill complex on Green Island. One year later the National Research Council took over the mill buildings west of the Rideau and their 1930 annual report announced that the Edwards mills were to become testing facilities for airplane engines. By 1943 the federal government owned the land extending from the site of the French Embassy to Earnscliffe. That year, the Edwards family lost their protracted bid to retain their family home, which is now 24 Sussex Drive, the prime minister's residence. From 1956–59 the NCC demolished most of the old industrial complex surrounding Rideau Falls.

Party at Government House, Rockcliffe (includes Thomas Ahearn) bound for the Chaudière by streetcar, April 18, 1906. City of Ottawa Archives, CA 1525.

Contemporaneous with its industrial development was New Edinburgh's development as a working class residential neighbourhood. Properties along its western boundary at MacKay and Rideau Gate were coveted because they overlooked Government House. In New Edinburgh large homes were in stark contrast to the modest doubles, single family homes, and apartment rows of clapboard, board and batten, and brick that lined the streets between Sussex and Beechwood.

Today the gentrification of the village is well underway. Population density is on the increase as infill destroys former gardens and multi-storey condominiums replace older structures. However, there are still many gems in this village, and many clues to its heritage still remain.

Mr. Henry Frances Sims at home with his wife, 79 Sussex Drive, which would have been located west of Rideau Falls, n.d. City of Ottawa Archives, CA 2041.

NEIGHBOURHOOD STYLES

There is an agreeable mix of buildings in the village. The old stone schoolhouse that Thomas MacKay first built for his workmen and subsequently turned into a school for labourers' children still stands. A few frame homes survive, some clad in clapboard, and one or two in board and batten. There's an eclectic mix of rambling Victorian farmhouses of polychromatic brick and classically inspired stone residences. And, always dominating New Edinburgh is Rideau Hall, "MacKay's Castle." Its carefully nurtured "natural" landscape is circumscribed by a wrought iron fence with limestone pillars. Governors General hold levees twice yearly and there are tours of the grounds in the summer, giving visitors an opportunity to appreciate this stately garden oasis.

Between Dufferin Street and Beechwood, the neighbourhood mood changes. Here, the community of Lindenlea begins, and there are more commercial buildings, more flat-topped apartment blocks and, on Beechwood, the welcoming doors of cafés, bookshops, and variety stores.

WALK TIPS

🚶 **4.5 km; 2 hours**

Park your car along one of the streets close to the corner of John and Sussex, then carefully cross Sussex and start the walk in the small lot at the foot of John Street, beside the French Embassy on Sussex Drive. (The small parking lot here is now reserved for visitors to the Canada and the World Pavilion.)

THE WALK

Follow the path heading west (left) at the north end of the parking lot, overlooking the Ottawa River. The **Canada and the World Pavilion**, which opened May 10, 2001 appears almost immediately, commanding a spectacular view over the Ottawa River north to Gatineau and the hills beyond. The postmodern pavilion showcases celebrated Canadians who have made a difference on the international scene in the arts, science, international trade and development. Admission is free so it's a good spot to linger if weather is inclement.

Back outside, stroll west a few metres and pause at the lookout to admire **Rideau Falls**, a tourist attraction since the earliest days of Bytown and the site of the city's early wool and saw mills.

Cross the footbridge over the Rideau River to **Green Island**, named after Patrick Green, who quarried stone for the canal. Green grew hay and pastured cattle on this twelve-acre island. By 1864 Muley's Saw Mill and Stave Factory had been built on the island, and on the north tip, in Confederation year, a foundry was opened, which operated until 1922. Today it is home to a large commemorative bronze statue depicting the world beneath the outstretched wings of an eagle. This is the **Commonwealth Air Force Memorial** (1959,) created by Art Price and dedicated to 800 Canadian airmen who died in WW II.

Mills on west side of Rideau Falls.
NCC, M. Newton file M12-004A&B.

Many of these men died when they were learning how to fly or while transporting planes made in Canada to bases in Europe and North Africa. Behind this memorial find a second installed in 2001 to honour the Mackenzie-Papineau Battalion. Named in memory of those who fought in the 1832 Rebellion of Lower Canada, the "Mac-Paps" were comprised of 1,546 Canadians who fought in Spain between the years 1936–39 to defend Spanish democracy. Opposite these a third memorial, unveiled by Governor General Adrienne Clarkson in 1999, commemorates men and women in the combined air forces of the British Commonwealth.

Cross the second footbridge to the west bank of the river and walk towards the **National Research Council, 100 Sussex**. Architects Sproatt and Rolph designed it in 1930–33, using the classical revival style popularized by the Parisian École des Beaux-Arts. Its monumental scale, massive columns and symmetrically balanced entrance pavilions declare solidity and importance. Prime Minister Mackenzie King personally selected the Biblical inscription about Truth carved above the doorway.

Cross Sussex Drive at the lights and head left (east) to view what were (until 2001) two versions of the **Ottawa City Hall** complex on Green Island. They form a juxtaposition of the old (1958) International Style city hall and Moshe Safdie's postmodernist 1992–93 creation which wraps around its predecessor and dominates Green Island. Today they are federal buildings. Note that you can explore inside this building and that there is a good cafeteria in the eastern wing (ask the security guard in the original building for directions, although if you enter via the doors facing Sussex and veer left, you'll probably find it).

Safdie's design is a composite of the geometric and classic architectural forms of cube, cylinder, triangle, and circle. Walking east from Sussex, you first see the northwest entrance tower, a pyramidal structure within a cube. To balance this, the southwest corner of the Bytown Pavilion (its western wing) has a cylindrical block base with a cone-shaped glass roof. This houses Victoria Hall, once the council chambers, which opened March 3, 1993. The pyramids of glass can best be appreciated if you enter the building: they bathe the interior atriums in welcome natural light.

Continuing east on Sussex, the International Style city hall now appears. It won the Massey Award of 1958 for architects Rother, Bland and Trudeau. Its repetitive rectangular design of glass, limestone cladding and aluminum is broken by the prominent three-storey massing over the main entrance. Safdie's newer design does not totally obscure the old; the sheer, buff-coloured walls offset the grey International Style building.

Now turn right (south). Find the pathway along the east side of the island, which follows the curves of the projecting "bubbles" of Safdie's Rideau Pavilion (the east wing). In the winter of 1992–93, the Rideau River overflowed its banks and froze right up to the base of the bubbles. Traditional spring blasting of the river ice to open up the flow of the waterway that year was a matter of grave concern for fear the building's foundations, walls and windows would be damaged during this annual event. (The blasting of river ice is announced by local media each year, lest the public became alarmed over the explosive sounds. It's quite a spectacle!)

As you emerge from the bubbles into the gardens at the rear of the complex, you see the Unity Tower. It is not Safdie's original design, which was too expensive to complete. This open steel truss is merely the frame of his concept, which originally included two elevators designed to transport visitors to a spectacular glass-covered, diamond-shaped observation deck. In 1993 the mayor of Ottawa, Jacqueline Holzman, and the Board of Trade started a fundraising campaign to raise the extra $750,000 needed to complete the tower. Take a look at this open metalwork to see what you think of it. Personally, I like its open effect and think that if it had been completed as designed, it could over-dominate the site. Look to your right to appreciate the fountain and interior "courtyard" created between the two wings of Safdie's design.

Now turn left (east) to cross the **Minto Bridges**, built in 1900 by the Dominion Bridge Company of Montreal. Lady Minto encouraged the erection of these bridges as a ceremonial route linking Rideau Hall to Parliament via King Edward Avenue. As you cross the iron and steel span over the easternmost branch of the Rideau River, you enter the Village of New Edinburgh. Before leaving the bridges, note the stylized crowns adorning their spans.

Before turning right on Stanley Street, pause to look at **92 Stanley**, a picturesque stone cottage built in 1862 by J. Dougal MacLeod, a Scot from the Isle of Skye. MacLeod was a miller who worked in MacKay's Rideau Falls flour mill. The fine stone home has a wooden porch with a trellis motif.

92 Stanley. NCC, M. Newton file H12-38, Box 44.

Walk south on Stanley. Number **97 Stanley, Gerard House**, built in 1867 was the first home of William Gerard, who later moved because of the regular flooding of the Rideau River each spring. Each year, basements of homes up to Crichton Street were filled with water despite the dyke residents built to arrest the floodwaters. The annual flooding continued until the city commenced the annual spring blasting and cutting of keys in the river ice. Even today basements throughout the city can get wet during spring runoff. Number 97 was originally a single family T-shaped dwelling, but it has been much altered over the years, and in 1949 Dr. R. E. Wodehouse converted it to a duplex.

Continue south to **110, 114,** and **116 Stanley**, pretty wooden clapboard homes with well-preserved gingerbread (bargeboard) trim beneath their steeply gabled roofs. Number 114 is the earliest, built in 1865 by Henry Avery, master carpenter and cabinetmaker for Thomas MacKay. He then built 110 for his son, Clinton, and then 116, in 1895, for his daughter, Margaret. A delightful picket fence defines the garden at 114. In bygone days, fences were a functional protection against free-ranging cattle, horses, pigs and chickens, which otherwise munched their way indiscriminately through lawns, vegetable plots, and flower beds.

Across from these houses is **119 Stanley**, the clapboard home of John Jones, mill worker, built around 1892 and restored in summer of 2002. Its cap-like mansard roof is characteristic of Second Empire style, relatively uncommon here in New Edinburgh. Farther south is **127 Stanley**, an example of unusual exterior finishing in wood: vertical board and batten. Nearby, note **132** and **136–140 Stanley** at the corner of Queen Victoria, examples of the popular 1960s bungalow style.

Continue south to **151 Stanley**, the **Bell House** built in 1868 for New Edinburgh physician Dr. W. R. Bell. *The Ottawa Citizen* of March 7, 1970 reported: "When Dr. Bell built the house on Stanley Avenue … his offices were next door in the red brick row (then frame) with a connecting passageway to the house. In about 1883, as the doctor's family grew, a wing was added on the east side that explains the rather odd shape of the house from the outside. Too, the house is now in reverse from the original — the front door used to face the Rideau River."

In 1883 the orientation of the Bell house was altered so that it faced Stanley Street rather than the river.

The Victorian detailing on this home includes polychromatic brick chimneys and alternating courses of scalloped and square shingle siding. Delicately carved dentil trim beneath the eaves of the porch roof and

151 Stanley, the Bell House. Oct. 1959. C. C. J. Bond.
NCC, M. Newton file M12-004 A&B.

the turret-like dormer in its main roof add an airiness to the façade. The porch supports feature inset panels of crocketed lattice trim, which adds a light touch to the home. Look at the bargeboard or gingerbread trim: you can see different designs emerge where additions were made to the original structure. Also note that most windows have their original rippled glass.

Farther along find **150 Stanley, Governor's Walk Residence**, once the Dominican father's residence, which was transformed in 2000 into a retirement home. The frescoes depicting the Stations of the Cross, painted in the chapel in the 1950s, have been removed and are on exhibit at the Canadian Museum of Civilization. Farther down the street find what used to be the City of Ottawa Archives at **174 Stanley**. A plain red brick building with stylized stone portico, it was transformed into loft apartments after the archives moved to Whitton Hall in the old City Hall building on Green Island. (**Note:** In 2003 they moved to a far more spacious location within the same building.)

Turn left (east) at Dufferin and almost immediately right on Crichton. This street is named after Thomas MacKay's wife, Anne Crichton. The New Edinburgh streets John, Alexander, Thomas, and Charles were named after four of their children.

On the left (east) side of Crichton is **St. John Evangelical Lutheran Church**, a white clapboard church built in 1895 by August Bochner, who also built the parsonage in 1903. Bochner was one of the many Lutherans who settled in New Edinburgh after fleeing religious and political persecution in Germany. Pointed arched windows with diamond-shaped panes, and a steep gable roof adorned by a hipped bell tower with Gothic arched openings are its main features.

St. John Evangelical Lutheran Church. November 1991.
K. Fletcher.

Farther down is **278 Crichton**, a still-beautiful 1908 Rogue Victorian brick home that is a study in competing shapes and forms. Its right side features a rounded tower two-and-a-half stories high extending from the basement. The bell-shaped dome is peaked with a rounded finial. The squared-off central doorway and the balcony alcove are later additions built when the single family home was turned into the Philip Apartments by the Betcherman family in the 1930s.

As you continue south along Crichton, you will notice the streetscape is filled with increasingly high-density buildings. Flat-top apartments dominate the west side of the street. Flat-topped roofs became popular in the 1860s in Ottawa as they allow full use of the top storey, unlike the angled attic imposed by gabled roofs. Utilization of all available space was a desirable design feature when building apartments or business properties.

278 Crichton, the Rogue Victorian. October 1991. K. Fletcher.

Numbers **309–321 Crichton** are flat-top units of wood frame construction with red brick veneer, sporting new copper cap canopies above each doorway. The flat roof is finished with a wood cornice. Note how the apartment block is built up to the sidewalk: there is no allowance for grass as the building itself takes up the entire lot.

Of similar construction, **323–337 Crichton** on the northwest corner at Beechwood features recessed doorways and porches, partitioned by tongue-and-groove curved wooden dividers for privacy. The cornice and porch entablature are painted pressed tin.

Contrast the streetscape of old apartments on the west side of Crichton with the complex of postmodern brick units across the street at **310-320 Crighton**, built in the early 1990s.

Postmodern complex at 320 Crichton. October 1991. K. Fletcher.

Turn left (east) on Beechwood and then left (north) again on MacKay. Note **25 Beechwood**, the 1990 **Royal Bank** building, a post-modern design by Alistair Ross and Associates. A precast concrete frieze depicting a crowd of people is set above the doorway, which is rounded at the corner. This is an inviting design feature, common to storefronts since the 1800s (see Lowertown walk, and Rathier House's angled entry).

The postmodern style makes clear reference to the historical precedents in commercial architecture. On the Royal Bank building, the architects included parapeted gables, a masonry stringcourse, and a concrete cornice with end brackets. The mansard roof punctuated by dormers and a rusticated brick façade complete the building's historical references. Across from the bank on the south side of Beechwood, a postmodern brick mall continues the historical detailing.

Now turn left (north) on MacKay Street. Find numbers **339, 341,** and **343 MacKay**, a series of modern homes that feature sharply broken rooflines. This allows light to flood inside the homes through the windows that face this roofline. The three modern homes crowding the single lot have a distinctly different relationship to the street than do the heritage houses. Notice how they present a completely blank face to the street. Their design deliberately shields their residents from the community; the architecture isolates residents from, rather than integrates them into, their neighbourhood.

Farther along MacKay is **St. Luke's Evangelical Lutheran Kirche**, built in 1915 at the corner of Noel. Known as Perpendicular Gothic, this style features a shallow "basket handle" arched doorway, with pointed arched panelling on its wooden door. The dark brick, square-steepled structure is well supported by prominent buttresses. Rectangular leaded paned windows set off by tracery add interest to this church, one of more than twenty Ontario Lutheran churches designed by architect W. E. Noffke.

Nearby, number **300 MacKay** is a Second Empire cottage which resembles 119 Stanley.

At the corner of Dufferin is **MacKay United Church**, built in 1909 by New York architect H. F. Ballantyne. In 1874, led by Thomas MacKay's daughter Annie, local Presbyterians started a subscription for what became known as the New Edinburgh Presbyterian Church. The original rubble stone church was designed by Robert Surtees in 1875 for $5,000. Annie financed the building of the adjacent manse during the previous year.

From this corner you can see the wrought iron fence marking the Rideau Hall estate. Turn left (west) on Dufferin and at Crichton head right (north) past **Crichton Street Public School**. The first two-room public school was built here in 1875, an addition in 1906, and a wing containing ten rooms in 1919-20. Architect William Garvock was responsible for the design of the 1919 addition. His untimely death in December 1918 left it up to his successor W.C. Beattie to supervise the construction. The flat-topped school is brick with an Indiana limestone trim and base.

Since 2000 it has housed the School of Dance. Enter it and opposite the office, find a plaque with a likeness of famous Canadian ballerina Celia Franca, founder of the National Ballet of Canada, and its artistic director for twenty-four years. A resident of Ottawa, it is fitting that her name is commemorated here.

Garvock House, featuring a turned wooden porch, contrasting quoins and twinned gables. Oct. 1959. C. C. J. Bond. NCC, M. Newton file H12-48, Box 44.

Farther north find **139–141 Crichton**, the **Alexander Garvock House**, a rare example of a once-common double stone residence (see Lowertown walk for another example). Ottawa once boasted many such stone doubles when canal stonemasons were building their own and rental housing. Its style is a mixture of Gothic, characterized by steep front gables, and classical features such as end gables with symmetrically placed chimneys. Stone brackets with a scroll design give sturdy roof support.

Turn right (east) on Keefer, named after MacKay's son-in-law and prominent Canadian engineer, Thomas Coltrin Keefer. Turn left (north) again to walk up Avon Lane. These lanes originally provided access for tradesmen delivering puncheons of water and coal by horse-drawn cart. A short walk down Avon Lane takes you to Queen Victoria Street.

Before turning left (west), walk to your right to view the stone Anglican church of **St. Bartholomew** affectionately called St. Bart's. Built in 1868, it was designed by Thomas S. Scott. St. Bart's is still a popular village church serving Lindenlea, New Edinburgh, and Rockcliffe. Its steeply pitched, dominant roof and rough limestone walls lend St. Bart's a medieval aspect. This was deliberate. Both St. Alban's (see Sandy Hill walk) and this church reflect the Anglican Church's reform movement, when a return to the old liturgy not only affected the service itself, but, symbolically, also Anglican architectural style.

St. Bart's has a colourful history. From its beginning, pews were free standing. Its solid stone walls lined with brick provided sturdy insulation, but the interior must have been chilly when heated with its original wood stove. Lord and Lady Dufferin were among the many governors general who attended the church — but the GGs were the fortunate few whose seats were kept warm due to proximity to the heat.

Now backtrack and turn right (north) on Crichton. Numbers **58, 60**, and **62 Crichton** are lovingly restored frame cottages, complete with tidy gardens in front. Each boasts a verandah and pretty bargeboard beneath a Gothic Revival gabled roof. Front porches of various styles became popular in the mid 1800s, as a place to "take the air" and appreciate precious leisure time.

Number **48 Crichton** is a tiny stucco building with an intriguing garage that sports a pedimented parapet roofline with corner "battlements" and pressed tin siding. In bygone days, sashes and doors were made here. Farther along is **51 Crichton**, the **Tubman Home**, at the corner of Union. It is a rambling clapboard "farmhouse," with a large garden on a corner lot. The Tubman family lived here from 1874 until 1986.

58, 60 and 62 Crichton: board and batten, clapboard, and stucco finishing. October 1991. K. Fletcher.

On the northeast corner at Union is **42 Crichton**, formerly the village shop known as **McCreery's**, but now a deli. McCreery's was a village institution, being an important community grocery since 1902. Unfortunately, when the shop was sold its new owners gutted the heritage premises. No longer can we view the old shop's shelves nor can we admire the original pressed tin ceiling, for both features were torn out.

Walk right on Union towards Rideau Hall's distinctive fence of pedimented stone pillars and wrought iron. Turn left (north) on MacKay. Here starts a row of distinctive homes of varying styles, from classical Georgian symmetry to whimsical Victorian Gothic built in the 1870s and 1880s. Each home has its special charm.

Number **87 MacKay**, **Maison Fréchette**, was the residence of Achille Fréchette, lawyer, and Annie Howells Fréchette, writer, journalist, and friend of poets Duncan Campbell Scott and Archibald Lampman. The Fréchettes held evening soirées and readings here. This home is a good example of the Victorian's love for asymmetry. Look at the two flanking dormers: their windows are completely different shapes and sizes. Also, the front entry is offset. Now walk a few steps north and look back at the front door. There is an assortment of windows of various shapes — round, rectangular and arched —

which are placed at staggered heights. The effect is one of movement and surprise — a far cry from the rigid precision of classical symmetry.

Number **73–75 MacKay** is a double Victorian Gothic red brick cottage. William Woodburn, a carpenter at MacKay's sawmill, built this home around 1874, and the whimsical wishbone bargeboard beneath its steeply peaked gables may have served as advertising for his woodworking skills. The picturesque design of this double, with its contrasting corner quoins, adds a romantic note to the streetscape. Symmetry is achieved by the twin front gables and emphasized by their crowning finials, the front porch, and bay windows.

Number **55 MacKay** provides an interesting contrast. Although Victorian Gothic in feeling, this large house possesses many features associated with the Italianate style. Note the sturdy porch columns and pediment and, beneath the front gable, the three-panelled Palladian window, its central pane topped with the characteristic curved moulding. Victorian detailing abounds in the left-hand turret which has peaked dormer windows. Its height is surpassed by the ornate red brick chimney on the opposite side of the house. Built around 1898, the house was the residence of lumberman Gordon C. Edwards. Note the lovingly preserved carriage house to the rear of the home, with its cupola atop the gambrel roof.

At the corner of Thomas is **35 MacKay–71 Thomas**, a two-and-a-half storey, classically inspired house, built in 1864–65 for James Allen, a New Edinburgh merchant and, by 1867, the village tax collector. The house is also said to have been built by Anne MacKay, wife of Thomas, for white-collar mill employees.

Originally a single-family home, it was divided into two apartments in the 1870s. Classical features include the central doorway on MacKay, which is repeated in the side entry on Thomas. Both doors are framed by a rectangular transom above and sidelight windows which allow light into the hall. The rough cut limestone is softened by smooth corner quoins and lightened by the delicate bargeboard trim. The pedimented front porches were added in 1925 by tenant Allan Keefer, son of T. C. Keefer.

All of these homes on MacKay overlook the viceregal estate. A close look at **1 Sussex Drive, Rideau Hall (Government House)**, is possible if you join a scheduled tour or attend a twice-yearly public levee. It is delightful to enter the estate grounds and stroll its shaded walkways or simply to see the exhibit on the role of the Governor General in Canada at the Visitor's Centre. To find it, turn right on Thomas Street, which becomes Rideau Gate. At the corner, find **Gate Lodge**, built in 1838 as the senior gardener's home. Today it serves as the Visitor's Centre.

If you continue left on Rideau Gate, you come to the main entry to Rideau Hall. An octagonal gatehouse just inside the grounds was built at the time of Lord Monck's residency, in 1868.

The original Regency style country house, built in 1837–38 by Thomas MacKay was locally known as "MacKay's Castle." The estate was purchased by the federal government in 1868 for $82,000 as a viceregal residence in perpetuity. A series of rambling additions commenced at that time have almost completely obliterated the original design. However, if you go inside the grounds, look for the curved bay projecting from the rear of the southwest façade, which is part of MacKay's original building. In 1913 an immense royal coat of arms was added over the front doorway.

Rideau Hall could and did inspire guests at dazzling viceregal functions. Annie Howells Fréchette (whose house you just admired at 87 MacKay), catalogued the guests of Lord and Lady Lorne and itemized the entertainments, including dinner parties, balls, "at homes," skating and tobogganing parties, and theatricals between the years 1879 and 1881. By far the most popular were the latter two events which saw

Rideau Hall with family of Viscount Monck, Canada's first Governor General, posing for camera, 1868. Photo taken by Sam McLaughlin, commissioned by Sir. John A. Macdonald. PAC-C5966.

2,000 guests each year attend the winter sports parties and 1,300 guests a year at the theatricals.[11]

Guests exclaimed in wonder at displays of fairy lights illuminating the garden walks and thoroughly enjoyed participating in the rather more informal idiosyncrasies of their Excellencies. These included the fun-loving, albeit hazardous, way of lighting Rideau Hall's interior gas lamps. Lord and Lady Lorne's guest Victoria Sackville West tells us how she lit them: "by rubbing [my] feet in the carpet all along the big corridor and putting my nose in contact, at the end, with the gas-burner."[12]

The approach to Rideau Hall is the short street called Rideau Gate, which is dominated by sedately classical homes. Number **7 Rideau Gate** was built in 1867 and is, since 1966, the official guest house of the Government of Canada. It is a solid Georgian-inspired home ideally situated between Rideau Hall and 24 Sussex.

Number **5 Rideau Gate, Edgewood**, the **High Commission for the Republic of South Africa**, was once the home of "Minto's Folly," the charming Lola Powell, mistress to Governor General Lord Minto in the heady young years of the last part of the 19th Century. The second storey of Edgewood is an addition to the original 1841 home.

Skating parties at Rideau Hall were extremely popular.
NCC, M. Newton file H12-052.

You can easily discern the joinery in the stonework between the addition and the original structure. This is yet another house touched by the architectural hand of W. E. Noffke, whose May 14, 1947, plans for this building exist at the National Archives of Canada.

Before heading west on Sussex, note the (2002) traffic circle outside the main gates to Rideau Hall. Built mainly for security reasons, it also serves to control traffic at this increasingly busy corner.

Look at **24 Sussex Drive**, the prime minister of Canada's residence, named **Gorffwysfa**, Welsh for "a place of peace." The original 1867–68 Gothic villa with a central doorway framed by an overhead gable, built for mill owner Joseph M. Currier, has long vanished, victim to a succession of alterations by the Department of Public Works (DPW). In 1943, Emmet P. Murphy of DPW recommended federal purchase of the property to prevent further commercial development of the river frontage. In 1950, after years of renovations, the house was offered to Prime Minister Louis St. Laurent as official residence. He always preferred his rented apartment in the Roxborough Apartments.

At the time of expropriation, DPW had no plans for the home, which lay vacant for over a year. On November 29, 1949, architect Gustav Brault thought repairs totalling $168,000 were adequate. As work progressed, Brault's figure rose to $410,000.

The interior was completely gutted: carved wooden panelling and a gently curving ten-foot-wide oak staircase were ripped out. The exterior suffered: gone is the original Gothic gabled home with its prominent oriel window, replaced by a sprawling house of rambling style. Successive prime ministers have added their own touches, including a swimming pool in 1975, during the tenure of Pierre Elliott Trudeau. Both this house and Stornoway, the leader of the Opposition's official residence in Rockcliffe, are routinely redecorated at public expense each time new residents move in.

Continue west on Sussex, on the south side of the street, then turn left (south) on Alexander. On your right is the remnant of a stone wall built by Isaac McTaggart that once supported a glass hothouse.

At the corner of Thomas stop to look at **34 Alexander, Henderson House**, built for John Henderson, manager of the Maclaren lumber company. This Second Empire design features fanciful wishbone gables on all four sides of its otherwise mansard roof. Notice the round-headed windows below the fire escape on the north side. These are echoed by the rounded pediment over the doorway. The home was originally painted white with black roof, porch, and trim, which proudly emphasized its design elements. Duotone colour schemes were extremely popular at the turn of the twentieth century: black and white provided the most dramatic contrast.

The square section on the west side of the house was originally the conservatory. But in 1937 the home was turned into apartments and the plant collection moved to Rideau Hall. Once famed for its beautiful gardens, today this house is a victim of infill and additions. Henderson House is now cramped on a lot too small for its scale. Gentrification of the village has its drawbacks.

Turn right (west) at Thomas and right again on John Street. Walk due north to cross Sussex to your car. On your right you pass **62–64 John**, the **Fraser Schoolhouse** originally built by Thomas MacKay in 1837 as a home for his millworkers. He later converted it to a schoolhouse where Montreal teacher James Fraser taught the three Rs. In 1848 the building reverted to rental premises. By 1959 the NCC had plans for the river waterfront and the northern limits of New Edinburgh, and 62–64 John was expropriated, but it was saved from demolition by public outcry.

34 Alexander, Henderson House, with its beautiful wishbone gables. Oct. 1959. C. C. J. Bond. NCC, M. Newton file, Box 44.

The classically symmetrical limestone exterior remains. But the NCC made many alterations in 1967: dormer windows and a rear extension were removed, a new shingle roof, modern doors, and windows were added, and the interior was gutted. Now it's a private business.

Walk to Sussex. On your right is a plaque to the memory of Thomas MacKay, founder of New Edinburgh. Cross Sussex to **42 John Street**, the granite **French Embassy**, which stands on the site of Isaac McTaggart's distillery. Built in 1936–39 by France's then chief architect of civil buildings, Eugène Beaudoin, it is the first embassy in Ottawa that was specifically built for that purpose. Note its dramatic, boldly framed windows.

MacKay and Burritt's sprawling mills have gone, as has McTaggart's distillery, but the new parkland has restored the beauty of Rideau Falls. Today, New Edinburgh blends old with new, struggling to retain its village texture. Gone forever, however, are some village memories. In his recollections of earlier times, former resident John Askwith wrote: "In those days the people of the Village could hear on a wintry night, the howling of the wolves which were concentrated between the East end of the present St. Patrick Bridge and the cemeteries. They came frequently on the winter nights."[13]

Rideau Falls showing extent of MacKay's Mill complex to east.
Photo predates the 1958 International Style city hall.
NCC, M. Newton file M12-004.

John Street School. 2002. K. Fletcher.

The French Embassy. 2002. K. Fletcher.

Canal

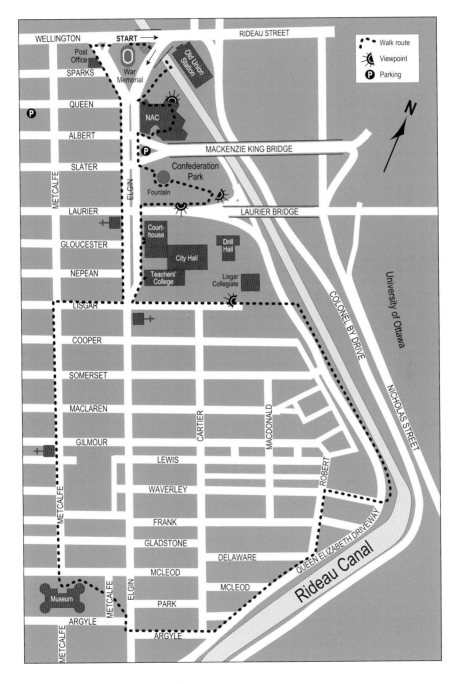

This Ottawa neighbourhood began its life in 1827 as Corkstown, located on either side of the Deep Cut. The Deep Cut is the straight stretch of the Rideau Canal alongside the Drill Hall and Lisgar Collegiate, extending to Waverley (see map). Deposits of highly unstable leda clay caused the canal walls to repeatedly collapse, and the workmen had much difficulty digging the canal here. Because of this, excavations had to be especially deep and well stabilized, hence the name "Deep Cut."

During the canal construction, Colonel By hired more than 300 Irish labourers. All needed housing but Bytown couldn't meet all their and their families' needs at once. In 1827 Lowertown was still a cedar swamp. A large, mosquito-infested beaver meadow existed where Union Station now stands. Many Irish labourers hewed their own rough log shanties out of the dense woods to create Corkstown, so called, some say, not because they came from Cork in Ireland, but because of all the whiskey corks popping from eagerly consumed bottles. Other settlers squatted in hastily built wooden shacks in Lowertown after the Bywash started to drain its low, wet land. After the Vesting Act of 1844, when the Ordnance relaxed its control of Lowertown, most labourers moved there from Corkstown.

It was here in Corkstown that Mother McGinty's popular tavern kept whiskey, beer, and a cordial known as "shrub" flowing. It seems she ruled her whitewashed log watering hole with a kindly but iron hand. Mrs. McGinty kept track of credit by making a short mark on a blackboard for half pints, a long mark for a gallon — and collected with a judicious blend of good humour and what one poet called "the athletic charms … of her bare arms."

Where Union Station and the National Arts Centre now stand was once the Canal Basin. The indented sides of the turning basin are filled in, but in early days there were landing docks for steamers delivering or receiving freight and goods from the crowd of wooden warehouses lining the canal. The traffic was so busy that the wooden boards of the docks needed continual maintenance and repair. On either side of the Canal Basin, steamers jostled for a berth. Boats such as the *Olive*, *Rideau Queen*, and *Pumper* docked here. And not all cargo was freight. Passenger traffic formed a respectable proportion of the canal trade. In the days before good roads or railways, water transportation was the way to go. Accordingly, steamers were outfitted

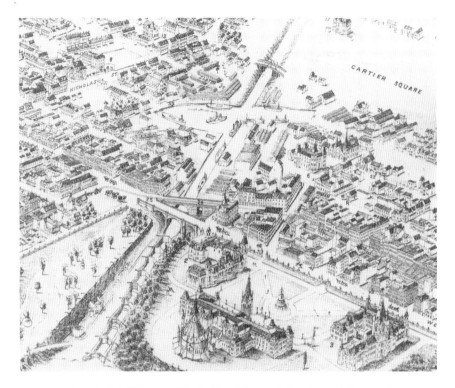

Detail of 1876 map, "Birds Eye View of the City of Ottawa,"
by Herman Brosius. Note the Canal Basin with several steamers at
its docks. The Laurier Avenue Bridge was then just a wooden
structure. NCC 172-301.

with overnight berths for passengers travelling between Kingston and
Ottawa, and beyond to Montreal.

The advent of rail effectively killed Rideau Canal water traffic.
Government control of the Canal Reserve — the strip of land bordering
the banks of the canal — was eventually relinquished. (Colonel By
had reserved the lands in case they were needed for military
fortifications.) The twin docks and turnaround areas of the basin were
filled in. In 1910 the Grand Trunk Railway was ceded land on the
east side of the basin, and in 1912 Union Station was built. The last
passenger steamer, the *Ottawan*, left its capital wharf on November 2,
1935, thus ending a century-long chapter in Ottawa's history.

Government control of lands was a constant issue. Nicholas Sparks
(after whom Sparks Street is named), an early Bytown resident,
purchased 200 acres of land bordered by Wellington, Bronson, Waller

The *Rideau Queen* heading north towards the canal turning basin c.
1908. Note the original Parliament Centre Block
on the upper left. NCC 712-284.

and Laurier. When Colonel By finally selected the present site of the
Rideau Canal in 1826, the Crown thwarted Sparks' intended
development of his eastern properties. Eighty-eight acres between Elgin
and Bank were seized for possible military defence, which prevented
Sparks from extending his street to Elgin. A long dispute ensued that
was finally resolved in 1845. Never one to waste time, Sparks immediately
divided his land into lots and sold them. But it took years for this
section of town to rival and then supersede the dominance of Sussex
and Rideau as the business core of the capital. In the 1860s Sparks
Street was gaining prominence, and by the 1880s brick and stone
buildings sprang up, reflecting the confidence of entrepreneurs in this
new business, professional and political centre of Ottawa.

As military threats died down after the Imperial troops left Ottawa
in 1870, increasing pressure was placed upon the Crown to free up the
Canal Reserve lands.

In 1832 By had purchased 600 acres for £1,200; today the canal,
Laurier, Bronson, and Gladstone Streets define the property. In 1876
three well-known Ottawa entrepreneurs — James Maclaren, Robert
Blackburn, and Charles McGee — bought part of his estate. The three
investors started the Ottawa Freehold Association in 1883 and the

development of the area into mixed commercial and residential quarters began in earnest. Increasingly, commercial buildings of the 1880s were built with permanence in mind. Buildings with brick load-bearing walls, wooden floor frames and a stone or brick exterior finish started to spring up. Styles such as Italianate, (the Scottish Ontario Chambers) Queen Anne (the Central Chambers) and Second Empire (the Langevin Block) competed for attention along the Elgin Street façade.

In earlier days, the Russell House dominated the Elgin-Sparks corner. It started life in 1845 as the Campbell House, a three-storey, tin-roofed inn. As Ottawa grew, so did the hotel's fortunes. In 1863 it became the Russell House, a popular meeting place for politicians, lobbyists, and journalists to argue and entertain one another with the latest gossip from the Hill.

The Russell's demise shocked residents. Its front doors were padlocked at 1:30 p.m. on October 1, 1925. It was destined to be demolished to make way for the creation of Confederation Square. While politicians and planners hemmed and hawed, two and a half

Russell House Hotel, corner of Sparks and Elgin.
Oscar Wilde once stayed here. S. J. Jarvis photo.
NCC, M. Newton file, Box 39.

years passed. During the night of April 14, 1928, a flicker of flame was seen in the old hotel: the Russell was doomed. For three months its blackened hulk haunted the streetscape it had once graced. Then the wrecking balls tore it apart in July of 1928. In the 1930s, Confederation Square took shape.

In 1899, Sir Wilfrid Laurier's Liberal government approved the creation of the Ottawa Improvement Commission. Its mandate was to plan the beautification of the capital. Frederick Todd's capital planning report of 1903 called for the effective landscaping of the industrial eyesore framing the Rideau Canal. Todd was deeply aware of how restorative natural scenery is to the human soul and so he encouraged the development of a picturesque landscape of trees, shrubery and floral beds.

Metcalfe Street was promoted by several governments and individuals as a ceremonial route to the Parliament Buildings. Framed by beautiful elm trees, gracious residences, and anchored by the splendid Victoria Memorial Museum (today's Museum of Nature), it seemed like a regal approach to Canada's seat of power. But because the land immediately south of the Hill was already built up by 1867, the costs of expropriation, demolition, and reconstruction were never approved. Finally, in 1939 Jacques Gréber proposed changes to the ceremonial

Rideau Canal, 1904, looking north towards
present site of Union Station. NCC 172-141.

route, but it was not until 1951, when his Master Plan was accepted by Louis St. Laurent's government, that his changes such as the oblique approach to the Parliament Buildings via Elgin Street were adopted. The dream of Metcalfe as a grand approach to Parliament was dead … Or, so the good people of Ottawa believed, until early 2000 when the NCC floated the idea of demolishing many buildings to create the grand approach to Parliament. Public outrage at the expense plus the loss of Ottawa's built heritage quashed the proposal … for now.

NEIGHBOURHOOD STYLES

The engineering marvel of Colonel John By's Rideau Canal lends visual continuity to this exploration of Ottawa. But many buildings of significance compete for attention. The National War Memorial provides a stunning start to the walk. Elgin Street — widened as far as Lisgar — boasts the colourful Italianate Scottish Ontario Chambers on the corner of Sparks Street Mall and Elgin, the Bell Block, and the Central Chambers, all Ottawa heritage gems. However, in 1993 architects Brisbin, Brock and Benyan started a massive downtown development project to incorporate all three into a modern office complex for Perez Commercial Corporation and Standard Life Assurance Limited. Today this heritage block is essentially a façade: the interiors of these buildings have been much altered over time.

The old limestone Teachers' College opposite the former residence of well-loved physician Dr. James Grant, now Friday's Restaurant, provides yet another important link to Ottawa's past. And architect David Ewart's Victoria Memorial Museum, now the Museum of Nature, is like a castle at the southernmost reach of this walk, deep in the heart of what was once Stewarton. The return route up Metcalfe Street evokes memories of past grandeur as you pass by the once-gracious mansions of Thomas Birkett and J. R. Booth.

The Canal-Metcalfe loop links symbols of national pride with seats of learning, private residences and commercial buildings. Tying it all together is the lovely parkland bordering the canal. The ring of picks and shovels has gone, as has the whitewashed tavern operated by well-loved Mrs. McGinty. Instead, paths through lawns and flowerbeds lure the walker.

🚶 4.5 km; 2 hours

You will be walking among parks, public buildings, and private residences. Feel free to explore the interior spaces of the National Arts Centre, the Ottawa Courthouse, and the Teachers' College, to name just a few of the public buildings on this walk. On Elgin Street you will find restaurants and shops to browse. As a special tip, it is well worthwhile visiting the War Memorial on November 11, Remembrance Day. Then, amid the crowds, the swirl of the kilts and the skirl of the bagpipes, Vernon March's sculpture takes on a life and symbolism of its own. (**Note:** In the description of this walk, the Queen Elizabeth Driveway has been abbreviated to "the Driveway.")

Installation of the War Memorial, Confederation Square, October 12, 1938. Now demolished Daly building visible at centre, rear. City of Ottawa Archives, CA 18623.

Start at the **National War Memorial** at the top of Elgin Street, southeast of Parliament Hill. Many buses arrive at this central location. If you are driving, find a parking space and make your way to the memorial.

The National War Memorial commemorates those who fought and died in World War I, World War II, and the Korean War. The allegorical figures perched on top of the monument are winged Victory and Liberty, who is holding a torch. Their flowing robes are reminiscent of the fluid, organic forms of the art nouveau period, and contrast markedly with the massive beaux arts style granite base. Through the arch of the granite, soldiers and horses look straight down Elgin Street. Notice the different races represented among these realistically detailed soldiers. A symbol of the pride and hope of a young Canada, the memorial dominates Elgin's busy streetscape. British sculptor Vernon March died before finishing his work. Completed by his brothers and sister, the sculpture was unveiled by King George VI on May 21, 1939.

On May 28, 2000 the Tomb of the Unknown Soldier was unveiled beneath the War Memorial. Constructed of granite from the Beauce region of Quebec, the sarcophagus is adorned with bronze maple leaves, a sword and helmet sculpted by Mary-Ann Liu, an artist from Mission, British Columbia.

The story of the Unknown Soldier is appropriately touching. The grave of an unknown Canadian soldier was disinterred from a cemetery near Vimy Ridge, and reburied here in Confederation Square. The tomb symbolizes the 116,000 or so men and women who fought during WW I and who lost their lives serving Canada abroad, and the sarcophagus represents the estimated 28,000 Canadians who have no marked gravesite.

Prior to the body being laid to rest here, it was honoured with a ceremony at Vimy Ridge, then flown to Canada where the remains lay in state in the Parliament Buildings. When the final internment was conducted at the War Memorial, soil from each of Canada's provinces and territories was buried with the coffin. The site is spectacularly lit after nightfall thanks to lighting designer Martin Conboy.

Look about you to note how the War Memorial site located diagonally opposite Parliament Hill, marks the symbolic heart of the capital. This asymmetrical approach to the Hill has bothered many Ottawa planners, who periodically threaten to demolish parts of the city so as to create a grand approach to Parliament. Previous prime ministers such as Laurier and King, through to official bodies such as today's National Capital Commission (and its precursors the OIC and FDC) have puzzled over how to realign Elgin and/or Metcalfe streets. Most recently, the NCC floated a highly unpopular notion: to tear down many buildings on Metcalfe to widen the approach.

Descend the broad flight of stairs on the east side of the War Memorial to admire Martin Conboy's lighting design on the underbelly of the Plaza Bridge. Walk left briefly, to see how he has created a theatrical touch (this is particularly appealing after nightfall, when you can view the canal water through punched-out holes in the supports of the bridge). If you continued north, with the canal on your right-hand side, you would reach the Bytown Museum (the former Commissariat — see Parliament Hill walk).

Now turn around and head south under the bridge with the canal on your left. Turn right to follow the pathway up across a lawn (look out for rabbits here, nibbling on the grass) to get to the east side of Elgin. To your left is the dark brown, gracefully Brutalist **National Arts Centre**, built 1964–69 by the architectural team of Affleck, Desbarats, Dimakopoulos, Lebensold and Sise. Find the staircase leading

The National Arts Centre, is "the most mysterious building in town," because no one can tell where the entrance is, according to architect Moshe Safdie. NCC 186-94.

up to the patios overlooking the canal. From here you can see the combination of hexagonal forms that describe the structure. Designed as a series of stepped terraces, which alleviate and animate its sheer walls, the building successfully integrates itself into the embankment overlooking the canal.

Its elevation affords an unexpected perspective on **Confederation Square**, and you can catch a glimpse of the Gatineau Hills to the north. While facing north you will see old Union Station (see Sussex walk) on the east side of the Canal opposite the Château Laurier. Keep to your right to walk to the south side, from which you can see the picturesque Drill Hall fronting Cartier Square. Note the dominating form of the Ottawa Courthouse standing on the corner of Laurier and Elgin, beyond Confederation Park. From this perspective, note the courthouse's modern equivalent of towers, topped with squared-off caps slightly reminiscent of châteauesque detailing.

Find the stairs by the sculpture on the south façade of the Arts Centre. Walk down and turn right to return to Elgin Street. Turn left (south) and cross Albert and Slater Streets. These two streets merge on your left to cross over the canal: this is the Mackenzie King Bridge. Turn left again at the angled pathway into **Confederation Park**, which was created in the 1960s by a series of expropriations and demolitions courtesy of the NCC. Among the demolished buildings was the eighty-two-suite Roxborough Apartment, a popular hotel-apartment for many politicians, including Mackenzie King. The eight-storey, eighty-two-suite apartment block built by Colonel James Woods was demolished in 1965. The space was supposed to be the new home of the Museum of Natural Science. However, after serving as a parking lot for years, the area was landscaped to create this welcome greenspace. A parking lot servicing the National Arts Centre was built beneath it.

The centerpiece of Confederation Park is the cascading fountain once located in Trafalgar Square, London. It was dedicated to Colonel By on October 5, 1955. Surrounding it — and dotted throughout the park — are many commemorative sculptures and artworks. At the southwest entry to the park find a massive bronze sculpture featuring bison, eagle and human figures honouring First Nations people who fought for Canada during the wars.

Angle through the park, keeping to your left until you reach the **Laurier Avenue Bridge**. Originally built of wood in 1872, when Laurier was known as Maria Street, the bridge provided a link to Sandy Hill and Lowertown. In 1900 a masonry and steel bridge replaced the original wood, and in 1943 the bridge was expanded again. In a spirit of heritage enthusiasm, the city has painted the turn-of-the-twentieth-century spans green. After undergoing even more construction in 2002-03, it reopened as a three-lane bridge.

Leave the bridge behind you to walk west on Laurier Avenue. On your left you will pass the 1879 **Cartier Square Drill Hall**, a vernacular hybrid, which incorporates touches of Italianate and Second Empire details. Its polychromatic façade is Italianate, as are its multiple round-arched windows and stringcourse. Yet a Second Empire feeling is imparted by its centre raised parapeted gable and flanking corner pavilions, which are topped with mansard caps. Apart from the addition of a new roof in 1981, and refurbishing of the brick façade in the mid 1990s, the building is basically unchanged. During the devastating Ottawa fire of 1900 it provided refuge for many destitute families.

West of the Drill Hall is the Regional Municipality of Ottawa-Carleton complex you will visit later on this walk.

At Elgin Street, turn left (south) to cross Laurier. You are now walking beside the 1986 **Ottawa Courthouse**. Architects Murray & Murray designed this severely Brutalist structure. The sheer walls of its imposing, almost windowless exterior feature fibreglass "boulders"

The Ottawa Courthouse, November 1991. Its massive form dominates the corner of Laurier and Elgin. K. Fletcher.

projecting from its Elgin Street façade. It is a dominating presence that demands attention and respect, and which also imparts faceless anonymity.

Enter off Elgin to go inside the courthouse. Its interior space reflects an inward-looking design. There are busy offices, oak-panelled courtrooms and public concourses. It is surprisingly light and airy, with a triangular-shaped central atrium that vertically connects all floors.

On your way out, on the first floor, locate Courtroom 24. Opposite, on the wall, is artist Jamelie Hassan's 1986 ceramic replica of Lieutenant Colonel By's 1830 map of the Rideau Waterway, "Water Communication." Hassan preserved By's original spelling of landmarks such as the "Gatteno" River and the Township of "Nipean."

Return to Elgin Street, turn left and find part of **Ottawa's City Hall** that now contains the Mayor's office and other administrative offices. The building was once the **Ottawa Teachers' College**, originally called the Normal School, which opened in 1875 at a cost of $81,000, and was one of the first of three such schools in Ontario. Architecturally eclectic, the cut limestone building is a mix of styles: Gothic, Second Empire, and Norman Romanesque. Second Empire is reflected in the building's overall massing, best evidenced in its Elgin façade. Note its central, mansard-roofed entrance pavilion. The doorway itself features a heavy looking rounded archway. Arched windows and colonnettes (small non-structural columns) are symmetrically positioned on either side of the door. Victorian Gothic touches such as the steep front gable with a trefoil motif, and steep-roofed belfries with pointed-arch openings add extra interest to this stylistic hybrid. In contrast to the postmodernist and Brutalist edifices along Elgin Street, this all-too-rare stone heritage building adds a humanizing touch to the streetscape.

If it is open, enter the Teachers' College to see its high and patterned pressed-tin ceilings, the Victorian scrolled and panelled detailing of the staircase at the rear east end, and the deeply inset window ledges which indicate the thickness of its old stone walls.

Return outside to Elgin Street and turn left (east) on Lisgar.

To your left is the **Model School** attached to the rear of the Teachers' College. It opened for classes in September 1880, and operated for thirty years allowing teachers-in-training a "model" school in which to practice their professional skills prior to graduation. Built of cut, rough-surfaced stone, it is similar to the Teachers' College in its stylistic mix. When it opened, there were six classrooms, an assembly room, a room for the head teacher, and a "recreation yard" more than 200 feet long.

Farther along Lisgar, and attached to the Model School, find **111 Lisgar**, a complex of public and administrative offices as well as City Hall (formerly the Regional Municipality of Ottawa-Carleton [RMOC] building). Completed in 1990 at a cost of $87 million, architect Raymond Moriyama here designed a postmodern building complete with steel lattice bell tower and sheer curtain walls. Go inside to view the council chamber. Its muted colours are in stark contrast to the hard surfaces of highly polished marble that dominate the building's interior public spaces.

Lisgar Collegiate. November 1991. K. Fletcher.

Continue east along Lisgar to **Lisgar Collegiate**, originally built in 1874 in the Gothic Revival style by architects W. T. Thomas and W. Chesterton. At first, the buildings were poorly heated, and students and teachers alike often sat huddled in their coats to keep warm. The problem was rectified in 1888 when a heating and ventilation system was installed. The school was seriously overcrowded by 1890. In 1892 James Mather designed an addition, but on January 30, 1893, the entire building burned. By mid-March, Mather had redesigned a completely new structure.

Like the original, the new building was faced in stone from Robert Skead's quarry in Nepean. Walk down the pathway on the school's west side to look at the projecting oriel window — the second-storey bay — on the north façade. As the student population continued to grow, so did the demands for additions: the years 1903, 1908, 1951, and 1962 all saw further additions designed by a number of architects. Return to the front of the building. The 1951 gymnasium by John Albert Ewart and A. J. Hazelgrove is connected to the front of the main building on Lisgar by an underground tunnel.

There are many scholastic motifs in the exterior carvings, including a set of books, a scroll, and the symbolic oil lamp of learning, whose motif is also found on the University of Ottawa's Simard Hall on Waller Street (see Sandy Hill walk).

Before heading on to the Queen Elizabeth Driveway, look west along Lisgar to appreciate the integration of 1870s' and 1990s' architecture. Lisgar Collegiate and the Teachers' College share the skyline with the vertical striping of Place Bell Canada and the postmodern glass-and-brick Barrister House.

Now proceed towards the canal. Cross the **Driveway**, built 1900–05 by the Ottawa Improvement Commission. Head south along its landscaped embankments. You will also see two "modern heritage" landmarks on the opposite side of the canal. One is the stylized cross of the University of Ottawa tower; the second is the op-art eyes painted on McDonald Hall, the physics and computer science building.

When first constructed, the Driveway was narrower. Travelling along it by horse and carriage allowed time to view the ornamental gardens that originally featured formal arrangements. Automobile traffic dramatically altered the landscaping. Streets were widened. Flower arrangements became less formalized because people couldn't appreciate the workmanship as they whizzed past in their cars. After World War II the designs changed again thanks to Holland's annual donation of thousands of tulips, a tradition still upheld today, and a source of national pride.

The canal now makes quite a dramatic "elbow" sweep to the southwest where you will find Waverley Street leading west. Go up it and immediately on your right you will find the **Embassy of the Federal Republic of Germany**. Its small windows seem to be punched-out of the sheer stone façade, recalling the Brutalism of the Ontario courthouse you viewed earlier (corner Laurier and Elgin). Walk west on Waverley to Robert Street.

Architect Peter Pivko designed **53–55 Robert** (1988), a dramatic postmodern rectangle on the corner of Robert and Waverley. Sheer white stucco exterior walls are relieved with angled teal blue and magenta windows. Much to the alarm of some neighbours (who tried to prevent this house from being built), this surprising residence shakes up the neighbourhood with its factory-like appearance in a sea of red-brick. The front is angled on its lot because of the imposed constraint of the property line itself, which is not square. Position yourself so you can look sideways along its façade to fully appreciate its windows, which project at angles from the otherwise smooth frontal plane. (This contemporary postmodernist home provides a fascinating comparison to the two modernist homes in Sandy Hill, on Goulburn and Range Roads.)

53–55 Robert. October 1991. K. Fletcher.

Turn left on Robert. On the right note the Rogue Victorian home, **65 Robert**. A rounded, bell-capped turret adorns this red brick residence with its asymmetrical, squared-off entryway, a sad later addition built when the single family home was turned into apartments. Unfortunately, this addition totally destroys the dignity of this otherwise beautiful home. (Its mate is 278 Crichton Street — see New Edinburgh walk.)

7 Delaware, the Embassy of the Republic of Armenia.
October 1991. K. Fletcher.

Turn right (south) at the Driveway and follow the paved pathway. On your immediate right is the Spanish Colonial Revival **Embassy of the Republic of Armenia** at **7 Delaware**. Prior to 1992, this house was a neighbourhood landmark because it was painted a brilliant robin's egg blue. Its present beige stucco façade is far less interesting. The 1900 residence was remodelled by W. E. Noffke in 1922 and still features beautiful diamond-shaped leaded glass windows and a red Spanish tile roof. Note the curvilinear gable and the sweep of the flared piers supporting the tiled, hip-roofed porch. Although crowded on a lot too small for its mass, the home adds charm and whimsy to the street.

Continue on the paved path now snuggled between the pretty back gardens of homes and a protective band of shrubbery lining the Driveway. In season you can catch the fragrance of roses and other blossoms; it's a nice spot to linger and examine how different garden plants are used for decorative effect. Next on your right is **102–108 Driveway**, at the corner of McLeod. Beautifully curved two-storey porches and flanking Palladian windows give this angled, flat-topped co-operative its charm.

Continue walking south until you reach Argyle Street. In summertime this walkway particularly appeals to gardeners, because flowers, shrubs, and landscape design are readily admired here, as is the fragrance of the roses and other blossoms.

Turn right (west) on Argyle and walk to Elgin Street. Here we can appreciate several postmodern red brick apartments (numbers **45–49 Argyle**) whose ground-floor patios are particularly attractive. As soon as the good weather comes, flower boxes, tomato plants, and patio furniture create an eye-catching, pretty addition to the streetscape. Numbers **51–59 Argyle** are older apartments, all of which have been spruced up recently.

At the corner of Elgin, cross at the lights and turn right. On your left at **424 Elgin** is the concrete and glass-bricked police station. Its sloped glass roof facing the street is attractive but can be a menace in winter when snow and ice cascade down onto the entryway. Every winter barricades are erected to guide people safely inside the police station.

The next block features the park grounds of the **Museum of Nature**, formerly the **Victoria Memorial Museum**. The museum was built for $1,250,000 between the years 1905 and 1912 by architect David Ewart. The builder, George Goodwin, employed 300 master stonemasons and stonecutters specially hired from Scotland. Walk around its magnificently ornate, castle-like exterior to view the detailed carvings and stained-glass windows. These windows are best seen from the interior: go inside, look up, and appreciate their exquisite detail. They are highly reminiscent of the style of the Arts and Crafts Movement, and have the feel of a William Morris design.

Ewart deliberately designed the museum to balance the Parliament Buildings in the days when Metcalfe Street was envisioned as a ceremonial route to the Hill. But, from the beginning, construction was fraught with complications. Because of unstable leda clay the foundations settled, and in 1915 the central tower started to pull away from the front of the building. The unstable clay forced Ewart to alter

The Museum of Nature: David Ewart's "castle."
November 1991. K. Fletcher.

his original designs — an example, like St. Alban's in Sandy Hill or the Parliament Buildings, of the natural environment's influence upon style. Workmen were affected, too. Some threw down their tools, refusing to work in the basement where shifting foundations shot bricks and stones at them.

The museum has served various functions. After the February 1916 fire destroyed the Centre Block of Parliament, the Senate and House of Commons convened here until 1920, when it reverted to its former function as home to the National Gallery and the Geological Survey of Canada. In 1919 the state funeral procession of Sir Wilfrid Laurier started here, his coffin in a carriage drawn by a jet black horse. By 1970 the settling and shifting of the museum's foundations could no longer be ignored: $6 million had to be spent on repairs, including a staggering $2.8 million to shore up the cracked, unstable foundations.

The land on which the museum sits was formerly the site of Appin Place, the 1868 residence of Kathleen Stewart, whose husband, William, was a prosperous early Bytown merchant and councillor. He died in Toronto in 1856, a champion of Confederation and a promoter of

Appin Place, built 1868 and demolished in 1902. NCC.

Ottawa as the new country's capital. In 1834 the couple purchased the land bounded by Gladstone, the Rideau River, and Bronson to just south of the Queensway. Kathleen Stewart built her home here after her husband's death. By the 1870s civil servants coming to the new capital started to purchase and build on the desirable lots, and in 1889 the City of Ottawa annexed what had become known as Stewarton along with its population of 400 residents. *The Journal* of May 18, 1888, still referred Stewarton as "the outposts" of the city. In 1902 the federal government purchased and tore down Kathleen Stewart's Gothic cottage to make room for the museum as a part of the OIC's plan for Metcalfe Street.

Now walk north on Metcalfe Street. Number **306 Metcalfe** is **Birkett's Castle**, a whimsical home of bright red brick. A red sandstone archway framing the front door is handsomely set off by a strongly contrasting rough cut limestone base. The baronial Gothic style is emphasized by its deeply crenellated roofline reminiscent of an old Scottish castle. Thomas Birkett was a successful hardware merchant in Ottawa, then mayor in 1891 and MP for Ottawa in 1900. He built the home in 1896, one of many VIPs to take up residence on the prestigious street.

306 Metcalfe, Birkett's Castle, is a residential interpretation of the castle theme. October 1991. K. Fletcher.

Today, Birkett's Castle is home to the **Embassy of Hungary**. Its interior still retains much of its Victorian detailing. Reminiscent of the *chinoiserie* popular in Victorian times is the vestibule's pressed-tin panelling figured with oriental designs of birds, dragons, and dolphins. The foyer boasts richly carved wooden paneling. A generous staircase sweeps into the hallway, and a bronze figurine of a fairy, Eau, graces the newel post.

Next find **296 Metcalfe**. The end-gabled red brick house features decorative terra cotta tiles depicting stylized thistles, maple, and lotus leaves.

Number **288 Metcalfe, First Church of Christ, Scientist**, is an example of the Palladian classical tradition. Andrea Palladio was an Italian Renaissance architect whose style enthralled British architects in the 1700s. This 1913 church, by architect J. P. Maclaren, represents a revival of this temple-like classical style. It features strong vertical lines emphasized by solid Corinthian columns supporting a dominating triangular pediment. Curved arches over doorways and windows soften the stepped roof visible behind the pediment.

288 Metcalfe, First Church of Christ, Scientist. October 1991.
K. Fletcher.

Number **233 Gilmour**, the **Public Service Alliance of Canada** (1968–69) at the corner of Gilmour and Metcalfe, is an oval tower faced in dark brick. It too is built on leda clay, but the architectural team of Schoeler, Heaton, Harvor and Menendez designed a raft-like, reinforced foundation that "floats" the building on this unstable deposit of clay. The building has evenly spaced windows whose glass is thicker in the top storeys to withstand the winds created by the building's shape.

Metcalfe Street continued to be a desirable address as the city grew, and so several apartment buildings were built here. **The Mayfair, 260 Metcalfe**, features carved wooden mouldings that nicely offset the ground and first floor windows.

Number **252 Metcalfe**, the **Laurentian Club** was designed by architect John W. H. Watts for millionaire Ottawa Valley lumber baron John Rodolphus Booth in 1909. Booth hired Swedish craftsmen to do the interior woodwork. Each room features a different species of wood that Booth personally selected. He died here in 1925, aged ninety-five. His son, Jackson, continued to live in this eclectic Victorian home until its sale to the Laurentian Club in 1947.

252 Metcalfe, the Laurentian Club, former home to Jackson Booth. Its irregular massing and eclectic use of materials and styles identify it as a late Queen Anne design. Aug. 1967. C. C. J. Bond. NCC, M. Newton file H12-122, Box 50.

A few steps farther north is **236 Metcalfe**, the **Chelsea Club**. This is one of the homes built on Ottawa Freehold Association property. Note the contrasting coloured hooded mouldings that frame the windows on this Italianate residence. Round-headed dormers are set into the shallow roof, and slightly overhanging eaves are supported by carved wooden brackets. Sir Alexander Campbell, a Father of Confederation, is listed as the first of many residents. He sold to brewer Sir John Carling, who sold to Louis H. Davies, chief justice of the Supreme Court of Canada. The Chelsea Club purchased the home from Davies' executors in 1926.

Continue north on Metcalfe. The streetscape becomes increasingly confused as you pass from the last of the grand residences of Metcalfe into a profusion of competing apartment buildings, commercial properties, and parking lots.

At **216 Metcalfe**, on the corner of Cooper, is **The Duncannon**, a luxury apartment built in 1931. Note the diamond-shaped leaded-glass window panes, the shallow Tudor revival stone arch over the entrance, and the patterned brickwork. As well, notice the apartment's overall design. Its gracious, welcoming entryway is deeply recessed, with two "wings" to the north and south. This popular apartment block design allows maximum light and air into the flats. In 1996 the building achieved heritage designation.

The Duncannon was designed as a desirable address: it was home to Martha Black, the second woman elected to the House of Commons, as well as Canadian photographer Yosuf Karsh.

Before turning right (east) on Lisgar, look north to **180 Metcalfe** to see Noffke's 1928 **Medical Arts Building**, a six-storey edifice featuring a stepped effect characteristic of many skyscrapers of this period, such as Toronto's 1928–29 Royal York Hotel. Noffke's art deco design includes decorative, geometrical brickwork and façade pilasters that feature a linear motif at the top.

Walk up to read the plaque by the entryway, placed here on October 15 1999. It informs us that Thomas "Carbide" Willson, one of Canada's most famous entrepreneurs, lived near here. Nicknamed "Carbide" because he discovered how to make calcium carbide commercially, Willson did much experimentation in the electrochemical field. The addition of water to calcium carbide creates acetylene gas, and it was Willson who "lighted the St. Lawrence" with acetylene buoys. (Willson also built the Ottawa Carbide Company Mill on Victoria Island in the 1890s as well as the super-phosphate fertilizer plant on Little Meech Lake in Gatineau Park, just below his summer residence.)

Return to Lisgar and walk east to **182–184 Lisgar**. Two flanking gambrel-roofed gables, softly flared at their base, and two porches with heavy brick and stone supports give a symmetrical look to this building. Its façade is enlivened by the polychromatic effect of the blond brick and grey stone. Horizontal planes are accentuated by the windows, by the cornice, and by alternate courses of stone and brick.

Number **180 Lisgar**, the **Royal York Apartments**, is next. Built in 1935, this is an unobtrusive building whose metal balcony railings feature a geometric art deco design. This motif is continued by the canopied entry with fluted, slightly projecting pilasters flanking the doorway, and by a stepped linear moulding above it.

Continue to Elgin Street, and turn left (north) towards the War Memorial and the start of your tour. To your immediate left is the tall postmodern **Barrister House, 180 Elgin**, by architect Alistair Ross. Located across the street from the Ottawa Courthouse, the building was opened in 1985 as office space for barristers. Go inside to contrast the postmodernist interpretation of art deco, a style you have just seen on the exteriors of 180 Lisgar and Noffke's Medical Arts Building. Pilasters with flared capitals that incorporate lights inside them compete for your attention with the loud geometric patterns in the floor of highly polished, reflective marble.

Next door is **Place Bell Canada**, a 1971 Olympia and York development. The tall light-coloured towers, striped with dark windows, bring a vertical dimension to the streetscape, and are especially effective at night.

150 Elgin, Dr. Grant's home, was still flanked by a now-demolished red brick residence on Aug. 16, 1967. To the right is the spire of the First Baptist Church. C. C. J. Bond.
NCC, M. Newton file, H12-135.

Number **150 Elgin**, **Grant House**, was Dr. Grant's residence. Sir James Alexander Grant, M.D. was a much respected medical doctor at the turn of the last century, being physician to Governors General from 1867 to 1905. *The Ottawa Citizen* of December 6, 1875, described Grant's new house: "Its style is that free and easy admixture of French Modern and Italian, which is fast becoming the vernacular of this county. The walls are of brick, Ottawa red, faced with Toronto white and with plain sandstone dressing to openings. It has a stone basement, measures 48 x 61 feet externally, and will cost about $11,000. The contractors are, for stonework, Messrs. Whillans. ... The architect is Mr. B. Billings." B. Billings was Braddish Billings III, the grandson of the Massachusetts settler who worked for Philemon Wright in 1817. He prospered and built the New England colonial clapboard home preserved as the Billings Museum.

Grant's home is an important survivor of the houses of the 1870s that once twinned Elgin with Metcalfe Street. Today the home is a restaurant. Go inside to see its interior layout, tall ceilings and the still-gracious staircase terminated by a sturdy newel post. Marble fireplaces still exist in most rooms.

Number **140 Laurier Avenue West**, **First Baptist Church**, graces the busy corner of Laurier and Elgin. Designed by architect James Mather in a Gothic style, the church was built in 1877–78. Tall lancet windows enhance the vertical thrust of the spire. Corner buttresses further emphasize this height. The cornerstone to Mather's cut limestone church was laid by Prime Minister Alexander Mackenzie, who worshipped here, as did Prime Minister Diefenbaker. The stained glass north window honours the industry that developed the Ottawa Valley. Two lumbermen stand beside an image of Christ, above the inscription: "The Trees of the Wood sing out in the Presence of the Lord."

Cross Laurier to the **Lord Elgin Hotel** built between 1940–41 by Ross and Macdonald in the châteauesque style with the copper turreted and dormered roof so favoured by Prime Minister Mackenzie King. In 2002 an addition was completed. Step inside the lobby to find marble busts of Lord and Lady Elgin.

Continue north to **90 Elgin**, the **Lorne Building** at the northwest corner of Slater. Named after the Marquis of Lorne, Governor General from 1878–83 and a great patron of the arts, this building "temporarily" housed the National Gallery for more than thirty years. A 1977 competition for a new design was won by architect John Parkin and Associates, but construction never commenced. A second competition, in 1982 and won by architect Moshe Safdie, resulted in the Gallery's new home on Sussex Drive (see Sussex walk).

Number **80 Elgin** is the **British High Commission**, an eight-storey building constructed in 1964 and designed by British architect W. S. Bryant. A façade of highly polished granite on the ground level reflects the light, making an interesting interplay of light and shadow. The building is set well back from the street, and so there is room for boxes of plants in front of it. Look closely and you'll spot some sculptures among them as you pass by.

Continue along Elgin to Albert. The first **Knox Church** was erected in 1872 on this corner but was demolished to broaden Elgin Street in the 1930s, when Confederation Square was built. (The "new" 1932 Knox Church by architects Sproatt & Rolph is sited across from the Teachers' College on the southeast corner of Elgin and Lisgar.) Building construction was supervised by J. Albert Ewart, and the builder was A. I. Garvock. The original design won an award from the Royal Architectural Institute of Canada.

This corner once overlooked the old post office, City Hall, and Russell Hotel prior to their destruction by fire and demolition. *The Ottawa Citizen* of February 14, 1872, remarked: "The plans and specifications of Knox's Church, which is to be built on Union Square, may be seen at Mr. Hope's stationery store. It will be an exceedingly handsome structure, and make quite an ornament to the city. If many more edifices be built in that neighbourhood, the old City Hall will crawl down to the Canal Basin and drown itself." This quote reflects the keen interest Ottawans had in the development of their city. Many architects' plans were advertised in the pages of old newspapers.

Between Queen and Sparks stands **46 Elgin**, the **Central Chambers**, a triangular building of special heritage significance. It was erected in 1889 as prestigious office space. The architect was John James Browne of Montreal, who chose the highly decorative Queen Anne style — unusual for commercial buildings which were more commonly Italianate. It cost approximately $100,000. The Central Chamber's is one of the first Ottawa buildings made with steel girders, which here rest on masonry supporting walls. The vertical composition of its bay windows represented another exciting design feature in its day. Here, Browne copied the idea from British architect Richard Norman Shaw, whose 1871–73 New Zealand Chamber in London, England, was avant-garde at the time. Today, such a design is hardly noticed, as we are used to large expanses of glass. However, newspaper advertisements of the day

Central Chambers c. 1920. Note the angled doorway, now removed.
NCC, M. Newton file, H12-221, Box 47.

boasted that the Central Chamber's windows were of the finest British plate glass.

The building was originally heated by steam, and tenants could choose whether to light their offices by electricity or gas. The *Ottawa Journal* of March 22, 1889, listed the Central Chambers advantages: "An Elevator of the newest and most approved design is in constant use. Special attention paid to ventilation and sanitary arrangements. Moderate rents will include janitorial service, thus relieving tenants of a very great annoyance."

Note the terra cotta detailing of oak leaves, thistles, and acorns along the building's polychromatic façade and the steeply gabled top windows that pierce the horizontal line of the flat-topped roof. This richly embellished building beautifully frames the west flank of Confederation Square. In 1964 the NCC purchased it. In January 1993, architects Brisbin, Brock and Benyan started work on refurbishing and integrating the Chambers into a large postmodern complex.

Adjacent to the Central Chambers is the **Bell Block** (1867) followed by the **Scottish Ontario Chambers** at the south corner of the Sparks Street Mall. Architect William Hodgson designed both in the Italianate style — then the most popular architectural style for commercial properties. Victorians loved asymmetry and colour, here interpreted by the massive stone base supporting upper stories of lighter-looking polychromatic brickwork. Note the narrow windows that are highlighted by segmented voussoirs, with prominent central keystones.

Streetcar on Sparks Street at Elgin, n.d.
City of Ottawa Archives, CA 0164.

Balancing it on the north corner of Sparks and Elgin is W. E. Noffke's 1938–39 **Central Post Office**, now **Postal Station B**, guarded by stone lions. Noffke's design effectively integrates with the other imposing stylistic precedents of the Langevin Block (Second Empire), East Block (Gothic Revival), Château Laurier (châteauesque) and Union Station (classical).

The post office boasts the beaux arts typical tripartite design, for it has three very discernible horizontal layers. A sturdy rusticated stone base sports two-storey high, rounded arch windows and is topped by a cornice above the second floor. Its mid-section features regularly spaced windows between flattened stone piers. This is surmounted by a copper châteauesque roof, its steep pitch relieved by dormer windows. Tying the vertical composition together is the curved corner. This is a successful *trompe-l'oeil*: it fools the onlooker into thinking it is a tower. Notice the angle of the corner curve as it extends upwards into the copper roofline. It has a triangular shape that resembles a corner tower.

Proud lion protecting the entrance to Noffke's Central Post Office, corner Sparks and Elgin. NCC 172.

Now you come to the **Langevin Block** built in 1883–89, designed by architect Thomas Fuller, who did the original Centre Block and Library of Parliament. This Second Empire building is of rich olive sandstone from New Brunswick. Its namesake, Sir Hector-Louis Langevin, was a Father of Confederation who represented New Brunswick. Like the post office, the Langevin Block is also a horizontally layered composition rooted by a rusticated stone base. Prominent stringcourses divide the floors. Stand back to note how a vertical feeling is imparted by the fenestration: windows diminish in size from large ones on the lower floors to small ones on the top storey. Such details help to carry one's eye upwards and visually reduce what could otherwise be an overbearing horizontal massing. Notice the rounded arched windows that are framed by colonnettes of highly polished pink granite and prominent mouldings.

On your right is the War Memorial: you have now returned to the start of the canal walk.

The Glebe

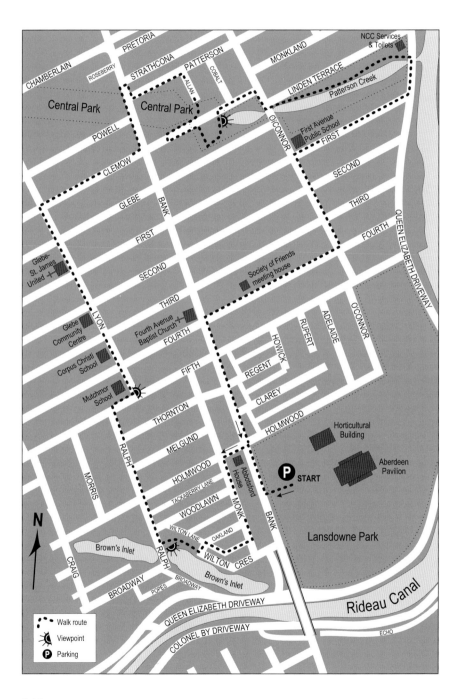

"New Toll Gate: The Ottawa and Gloucester Macadamized Road Company intend erecting a new toll gate house on their road opposite the residence of Mr. Mutchmore [sic]. This is done to catch those who evade the toll by branching off to Elgin near the Agricultural Show grounds."[14]

These two brief sentences from *The Ottawa Citizen* of 1875 open a window onto the land south of the McLeod Street "boundary" that on an 1874 Ottawa map is identified as the City Limit. Until the 1880s, the McLeod toll gate officially delineated "country and city." In later years, J. R. Booth's Canada Atlantic Railway similarly cut off the Glebe from Ottawa proper until it was replaced by the present Queensway in the 1950s.

In Ottawa's early years, the Glebe was farmland, much of it being part of the Clergy Reserve of St. Andrew's Presbyterian Church. In 1826, George Patterson, Colonel By's chief of the Commissariat, was also granted land in the area. But it was not until the 1870s that the farmland was deemed to be within reasonable distance from the city centre. Pioneer Alexander Mutchmor built his stone home, Abbotsford House, here in 1872 in open farmland.

The Ottawa Citizen of May 15, 1874, listed a house for sale in the Glebe: "There are also excellent out-houses and every accommodation requisite for a comfortable rural residence ... an excellent opportunity for persons of limited means who desire to secure a pleasant Residence within a convenient distance of the city."

The exhibition grounds at Lansdowne Park became the ideal site for an agricultural fair, removed as it was from the city centre. From Buffalo Bill to the steeplechases and the first running of the Queen's Plate, the fairs at Lansdown have long been a dominant feature of the Glebe. Buffalo Bill Cody's "Wild West Show" first came to Ottawa in 1893 to thrill an astounded audience with its version of Custer's Last Stand at the Battle of Little Bighorn. The troupe staged the show on the east side of the canal at the old Metropolitan Grounds past today's Pretoria Bridge. In 1900 the famous scout returned to stage a second show to sell-out crowds in the Glebe.

Mutchmor Driving Park was located west of Bank Street between First and Fifth, extending to Bronson. (Bank Street was first known as Esther Street, named for Colonel John By's wife.) Here, spectators bet on their favourite horse while watching the steeplechases. It was also home of the first running of Canada's premier horse race, the Queen's

Plate, in 1872, and again in 1880. By the 1870s, residences started to pepper the mixed landscape of farmland, large gardened properties, and fairgrounds south of the city limits.

As the city grew in the 1870s and 1880s, its southern expansion was inevitable. The attraction of the agricultural fairgrounds encouraged the development of the Bank Street road and Elgin Street, which were extended, and bridges over Patterson Creek were built.

The Mutchmor estate, an eight-room, one-and-a-half-storey house, was built near the racetrack. In 1889 it came up for sale and was purchased as the Protestant Home for the Aged. A press release of the day announced the streetcars would soon make it accessible, and by 1891 this was true. Thomas Ahearn drove the first tram from the Albert Street sheds of the Ottawa Electric Street Railway Company to Lansdowne Park. Thousands of spectators turned out to see this new contraption, the streetcar.

First streetcar to pass beneath the Bank Street "subway,"
and the Canadian Atlantic Railway right-of-way known
as the "Cross-town Track." (Today's Queensway.)
City of Ottawa Archives, CA 1573.

Although the streetcar was an undeniable boon, the design of the tracks — raised well above street level, not flush as they are in today's city streets — presented hazards to carters, pedestrians and horses throughout the city. Contemporary newspapers are full of complaints over the danger they represented to life and limb.

But the advent of these streetcars — the first in North America to be heated — meant people could now live in areas previously considered to be remote countryside, such as the Glebe. But it only became a fashionable new neighbourhood after 1906, when the Governor General's secretary built his home here, at 126–128 Fourth Avenue.

At the turn of the twentieth century, there were many homes between the canal and Bank Street, and First Avenue Public School had been built at First and O'Connor streets. However, on the west side of Bank through to Concession Street (Bronson) market gardens, pine trees and brush were punctuated by only a few buildings such as the Fourth Avenue Baptist Church and the Mutchmor Street School.

The Driveway, built by the Ottawa Improvement Commission (OIC) in 1900–05, allowed people to drive first by horse and carriage, then by motorcar, to the developing residential area approaching Dow's

View of Brown's Inlet and Wilton Crescent from south side of Canal. Note the horse-drawn conveyance. Circa 1913.
City of Ottawa Archives, CA 0261.

Lake. The numbered streets (First to Fourth — Fifth Avenue was known as Mutchmor) were laid out by 1890, and by 1914 most Glebe streets were built. The area developed steadily, especially in the post-World War I years, when returning soldiers urgently required housing.

As the city grew, the OIC gave more attention to the creation of public parks. Parks were increasingly considered critical open spaces. OIC planner Frederick Todd was responsible for saving the land on either side of Patterson Creek from construction, and for turning it into a park in the early 1900s.

After World War I, the Glebe prospered, and properties adjacent to the OIC's landscaped drives became desirable residential locations. Clemow Avenue, Brown's Inlet, and Patterson Creek were the locations of choice for estate houses designed by architects such as W. E. Noffke, who was hired to design a planned community of houses nestled around Central Park.

But the Glebe's residential development was dominated by members of the new, increasingly sophisticated middle class, who had specific needs but not the money to engage a personal designer such as Noffke. Nor did they have the income to hire servants. This need spawned a new breed of architect, a new design philosophy, and a new type of housing that incorporated such comforts as interior bathrooms, central heating, and electricity.

In the late 1920s and the 1930s, developers such as David Younghusband purchased large blocks of property in the Glebe, building "Glebe charmers" such as 394 Third (not on this tour). Now that the Glebe had become a trendy part of town instead of sleepy rural countryside, the city started to impose restrictions upon what type of structure could be built.

After World War II, mass production, the development of prefabricated construction techniques, and other technological innovations swept the building and architectural professions. The new fashion became the bungalow; so it was that the Glebe lost its attraction as a residential area during the 1950s. People looked for newer homes, larger lots, more modern schools and shopping plazas. The Billings Bridge and Alta Vista suburbs were developed in the 1950s. Many Glebe homes were converted into apartments.

At the same time, the Glebe's population changed from being largely British Protestant to a mixture of ethnic groups. Fashion swings being what they are, the Glebe enjoyed a rediscovery in the 1960s and 1970s, as owner-residents moved in to "gentrify" the neighbourhood.

Older homes were purchased, renovated, and often restored to single family dwellings. But the Glebe's new popularity has brought the headaches of traffic control, high-rise development and heritage conservation.

View of Central Park showing First Avenue Public School, c. 1911. NCC 172.

NEIGHBOURHOOD STYLES

The Glebe is a community of middle-class homes characterized by closed-in front porches, red brick walls, and gambrel and gable roofs. Most are two-and-a-half or three stories high. Interspersed among these typical houses are examples of Prairie and Spanish Revival designs, with their horizontal planes and red roof tiles. Tall apartment towers dot the streetscape, but are kept to a minimum by strict zoning by-laws. The Glebe, like many other Ottawa neighbourhoods, possesses an active community association that keeps current councillors in tune with the varied residential, schooling, and commercial interests of the neighbourhood.

Density and traffic control are key issues as witnessed by the special studies of architects and planners such as Glebe resident John Leaning. Heritage is another reoccurring concern, which climaxed in the 1968 fight to save Pretoria Bridge. This cause coalesced the efforts of several community groups throughout the city, which united in an effort to prevent a traffic corridor from further separating the Glebe from Ottawa South.

In the early 1970s, Glebe residents banded together to protest the rapidly advancing high-rise apartment buildings marching down the west side of the Canal. In August 1974, the Ontario Municipal Board approved a downzoning of several blocks between Patterson Creek and Fifth Avenue. The decision did not prevent William Teron's hotly contested tower at 300 the Driveway (1974), but it did stop the demolition of the picturesque Rogue Victorian row house complex to its south.

Of similar heritage concern has been the fate of Moses C. Edey's Aberdeen Pavilion and Francis Sullivan's Horticultural Building. These buildings have been the focus of an ongoing preservation battle. Although the Aberdeen Pavilion was stabilized, restored and reopened in 1994, the fate of the other building is undetermined.

Natural cedar summer house handmade by OIC carpenter Thomas Craig, was located near Pattison Creek. c. 1911. NCC 061-38.

Detail of the Aberdeen Pavilion, south entry. Note the laughing horse's head (top) and the lion's head (bottom). October 1991. K. Fletcher.

WALK TIPS

🚶 **4.5 km; 2 hours**

The Glebe walk takes you past urban parks, waterways, and shaded streets. Bank Street is the main north–south artery bisecting the neighbourhood. It is a commercial street, made up of shops, libraries, churches, neighbourhood cafés, and pubs. Washrooms exist in the many restaurants and businesses along Bank. Fifth Avenue Court at Fifth and Bank Streets has a public washroom and a pleasant interior courtyard, a welcome refuge in inclement weather.

Front cover of 1879 Canadian Illustrated News depicts first Dominion Exhibition (Lansdowne Park). October 4, 1879. City of Ottawa Archives, CA 18804.

Park near Lansdowne Park, the original exhibition grounds and the heart of the Glebe, and walk east to the 1898 **Aberdeen Pavilion**, the **Cattle Castle**. It is easily recognizable by its rounded roof topped by a cupola ringed with snarling lion's heads. Designed by Shawville, Quebec, architect Moses C. Edey, the Aberdeen Pavilion is a rare surviving example of exhibition halls inspired by the Crystal Palace, built for the 1851 London Great Exhibition. Edey's design took only two months to erect, an event that amazed Ottawans.

The Maude and two other side-wheel steamers unloaded fair-goers where Fifth Ave. now joins the Driveway. From Canadian Illustrated News October 16, 1879. NCC file 172.

The building is an important engineering achievement in Ottawa. It represents the first use in the city of long-span steel arches, which create an open interior eminently suitable for its agricultural displays. Steel's structural strength allowed Edey to design an interior enclosure 310 feet long with a span of more than 130 feet. Whereas earlier fair buildings were built of wood, Edey's use of steel with pressed-tin cladding indicates that he was building with permanence in mind. In 1899, during the Boer War, Lord Strathcona's Horse Regiment camped inside the building for two weeks before being sent to the front. And it was here the Silver Seven won the 1903 Stanley Cup.

On the outside, the two cross-gabled side entries to the north and south are particularly decorated, highlighted by corner towers that are topped by cupolas. The southern entrance has the projecting head of a laughing horse over the central doorway; the balancing north door sports a cow's head. The east and west doorways are less fanciful but their pediments and round-arched windows still evoke a sense of whimsy.

Of a completely different style is Francis C. Sullivan's **Horticultural Building**, just north of the Aberdeen Pavilion. Sullivan worked for Edey for several years. Stand back to appreciate this building's stark horizontal lines, a good example of Sullivan's interpretation of the Prairie design of Frank Lloyd Wright. Horizontal planes are accentuated by the flat roof and its broad eaves, as well as by flanking wings that carry the eye outwards. Exposed spandrels, or load-bearing beams, of concrete serve to emphasize the linear motif. Note, too, Sullivan's detail in the façade and window treatment. Built in 1914, the building is an important example of a commercial structure after the Prairie School style.

Walk back to Bank, head right (north) and cross the street at the stoplights at Holmwood. Stop at the old stone house at **954 Bank**, **Abbotsford House**, now part of the **Glebe Centre**. This lovely stone residence, built in 1872 for Alexander Mutchmor, was named after Sir Walter Scott's birthplace. In 1889, the house became the Protestant Home for the Aged. *The Ottawa Journal* of August 23, 1889, reported that the home, on its two-and-a-quarter-acre property, "is capable of accommodating about 75 inmates, and is surrounded by a beautiful growth of shade trees. … About $10,000 will be required to pay for the property and place it in a proper condition for occupation." On September 3 that year the paper reported that Moses C. Edey had been asked to prepare an estimate of the cost of repairs.

Under threat of demolition for years, Abbotsford House is now recognized as a heritage property. Its Victorian Gothic design features steeply pitched gables set off by delicately turned bargeboard. The projecting bay window fronting Bank Street and the multiple gables add a note of charm to the streetscape.

Turn left (west) on Holmwood to view the recent extension of the Glebe Centre. Proceed to the first street, Monk, and turn left (south). Keep watch for **Wilton Lane** (*not* Wilton Crescent), which leads off to the right, one building past Oakland Street. Walk up the lane to appreciate the Glebe's back-garden atmosphere. Fences define and segregate the gardens, but most are low enough to foster the neighbourly conversation that binds a community together.

Also note here the sometimes angled lot sizes, which define the shape and massing of homes. Perhaps the best example of an "Iron-shaped" home is the large three-story gambrel-roofed residence at 20 Oakland (the last house on your right before you emerge onto that street). The wedge shape takes full advantage of the narrow, pie-shaped lot.

Stop at the corner of Oakland for a moment to note the clapboard garages and the horse and sulky weathervane atop **25 Oakland's** garage.

Turn left on Oakland and almost immediately right onto a walkway bordering **Brown's Inlet**. Houses crowd the edge of the inlet, each with a splendid southern view. In mid-August yellow water lilies (bull head lilies) carpet the inlet, in autumn the water reflects the season's glorious colours, and come winter young hockey players shout and dash about on the ice. Walk to Ralph Street, directly ahead. Pause to look southeast to the **Bank Street Bridge** designed by Newton J. Ker in 1912. You can also spy the silver dome of the 1914 former **Monastery of the Precious Blood**, built upon "Ray's Hill," once a popular tobogganing run. J. Albert Ewart's 1931 **Southminster United Church** is also visible, as is his companion piece across Bank, the Ottawa Library South Branch.

Turn right on Ralph, walking north to see your first W. E. Noffke Glebe design, **86–88 Ralph**, the **Baker Residence**. The urns carefully

86–88 Ralph, October 1991. The Baker residence is now a double, overlooking Brown's Inlet. K. Fletcher.

placed at intervals along the front entryway, the Spanish tiled roof, and the sheer stucco walls are vintage Noffke. The townhouse complex at 92–94 Ralph today obscures the view of Brown's Inlet from this elegant house. This is a good example of how lot severance permanently changes the face of a neighbourhood. Typical of his best work, Noffke's design of 86–88 Ralph created a house whose design was well-proportioned to its lot. Today's infill buildings destroy the original grace of the house.

Now find **36 Ralph, Marsham Manor**, dated 1899. Tucked behind a cedar hedge, this is a large rambling Queen Anne style residence with a semicircular driveway. Its size indicates that like the Noffke home, it was built for a person of some prominence.

Continue to **20 Ralph, Berwick Cottage**, built in 1895. The cottage's original façade is now much altered. At the corner with Fifth Avenue, find **200 Fifth**, a modest brick home with a deep Mansard roofline. Its gardens and lawn are well defined by a cast iron fence whose attractive detailing mirrors the turning and paint work done on the wooden porch.

At Fifth Avenue, cross the street and go right (east). **Mutchmor School, 185 Fifth**, gets its name from the first owner of Abbotsford House and was built in the same year as Berwick Cottage. Originally a four-room schoolhouse, it was designed by architect E. L. Horwood and cost $10,470.

The school is an example of Romanesque Revival design. It features squared-off towers, horizontal massing accentuated by the low-pitched roof, symmetrical alignment of windows, and contrasting broad horizontal stone stringcourses beneath the second-floor windows. The central doorway's massive rounded archway is the school's most identifiable Romanesque feature. The rounded second-storey windows above the entry echo this dramatic arch. Note, too, the Romanesque terra cotta capitals on either side of the doorway piers. Terra cotta became increasingly popular in the 1870s in North America, and was locally available to Ottawa builders from Thomas Clark's brick and terra cotta yards in New Edinburgh.

From here, look east down Fifth Avenue towards Bank Street. Note the tongue-and-groove enclosed verandahs that front some of the red brick, three-storey gambrel and gable roofed homes: this is a typical Glebe streetscape. The verandahs provide welcome additional living space. Storm windows can be removed during summer to create screened porches.

Turn left (north) on Lyon Street. Between Fourth and Third, on your left (west) is **Corpus Christi School**, built in 1926.

Note the solid massing of **690 Lyon**, the **Glebe Community Centre**. Built in 1914 as St. James Methodist Church, it became the St. James United Church in 1925 until becoming a community centre in 1973. A classical design typical of the early twentieth century revivalist movement, this Roman temple-like structure features monumental Doric columns topped by a triangular pediment around its original main entrance on Second Ave. The domed roof is a Glebe landmark.

The revivalists sought change. They espoused a return to cleanly defined lines, in stark contrast to the fanciful, ornate detailing of Queen Anne and Victorian Gothic styles. Yet, in the years just before and after World War I, most architects continued their backward glance for inspiration. There were not many who strode forwards as progenitors of the soon-to-emerge modernist movement. The Glebe Community Centre is a stylistic contemporary of the 1909–12 Union Station (see Sussex walk); the 1904 Tabaret Hall (see Sandy Hill walk); and the 1913 First Church of Christ, Scientist (see Canal walk). Each is an important reminder of its architect's struggle for purity of structural expression. If it is open, go inside the Community Centre to see the interior of the dome and, perhaps, to find a welcome rest, lunch, or cup of tea at the Glebe's "secret" restaurant, The Pantry.

Back outside, continue along Lyon. Number **221 Second Avenue** (completed 2001) is a postmodern complex built when its heritage neighbour at **662 Lyon** was renovated. This latter building was constructed in 1912–1914 as the **Ottawa Ladies' College** (originally located at the Ottawa Technical School on Bay and Albert Streets in Uppertown). During the Depression years the residential school suffered declining enrollment, and in 1942 the building was expropriated. During World War II it served as the Glebe Barracks for the Canadian Women's Army Corps. In 1957 this was the original site of Carleton University, but two years later the university moved to its present location near Dow's Lake. Subsequently, in keeping with its educational raison d'être, it became administrative offices for the Ottawa Board of Education (OBE). Times change, however, and in the late 1990s the building lost its purpose.

In 1999–2000 it was gutted and apartments created along with the afore mentioned residences that were built on the former OBE building's parking lot. Happily, the builders constructed underground parking facilities for the new residents, thus minimizing the impact such a large influx of residents could have upon the neighbourhood.

The steeply pitched roof of 662 Lyon still retains its Spanish Revival style. Of note are the overhanging eaves with their bold wooden bracket supports. A covered portico extending over the semi-circular drive entryway off Second Avenue announces to passersby that this is supposed to be an address of note. Step inside the lobby to read the heritage plaque and to appreciate the renovations that transform the interior.

Glebe-St. James United Church, October 1991. K. Fletcher.

Directly opposite, at **650 Lyon**, is **Glebe-St. James United Church**. Designed by architect J. W. H. Watts, it opened its doors in May 1906. Its fanciful turrets of shingled siding are painted moss green and beautifully complement the soft grey trim and limestone walls. Note in particular the transept tower: this is a Romanesque feature both in its positioning and massing.

It was originally Glebe-St. James Presbyterian church prior to the amalgamation of the Methodists, Congregationalists, and Presbyterians into the United Church in 1925. After the union, this corner of the Glebe had two United churches separated by only one city block. In December 1970, the two congregations joined forces. One church became the Community Centre at 690 Lyon, while the other, now Glebe-St. James, continues as a United Church.

Walk two blocks farther north to Clemow Avenue, named after Francis Clemow, managing director of the Consumers' Gas Company in the mid 1800s, and a senator from 1885 to 1902. It was Clemow who urged that Ottawa's first waterworks be constructed.

Turn right (east) on Clemow. Here the large residences are fronted by deep gardens, removing them from the curious eyes of sidewalk amblers. Tastefully designed traffic barriers barely concealed as plant boxes restrict car access from Bank Street. Clemow is another enclave of embassy residences. As you walk towards Bank Street various styles compete for attention, from the Palladian classicism of **211 Clemow**, to the bell-capped copper turret of **164 Clemow**. The globe street lamps along Clemow, rather than creating any stylistic conformity with its houses, are meant to provide visual continuity to the streetscape.

Clemow was one of Frederick Todd's planned boulevards of distinction for the capital. He was a stickler for detail and included such minutiae as the height of fences, planting of trees, and size restrictions for billboards in his plans.

Turn left on Bank, remaining on the west side. Cross the bridge spanning the filled-in westerly extension of Patterson Creek — Central Park.

On the west side of Bank, north of the Park, find **672 Bank, Ambassador Court**, designed by W. E. Noffke for developer David Epstein in 1928. The wedge-shaped building is flush with both Central Park and Bank Street, and the end-corner is squared-off with small projecting balconies. There is a strong cornice with a pedimented parapet that breaks the flat roofline. Concrete stringcourses between stories contrast with the yellow brick walls, and the arched front entryway adds visual interest. When it was first opened, an advertised feature of the Ambassador Court was that every apartment had its own electric fireplace.

Cross Bank Street at the lights and backtrack south to walk left (east) on Patterson, one of the oldest streets in the Glebe. There are several flat-topped row houses near Bank Street on the north side of Patterson, and above number 219 you can see how residents have cleverly expanded their space by adding a rooftop patio.

On the south side of Patterson find the two-layered infill complex called **Central Park**, at **204–226 Patterson**. Farther along, row housing gives way to vernacular red brick houses with the steeply gabled roofs so typical of this neighbourhood. Some of these homes feature the irregular massing characteristic of the Queen Anne style, especially where Patterson continues east towards the canal, a section this tour does not include.

Turn right on Allan Place. Number **6 Allan Place** is attributed to architect Francis C. Sullivan. The original design has been much altered by a front addition, which was sensitively designed to blend into Sullivan's concept.

Number **12 Allan Place** is W. E. Noffke's 1913 Prairie Schoolhouse designed for Ernest C. Powell, (brother of W. F. Powell, the developer of Patterson Creek). This house takes full advantage of its raised elevation overlooking the east portion of Central Park. The home has a slight Japanese feel, which is derived from its wide, low-pitched eaves with carved, flared rafter ends. This is no fanciful coincidence: Frank Lloyd Wright spent several years in Japan and was heavily influenced by that country's architectural styles. Thus, Japanese motifs crept into Wright's plans. Because Noffke (and Sullivan) were influenced by this great American architect, their own designs, in turn, reinterpreted Japanese forms so that today we can observe them here in the Glebe.

Descend the few steps into the park. It is here, in the carefully landscaped parkland of **Patterson Creek** and **Central Park** that Noffke made his major impression upon the Glebe. Developer W. F. Powell and his aunt, Adelaide Clemow, hired the prolific Ottawa architect to design an integrated, prestigious development here. Noffke's 1913 plans, still extant, reveal his sensitivity to site.

On your immediate left at the foot of the stairs is **13 Clemow**, a grey stone "castle" residence. Notice it sports the typical roofline battlement feature, a corbelled parapet, and that it has two corner towers, one round, the other octagonal. Its lovely front door has a beautiful oval, bevelled glass inset.

Keep to your right on the park footpath. Then climb the steps beside **27 Clemow**, the Tudor Revival house Noffke designed for William F. Powell. The house integrates well to the hillside. Half-timbering indicates the Tudor inspiration, a style emphasized by the leaded glass windows with their wrought iron detailing. Twin chimneys with copper flashing lend the house its old English cottage appeal.

Opposite is **26 Clemow**, the dramatically different house Noffke built in the Spanish Colonial Revival style in 1926 for Levi W. Crannell. The southwestern US ambiance of the home is unmistakable, accentuated with a sheer white stucco finish, spiral colonnettes, and red tiled roof. Note its round-headed windows and the dramatic off-centre chimney with flared base that is the dominant feature of the front façade. A curved parapet gable over the main door completes the ornate façade.

27 Clemow, the second home Noffke designed for developer
W. F. Powell. October 1991. K. Fletcher.

Turn left to view **20 Clemow**, Noffke's own home, which he built
in 1913. Noffke left his "cottage" home at 209 Wilbrod in Sandy Hill
to reside here for several years. Perhaps he designed this to advertise
his considerable design talents: it is certainly a potpourri of styles.
Basically, it represents the bungalow style which was increasingly
popular at the time, with a broad front porch and wide, gable dormer
above it. Yet there are Tudor touches in the arched, buttressed and
battlemented front entrance. And Noffke reminds everyone of his
competency in Spanish Colonial Revival style by adding familiar red
roof tiles and a massive chimney. Note, too, the geometric designs in
the brickwork.

Number **18 Clemow** is Noffke's 1923 design for Ethel Chamberlain's
home, another Tudor Revival, which nicely balances 27 Clemow across
the street.

Now turn left (east) towards Patterson Creek and walk up the
gentle grassy slope on your right. From here you can view what is
perhaps Noffke's most successful, if not most famous, residential design,
85 Glebe Avenue, W. F. Powell's first home on the park, built in 1913.

85 Glebe, January 1992. Note its flaring porte-cochère.
E. Fletcher.

An Ottawa landmark, this house is best seen from Glebe Avenue, a few paces ahead.

The house's flaring buttresses and horizontal planes deliberately carry the eye from the line of the house into the surrounding trees and parkland. The home is truly part of its setting. Note the porte-cochère, or covered entrance, that shelters the front door on the semicircular drive. In contrast, the row of steeply pitched, gable-roofed homes on the southern side of Glebe Avenue dominate the streetscape rather than fitting into it.

Now retrace your steps, returning to Patterson Creek and the south side of Clemow. Spend a moment to look east past O'Connor Street to the canal to savour the precious open space preserved in the heart of the city.

Continue east to **11 Clemow**, the **Benson C. Beach House**, at the corner of Cobalt. Noffke designed this house in 1915 for the president of the Beach Foundry. (The foundry used to be located on Spencer Street in LeBreton Flats but was demolished in the mid-sixties by the NCC). The yellow brick used here lightens the mass of this stately residence. Note how the projecting porch piers and the chimney introduce strong vertical lines into a structure which otherwise appears solid and massive. Proceed to O'Connor Street, where you will view the last three Noffke designs of Patterson Creek.

Fittingly, because the Patterson Creek area was designed as an upscale residential neighbourhood, this part of the Glebe boasts many High Commissions and Embassies. Number **1 Clemow**, the **High Commission of Ghana**, was Noffke's 1915 design for Francis X. Plaunt, a railway tie contractor. Noffke historian Shannon Ricketts describes 1 Clemow as being Mediterranean style after a turn-of-the-century, exclusive Florida resort named Coral Gables. This house features sheer white stucco, unembellished windows, and the remnants of its original red tile roof.

Number **7 Clemow** is the **Malawi High Commission**.

Across the street is **515 O'Connor** at the corner of Monkland, the 1913 Noffke design for Austin E. Blount, Prime Minister Sir Robert Borden's private secretary. The house is now the **Embassy of the Republic of Tunisia**.

Monkland Avenue, summer 1911. Prior to the Noffke-Powell development, these landscaped drives had few homes. NCC 062-8.

517 O'Connor. October 1991. K. Fletcher.

Nicely complementing Blount's home is **517 O'Connor**, the G. Frederick Hodgins home, also built in 1913 by Noffke. Whereas 515 is a solid looking stone structure, quite different in feeling from the other Noffke designs on Patterson Creek, Number 517 possesses a few features that suggest Frank Lloyd Wright's Prairie Style. Horizontal planes are highlighted by a masonry base topped by a narrow stucco strip on the upper level. The effect is finished with a low pitched roof. One-storey wing extensions on either side of the house carry the eye even more linearly: on the left is another porte-cochère, in the middle is a covered doorway, and on the right, an enclosed porch. Together, all three serve to emphasize Noffke's linear design. Also reminiscent of Prairie Style are the projecting vertical piers topped with a spherical ornament. However, what is definitely "un-Wrightian" are the parapeted end-gables with chimneys.

Now turn right on O'Connor. Just south of Linden Terrace find the path beside **Patterson Creek**. Walk east toward the **Driveway**. Note the large homes lining Linden Terrace, some of which have massive column supports to their front porches. On the south side of the inlet, you can see the backs of infill homes on First Avenue. As you get closer to the Driveway, you can see the tile-roofed **NCC service building and public washrooms** (still functioning) just below the bridge. Built in the days of the Federal District Commission (heir to the Ottawa Improvement Commission) circa 1928, its design is attributed to Francis Sullivan. Similar structures are found in Rockcliffe Park.

Climb the stairs. Turn right (south) on the Driveway, crossing the little bridge over Patterson Creek, also credited to Sullivan. In 1904 the American historian, raconteur and traveller, Anson A. Gard revealed a hidden feature of the uppermost iron tube rail along the canal. An invention of local iron worker J. L. Flanders, the rail doubled as a water pipe, complete with attachments for hoses. It was an ingeniously designed sprinkler system.

Number **300 the Driveway** is a tall apartment building put up in 1974 by William Teron's firm, Urbanetics. It features dark brown brick and horizontal, angled pre-cast concrete balconies. This high-rise was bitterly opposed by many Glebe residents who sought to prevent the march of high-rises southwards along the canal. Beside its western face, along First, are low townhouses, overlooking Patterson Creek.

Directly across from number 300, on the south corner at First Avenue, is **304–312 the Driveway, Queale Terrace**. This whimsical row house development was built for William Queale, an Ottawa businessman. It was spared demolition by the Ontario Municipal Board's down-zoning ruling of August, 1974. The 1906 design continues the Victorian love for asymmetrical juxtaposition of forms. Here, porthole windows compete with arch-roofed and bell-capped turrets, and a staggered, zigzag ground floor plan not only gives a modicum of privacy to each entry, but also exploits to excellent advantage the awkwardly narrow, angled lot. Unit 312 has a heritage plaque.

Walk a few steps past this building to look at its postmodern neighbour, an appropriately whimsical companion to Queale Terrace because its architect played with angles and colour. This newcomer's royal blue and scarlet window surrounds add just as much interest to the streetscape as does the asymmetrical 1906 terrace.

Retrace the few steps to turn right (west) on First. As you pass by 304–312 on your left you can see more clearly the zigzag pattern of its plan.

Farther along are **49A** and **49B First**. These 1988 infill houses are a "second layer" of buildings behind the older homes fronting the street. Number 300 the Driveway, its neighbouring townhouses, and this double layer of homes along First are all evidence of the resurgence in popularity of the Glebe as a residential neighbourhood.

Numbers **70** and **74 First** are two charming clapboard homes. Their simple façades and attractive verandah detailing provide visual relief from the red brick that distinguishes Glebe streets.

49A and 49B First Ave. are second-layer infills facing Patterson Creek, behind 49 First. October 1991. K. Fletcher.

Number **73 First, First Avenue Public School,** was built in 1898 as an eight-room schoolhouse. At that time, Patterson Creek was wooded. Designed by J. Albert Ewart, son of architect David Ewart, the school cost $20,484. The completion of this school and the 1895 Mutchmor School within four years of one another attests to the growing population of the Glebe area at the turn of the twentieth century.

The school features a massive Romanesque arched entryway and terra cotta faces of the West Wind on either side of the portal. The building has weathered many alterations, including the addition of a ventilation system in 1907 and, in 1936, the twin conveniences of new wiring and urinals in the washrooms. It survived threats of demolition and in the 1980s the firm of Alistair Ross and Associates was hired to design a gymnasium. Located at the rear, it was faced in red brick so that it blends in well with the original designs.

Terra cotta detailing of the West Wind on First Avenue Public
School. October 1991. K. Fletcher.

585 O'Connor, the
Prince Rupert
Apartments.
October 1991.
K. Fletcher.

Turn left (south) on O'Connor Street. Pass the imposing red brick Edwardian classicism of the **Prince Rupert Apartments, 585 O'Connor**, built around 1915. It features symmetrical four-storey bay windows and deeply recessed balconies with prominent wooden railings. Ornate brackets support the cornices of this flat-topped, four-storey walk-up.

Now turn right (west) down Fourth Avenue. Here you find several end-gabled red brick homes typical of the Glebe neighbourhood. Many feature turned wooden porches fancifully decorated with motifs such as sunbursts, moons, and stars.

Number **91A Fourth** is the **Religious Society of Friends** (Quakers) meeting house. The second church in the Glebe, the original 1892 structure was wooden. In about 1910, it became the Zion Congregational Church, and around that time was clad in brick. In 1969, the Society of Friends purchased it and used it as their meeting hall. In the late 1980s the Friends sold off the eastern section, which was subsequently redesigned by architect Wolfgang Mohaupt, who developed the site with infill housing. The congregation now meets in the eastern, rear brick extension.

At the northwest corner of Bank and Fourth look across to the **Fourth Avenue Baptist Church**. Two lots were purchased here around 1898 for $2,200 and soon a small wooden church opened its doors. It was a lonely building, just about the only one built at that time between Bank and Bronson. This red brick church was erected in 1904.

Now turn left (south) on Bank towards Lansdowne Park and the start of this walk. You pass **Fifth Avenue Court** on your left, at the corner of Bank and Fifth. This complex integrates old shop fronts with a new rear, interior covered courtyard. It won an Award of Excellence for Minto developers in 1980. Despite Ottawa's long winter, sadly this covered courtyard fails to capture the imagination of shoppers and it has never caught-on as a neighbourhood meeting place. Possibly the granola and java-loving Glebe-ites consider the interior space of sheer red brick rather gloomy and uninviting, proving that a building needs more than an award to be accepted by its community.

Continue south on Bank to return to your car and the start of this walk at Lansdowne Park.

Sandy Hill

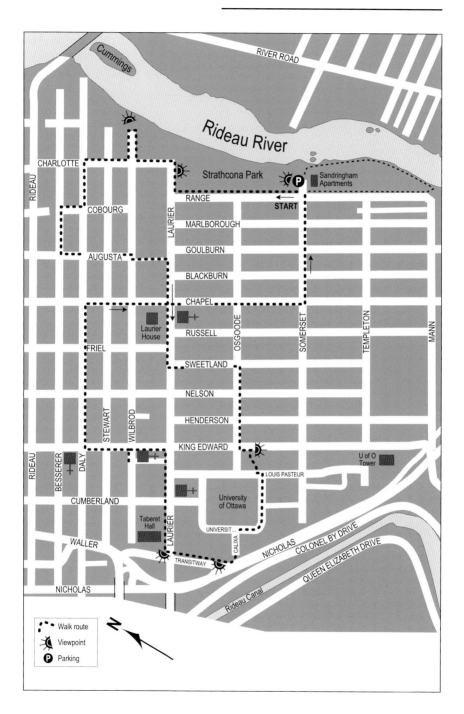

Cummings

RIVER ROAD

Rideau River

CHARLOTTE

RIDEAU

COBOURG

AUGUSTA

Strathcona Park

Sandringham
Apartments

RANGE

START

MARLBOROUGH

GOULBURN

LAURIER

BLACKBURN

CHAPEL

Laurier
House

RUSSELL

OSGOODE

SOMERSET

TEMPLETON

MANN

FRIEL

SWEETLAND

STEWART

WILBROD

NELSON

HENDERSON

KING EDWARD

U of O
Tower

LOUIS PASTEUR

RIDEAU

BESSERER

DALY

CUMBERLAND

University
of Ottawa

Taberet
Hall

LAURIER

UNIVERSIT...

CALIXA

NICHOLAS

COLONEL BY DRIVE

WALLER

TRANSITWAY

QUEEN ELIZABETH DRIVE

NICHOLAS

Rideau Canal

Walk route

Viewpoint

Parking

N

Sandy Hill's building boom started in the 1860s after Ottawa was declared the capital of Canada. Middle and upper class Canadians moved to the city to take up civil service jobs, and, very soon, the city ran out of suitable housing for them. In 1876 the land south of Laurier Avenue East, lying between King Edward and Chapel — part of Colonel By's estate — was surveyed. From the outset, lots were kept large to accommodate "villa residences" and only sold by private sale to create an exclusive domain for the wealthy.

Yet there were problems. Among the most humbling was the stench of the drains, which disgusted Sir John A. Macdonald at Stadacona Hall as much as it did the ordinary mortal. His next-door neighbour, architect Colborne (Coly) P. Meredith, provided a sobering glimpse into the Sandy Hill of the 1870s in his unpublished memoirs. Commonly, drains were of the primitive wooden box variety. Even if they were made from tile, most joints were of clay, not cement. As a result, they often failed, sometimes forcing families to vacate their homes. Meredith observed that children continually suffered from sore throats, and that the relationship of health to inadequate sanitation was not properly understood.

Rats were another pernicious problem. Backyard stables provided a handy food source for these vermin, and basements were often floored with cedar sleepers, allowing space beneath them for the rats to create runways and nests. (Interestingly, the 1990s environmental phenomenon of the backyard compost pile has lured rats back into many Ottawa residential communities.)

Streets and sidewalks posed their own hazards. Plank sidewalks heaved and created a jumble of levels. Just as today, residents were responsible for shovelling the snow in front of their own home. Even back "in the good old days," human nature being what it is, some people were more diligent than others, resulting in a haphazard pattern of cleared space and deep snow. Frequently, pedestrians on snowshoes competed on the roads with horse-drawn sleighs and wagons. Winter's packed snow provided a far preferable road surface to the muddy potholes of spring and blowing dust of summer.

Sandy Hill may not have been ideal, but lots were of good size, and during the 1860s and 1870s many houses were built. Coly Meredith recalled his family's 1874 home at the northwest corner of Augusta and Wilbrod as being on the fringe of Ottawa. It bordered unfenced meadows extending to the Rideau River, which provided grazing for residents' cattle.

Ottawa's last smallpox epidemic was in 1874. Irish labourers were decimated by the disease, which spread with lightning speed through their log shanty homes bordering the Canal and into Lowertown. The epidemic touched all parts of the city, and Sandy Hill was no exception. In 1875 *The Ottawa Citizen* carried a story about the Sandy Hill hospital operated by the Grey Nuns, which "has been converted into a small pox ward. The old wooden building should be destroyed as soon as possible."

The need for a hospital was great, and the nuns were determined to erect a new hospital in the community. But many residents were opposed, and newspapers of the day reflected their strong feelings. The July 8, 1875, *Citizen* tried to quell concerns about contamination, but was unsuccessful. Construction commenced on the new hospital, but on July 15 a passionate objector, who understood little about explosives, tried unsuccessfully to blow it up.

There were other protests when the old wooden hospital in Sandy Hill was torn down. The wood was supposed to be burned but instead was sold to someone who intended to build. Again the Sandy Hill community united and successfully forced the hapless buyer to burn

Strathcona Park, c. 1905. Note the park's ornate pathways and artificial streams with ornamental bridges. NCC 061-28.

the "infected timbers." Residents repeatedly took matters into their own hands regarding the Nuns' hospital. As late as November 22, 1879, the story resurfaces: "residents of the locality" burned the 1875 hospital to the ground.

Today, Sandy Hill residents continue to participate in protecting their community — but modern methods exclude explosives. Instead, protection through by-laws seems to do the trick, in combination with an active community organization. The 1982 City By-laws list four by-laws that mark the creation of several Sandy Hill heritage districts. The designated areas vary in size from a single lot to many blocks.

Another contentious issue was a 1991 proposal to build a shelter for homeless women at 229 Chapel Street. Sandy Hill residents opposed this proposal vigorously. They were able to convince the Ontario Municipal Board that their neighbourhood has its share of housing for the needy. *The Ottawa Citizen* of February 20, 1993, reported that owner Eric Cohen might have to convert the residence to a "rooming house for as many as 42 tenants." But residents opposed this on density grounds, arguing that the neighbourhood would suffer with increased parking problems. Today the fine old home — formerly the Frederick Toller house — is the **Embassy of the Republic of Croatia**.

NEIGHBOURHOOD STYLES

Vernacular Victorian Gothic cottages, personal residences that several Ottawa architects (Noffke, Ewart, Sullivan, Meredith) designed for themselves, and the micro-community of University of Ottawa are among the landmarks greeting the Sandy Hill walker. As well, Sandy Hill presents two uncommon modernist residences for explorers to enjoy towards the end of this delightful ramble.

It is a diverse neighbourhood of museums, embassies, private homes and apartments. At its southern extremity, Mann Road, are a series of CMHC public housing units that border the noisy Queensway. On the restful banks of the Rideau River, Strathcona Park provides shaded pathways and pretty views. Bordering this park are the Embassy residences that were once single-family homes. And, on top of the rise of land overlooking the Park is the much altered, once stately Munross House, former home of lumber baron John Mather and now home to Le Cordon Bleu Culinary Institute: the only such institute in North America. East of it are a series of heritage structures including Laurier

House, former home to Prime Ministers Sir Wilfrid Laurier and Mackenzie King.

As its name suggests, Sandy Hill sits on underground deposits of sand, which challenged the architects and builders of this neighbourhood much as the leda clay made building difficult in old Stewarton (see Canal walk).

WALK TIPS

🏃 6 km; 3 hours

Strathcona Park's beautiful landscaped lawns make it a delightful start and end to this walk. In summer, the low water level of the Rideau River entices many to cross to the far side where the bubble tennis courts of the Rideau Tennis Club are located. Sandy Hill has many corner stores and public buildings, so you will find a spot to rest and linger over a coffee. And be sure to go inside Laurier House Museum for a peek into the private lives of Prime Ministers Laurier and King.

THE WALK

Park your car in the lot at the easternmost extension of Somerset East, in Strathcona Park.

Walk north on Range, keeping the sparkling Rideau River to your right. (The lovely paths of Strathcona Park provide a shady, lovely start to the walk. You can walk through the park rather than the street, and look over at the homes fronting Range.)

Strathcona Park has enjoyed various former lives. At first it was the neighbourhood commons and cow pasture. Coly Meredith's memoirs reveal he changed the name Salisbury Road to Range Road, to honour the park's second life as the Dominion Rifle Range, which opened in 1873. By 1891 it was a fifty-acre, nine-hole golf course developed by Hugh Renwick. As you walk north, look at the homes framing the park.

A match ending — a range officer checking firing tickets at rifle meet. Strathcona Park, circa 1900. NAC PA-134821.

Number **38 Range** is the **Embassy of the Kingdom of Morocco's Chancery**.

Number **32 Range**, the **Embassy of Venezula**, was built in 1930 by the firm of Noffke, Morin and Sylvester as home for a Gerald Bate, Esq. It is a two-storey, gable-roofed stone cottage, complete with stone walls delineating the property line. Its two chimneys highlight the end gables, and its central entryway is framed by sidelight windows and an Adamesque elliptically shaped fanlight over the door. To accent the symmetrical design of the house, an oval "porthole" window is centred above the fanlight.

Number **28 Range** is the 1924 **J. R. Booth Jr. residence**, a Spanish Colonial Revival design by architects Burritt and Kingston. Currently it is the residence of the High Commissioner of Sri Lanka. Number **18 Range**, the **Street residence**, is a W. E. Noffke design, built in 1920 for Colonel Douglas Richmond Street, commander of the Governor General's Footguards and director of the Ottawa Car Company. If you look at the house carefully you can still detect Noffke's side porch, later filled in to provide extra interior space.

Now start to climb the rise to Laurier East. At the northwest section of the park, note Stephen Brathwaite's children's play area built in the summer of 1992. A later addition is a children's wading pool, which sparkles turquoise in the summer sunshine. Brathwaite's concept features architectural remnants rescued from previously demolished Ottawa buildings. The art deco female heads hail from a Bank of Montreal. Brathwaite calls the sandbox "Strathcona's Folly," saying: "It's intended to provoke imagination and play. The theme is time — so children can imagine their future by seeing the ruins of the past."[15]

At the top of the hill find **453 Laurier**, built for John Mather, lumber baron. For many years it was **Le Cercle universitaire d'Ottawa**, changing in the late 1990s to become **Le Cordon Bleu Cooking Institute**. The original structure is vastly altered, both in design and in function. Its second owner, Dr. Henry Ami, a geologist, had the castle-like turret added. W. E. Noffke's 1928 architectural drawings reveal he was hired to design the then-fashionable Tudor half-timber addition for the third owner, entrepreneur J. Ambrose O'Brien.

Head right on Laurier and then curve north on Charlotte. Number **285 Charlotte**, the **Embassy of the Russian Federation**, built in 1956, is another Noffke building. Originally dubbed "Stalinesque Brutalism" in style, it once presented a stolid, bleak image to the streetscape. However, during the summer of 1992 the façade was given a lift: the windows are now surrounded by exaggerated, inverted U-shaped mouldings of reflective glass. These pseudo-mouldings add sudden drama to the otherwise weary-looking building. According to Noffke historian Shannon Ricketts, the walls are "2 feet thick with a 14 inch concrete inner leaf, a 2 inch air gap in the middle and a 4 inch stone facing on the exterior."[16] Noffke's original plans show his signature urns on either side of the door.

Turn right (east) at Wilbrod to view **500 Wilbrod**, the **Andrew Fleck House**. This is a romantic Nepean sandstone house showing the irregular massing characteristic of the eclectic Queen Anne style. However, its rugged stonework of blond and red sandstone (sandblasted in 1992) and its unadorned arches recall American architect H. H. Richardson's Romanesque Revival style so popular on the North American continent at the turn of the twentieth century.

Architect J. W. H. Watts designed this whimsical residence in 1903–05 for Andrew Fleck, the owner of the Vulcan Iron Works. English born, Watts came to Canada in 1874 when he was twenty-four years old. Here he designed a romantic mansion featuring a

View up the Rideau River, showing the foot bridge to the Rideau
Tennis Club from A. W. Fleck's gardens, Rideau St., Ottawa.
n.d. NCC 061-53.

prominent castle-like rounded turret, a Spanish tile roof, and an offset
entryway complete with stained-glass windows and a massive oak door.
In their medieval romanticism — and exquisite craftsmanship — such
features are reminiscent of the Arts and Crafts Movement. Detailing
on the door includes the date "AD 1901."

The home and its well-preserved carriage-house offer a strikingly
whimsical contrast to the severe Russian Embassy you have just seen.
Also known as the **Paterson House** after Senator Norman Paterson,

its second owner, the house was sold in July 1992 to start its new life as a headquarters for an international transcendental meditation organization that also operated a B&B here. Currently the home is the **Embassy of the People's Democratic Republic of Algeria**.

Walk to the end of Wilbrod for a splendid view of the Rideau River. If you wish, descend the rather steep stairs beside **550 Wilbrod, Wilbrod Place**, for another view of the river. **Cummings Bridge** spans the water on your left. First built of wood in 1836, the bridge is named after settler Charles Cummings. The city named a replacement bridge built in 1893 after Samuel Bingham and erected plaques proclaiming the "Bingham Bridge." But feisty Sandy Hill residents felt strongly about retaining the name, and according to local lore someone tore the plaques down and threw them into the river.

Now backtrack on Wilbrod, keeping the 1980 solar-heated townhouses designed by Ecodomus to your right. The translucent fibreglass shapes on the southern slopes of the roofs are solar panels. Basements are said to be ninety per cent filled with rocks for passive solar heat storage. Turn right (north) on Charlotte to walk along "apartment alley," between a series of high-density dwellings built in the early 1900s in response to the demand for more housing adjacent to downtown.

Turn left (west) on Daly and stop at the corner of Cobourg to admire **363–383 Daly, Philomène Terrace**. This is the oldest example of nineteenth-century stone row housing in Ottawa.

Antoine Robillard established a limestone quarry around 1840 on Montreal Road. Antoine worked for Thomas MacKay on the first eight entrance locks of the Rideau Canal, and also as a contractor for Rideau Hall. It was Antoine's son, Honoré, who built Philomène Terrace in 1874–75 in limestone from the quarry, and named it after his wife. Since then the six units have experienced successive alterations, owners, and tenants. In 1888 verandahs were added to the three westernmost units, and in the 1890s the kitchens, originally in the basement, were relocated to three-storey rear brick additions.

Lumber merchant Isaac Moore lived in unit 363 prior to building his own residence at 240 Daly. Canadian poet Archibald Lampman lived in unit 369 between the years 1893 and 1896. His close friend, poet Duncan Campbell Scott, observed that the house was cheap and damp. Nonetheless, Lampman was enthusiastic about the house as it was the first time he'd had a room of his own in which to write.

Stand back on the south side of Daly to appreciate the different front porches of the terrace. The Eastlake style of the two paired central wooden porches is named after Charles Locke Eastlake (1836–1906), an English interior designer, writer and architect. These porches feature beautifully ornate turning that gives a completely different ambiance to the Terrace than the plain squared, classically inspired porches of the two westernmost units. Notice their fanciful twists, turns and elaborate and delicate sunburst patterning with chamfered posts. In 1977–78 the City of Ottawa bought the two easternmost units and replaced their paired porches, but their attempt to emulate the Eastlake central four does not quite measure up. Notice, for example, how the central porches have turned supports, while the newer east porch supports are square. Together, the porches add a playful quality to Robillard's sturdy limestone structure, well matched by the picturesque pitched dormer windows.

464 Besserer, David Ewart's home. The extension to the right was added later. October 1991. K. Fletcher.

Now turn right (north) on Cobourg and immediately left (west) on Besserer, named after the original property owner. Stop at **464 Besserer**, which **David Ewart** designed as his own home in 1873–74. It is utterly different from the fortress-like public buildings he designed. This house has no Scottish baronial overtones. Instead, it is an English Victorian Gothic cottage, which features prominent wooden brackets supporting its shallow, hat-like roof. The scrolled brackets look as if they are melting. Trefoil-arched dormers protect Gothic window frames that are today almost obscured from view by modern, squared-off double-paned windows. A projecting bay window, centre front of the main façade, adds interest, as does the bell-curved balustrading of the front porch.

Turn left (south) on Augusta, noting the use of the modern but unusual exterior finish of board-and-batten, and the brick "cottages" framing the street. Number 226 was built in 1880 during Sandy Hill's building boom.

You now pass **336 Daly**, **Patterson House**, a pretty L-shaped Victorian Gothic cottage on the corner of Augusta. This treasure was built in 1870 for Thomas Patterson, grocer. That year he procured a mortgage of $6,000 to build this charming vernacular home. The house has a cheerful and highly decorated exterior which exhibits much of the asymmetry popular with Victorians. Its yellow brick corner quoins are connected to the body of the house by a prominent yellow brick stringcourse, and the quoins are echoed in the differently shaped yellow brick window mouldings. Although the two roof gables are sharply peaked, here their similarity ends. One gable has a trefoil design, while the other, over the western wing, has extremely delicate wooden gingerbread trim (bargeboard).

In 1906 architect Louis Fennings Taylor purchased the house and converted the interior to two apartments with a rear addition. Today its cottage ambiance is emphasized by the crowd of lilacs at the rear entry.

Number **286 Stewart**, **Grayburn/Pope House**, on the southwest corner at Augusta, is a completely different style. It is a Second Empire house built in 1875 for Christopher Grayburn, featuring tall, hipped wall dormers with peaked wooden caps. In 1907 Sir Joseph and Lady Pope moved in. Sir Joseph was private secretary to Prime Minister Sir John A. Macdonald. A verandah once stood where the brick addition is now located.

Across the street there is a plaque identifying the heritage architectural importance of Sandy Hill. Beside it find **245 Augusta**, built around 1870. It is a cream-coloured stucco Gothic cottage, the former home of Prime Minister Lester Pearson during the years 1947–54. Like Ewart's residence, the vernacular design of this house features wooden bargeboard beneath its eaves.

Continue down Augusta, once called a "treeless wasteland of mud," by Coly Meredith, to Wilbrod. Turn right (west) and then immediately left (south) down a narrow laneway that residents obviously enjoy using. Once congested with vegetation, it is now well lit and the shrubs have been cut back. The laneway first passes **400 Wilbrod**, a large brick mansion Coly Meredith designed in 1910, now the residence of the **Ambassador of Brazil**.

Next to it is **395 Laurier East**, **Stadacona Hall**, then the residence of the ambassador of Belgium, and currently it is the **High Commission of Brunei Darassalam**. Originally built for lumber merchant John A. Cameron in 1871, the Gothic limestone cottage has undergone several transformations, including the addition of a garage built in 1945. Lilian Scott Desbarats, former Sandy Hill resident of nearby 274 Daly, observed the Camerons needed "a very big house because they had 11 children."[17]

Cameron rented to a series of tenants including, in 1877—83, Sir John A. and Lady Agnes Macdonald. During their tenure peacocks strode the lawns, attracting curious children to the gates of the estate with their haunting cry and iridescent plumage. Explanations of the residence's name vary. One story says that Sir John A. christened it Stadacona Hall after his Kingston political club; yet another claims that a later tenant, Hon. Joseph-Edouard Cauchon's wife, named it after the Iroquois name for the village that once stood where Quebec City now is.

Speaking of cutting back shrubbery, the current residents were arguably a tad excessive, as several gracious old trees and shrubs were completely removed. Security for a laneway is one thing; it's a pity when established trees are cut down for such reasons.

Now turn right (west) on Laurier. On the opposite side of Laurier, at the corner of Blackburn, find the rambling Queen Anne style red brick mansion that is home for **Heritage Canada**, 1 Blackburn.

Across from All Saints Church is **335 Laurier House**. Bequeathed by Lady Laurier to Prime Minister Mackenzie King in 1921, the home was originally built in 1878 for wealthy Ottawa jeweller John Leslie, whose shop was on Sparks Street. This house was the second on Laurier Avenue designed by James Mather: the first was Munross (now Le Cordon Bleu Culinary Institute), overlooking Strathcona Park. Prior

Laurier House in October 1902. Note the original ironwork cresting, and the original porch predating Noffke's 1913 design for Sir Wilfrid Laurier. PAC-PA-8979.

to its many additions, the original Munross house was the mirror image of this home, having its bay on the left side, not on the right. Laurier House is now a museum. Go inside to enjoy its richly furnished interior, notably King's third-floor, wood-panelled library and study with its cozy fireplace.

This rambling house is a good example of the crossover of architectural styles. Its massing, with its five-sided wings and bays, as well as its mansard roof, identify it as Second Empire. However, some details such as round-topped dormers and window moulding is pure Italianate. The yellow brick of the exterior was traditionally referred to as "white brick." W. E. Noffke designed the wraparound verandah in 1913 for Sir Wilfrid Laurier, who lived here from 1897 until his death in 1919.

In 1922 Mackenzie King altered the interior space to suit his personal taste as well as public demands. The design by the firm of Sproatt & Rolph included a personal retreat for the prime minister on the top floor.

312 Laurier. November 1991. Curved bay windows and projecting wings soften George Goodwin's massive brick mansion. K. Fletcher.

The blond brick of Laurier House is echoed in the sprawling thirty-three-room mansion now dwarfing its lot on the corner of Russell, **312 Laurier**, the **George Goodwin mansion**. The 1900 home features prominent rounded bays with symmetrical twin wings on both its east and west sides. It has a fascinating past. Built for George Goodwin, a railway contractor, it has served as headquarters of the St. John Ambulance. During World War II it served as the Kildare Annex, barracks for the Canadian Women's Army Corps. Six cells were built in the basement for those who transgressed strict army rules. The basement also contained a huge rainwater reservoir, reportedly the size of a swimming pool.

Turn left (south) on Sweetland, and enter the part of Sandy Hill that Colonel By surveyed.

16 Sweetland. November 1991. Brick corner quoins, delicate wrought-iron balconies and polychromatic brickwork enliven this flat-roofed triplex. K. Fletcher.

Find **16 Sweetland**, on the west (right-hand) side. Built in 1886, this brick flat-top apartment building's front lawn is defined by a wrought-iron fence. Its gate announces "J. Harry, 1886." Such fences are mostly decorative nowadays, though they thwart enthusiastic dogs in this new millennium just as effectively as they originally served to keep neighbours' pigs and cattle out of the garden.

Pass **24–34 Sweetland**, beautiful brick row houses, which feature rounded false parapet gables projecting above their flat-topped roofs. Note the detailed dentil cornice and bracket supports. Ornate porches with turned posts and windows framed by arched brick voussoirs create

The iron gate at 16 Sweetland. November 1991. K. Fletcher.

an elegant façade to the street. Inset porch entryways are shared, but beautifully arched tongue-and-groove dividers provide a degree of privacy. The row houses at **38–48 Sweetland** feature highly detailed spooling on their front porches.

Across the street, don't miss **31 Sweetland**, **Simard House**, the oldest home on the street. It is a typical worker's Second Empire style with a Mansard roof. Tongue-and-groove wood exterior features a mock Italianate-style tower entryway.

The street is named after Dr. John Sweetland, sheriff of Carleton County in 1867. Find **62 Sweetland**, currently the **Home Sweetland Home B&B**. The City of Ottawa awarded it heritage designation as a superb example of a nineteenth-century home. Built for Sarah and

Andrew Mitrow in 1895, the steeply gabled, L-shaped red brick home features an ornamental verandah with scrolled and turned woodwork. Note the projecting finial at the peak of the home's front-end gable.

Now look at **61 Sweetland**, another clapboard cottage amid a sea of red brick homes.

24–34 Sweetland. November 1991. K. Fletcher.

École Francojeunesse. Contrasting colours enliven the school's
façade. November 1991. K. Fletcher.

Now turn right (west) on Osgoode. At the corner of Osgoode and
Henderson Streets is the **École Francojeunesse**. Strong horizontal
lines are emphasized by the contrast between rough-hewn grey limestone
layers and the rich red brick façade. Highly detailed terra cotta capitals
with a typically Romanesque organic motif adorn either side of the
arched entryway on Osgoode. This detailing is characteristic of the
solid Romanesque Revival architectural style so popular for late
nineteenth century schools. Architectural mates to this school include
First Avenue and Mutchmor schools (see Glebe walk).

Opposite the school, have a look at four buildings: **140–138, 136
(Antrim Terrace), 134–132**, and **130–128 Osgoode**. At first glance
these may appear unremarkable. Look again: can you see the oddly
indented bricks that are incorporated in each building? Evidently
erected by the same builder/contractor, it's this type of attention to
detail that makes a neighbourhood unique.

In order to get a close-up look of a now rare, pressed-tin façade to
a building, take a few steps south to see **93 Henderson**. Barely hanging
on to life, this old garage's front façade has a different pattern from
that on its southern side.

Continue along Osgoode until you reach King Edward. You are now facing the entryway to the **University of Ottawa**. Its postmodern residences form a visual continuum south, down the western façade of King Edward Avenue.

The tall tower you can see to your far left forms a stylized cross. It is a "modern heritage" landmark of Ottawa which symbolically recalls the university's 1848 founding by Bishop Guigues as the Collège de Bytown (see Sussex walk). The tower marks the southernmost extent of the main campus and is actually a chimney for the heating plant of the university. In 1972 Murray & Murray, with associate architect Louis Lapierre, won an award for this innovative design.

Now take a few steps to your left on King Edward, and then an almost immediate right, to enter the walkway through the **Brooks residence**, at **620–622 King Edward**. Here the quarters for married students feature a colourful children's playground.

Montpetit Hall, University of Ottawa. Brutalist lines present smooth, sheer walls and regularly spaced smoked glass windows. November 1991. K. Fletcher.

At the end of this short walkway is Louis Pasteur Private. The word "private" means that this street is not maintained or owned by the city. Take a seat and soak in the atmosphere of the university. A campus has a life of its own, being a city within a city, and the challenge for the designer is considerable. Inexpensive yet functional residences for faculty and students are mandatory; well-lit walkways safe for students who are burning the midnight oil must be landscaped; and visually stimulating yet functional, cost-effective structures such as laboratories and libraries that balance communal areas with private study carrels must be designed. Between the years 1969–71 a master plan for the university was devised by the architects Martineau, Lapierre, and Murray & Murray Associates.

At Louis Pasteur turn left and then immediately right onto University Private. Note the daringly angled planes of the 1973 **Montpetit Hall's** smoked glass windows. Stay on University Private as it turns right (north), and pass the twin brick high-rise residences of **Marchand Hall** and **Stanton Hall** before turning left again on Calixa-Lavalée (named for the composer of Canada's National Anthem) and then right alongside the Transitway, which hurtles buses from Highway 417 to the city centre. From here you get a splendid view west of the Rideau Canal and Centre Town; note the juxtaposition of the old Cartier Square Drill Hall, the copper châteauesque peaks of the Lord Elgin Hotel (see Canal walk), and the shining silver orb atop the 1991 World Exchange Plaza, which actually was designed as a clock. The ball travels along the parallel, curved tracks on top of the Plaza, and its position indicates the time of day — with noon being the centre (top) point.

Continue alongside the Transitway. Directly ahead of you is the flamboyant 1883 **Odell House** at **180 Waller**, now a real heritage island in the stream of traffic. Horace C. Odell, brick mason and brickyard owner, built the house as a wedding gift for his son Clarence. It exhibits many features of the Second Empire style so popular in the late 1800s. Incorporated into the jaunty tower and mansard roof are round-headed dormer windows. The first-floor windows are framed by draped hood mouldings with prominent keystones. There are two entryways to the home: one has a lovely wishbone gable atop its porch; the other is centred in an Italianate tower, the inset windows in its double-door making it a gracious entry.

Perched today between Waller, the Transitway, and Laurier East, the home has forever lost its original garden setting. But its colourful

180 Waller. Horace C. Odell's Second Empire present to his son Clarence. November 1991. E. Fletcher.

whimsy adds a touch of glamour to the busy campus. The University of Ottawa bought it in the 1970s.

During November 2002, while a high-rise condominium was under construction, two late 1800s brick homes adjacent to Odell House collapsed, causing considerable consternation amid Sandy Hill's heritage conservationists. Both homes were demolished, permanently changing the scale and style of this gateway to the community. Their removal, in combination with the construction of the tall apartment-style condo (the first of its kind in this area), irrevocably dealt the heritage corner a mortal blow. Today, the Second Empire Odell home is a forlorn orphan, while buses zoom past it on the transitway.

Across from 180 Waller is **Simard Hall**, the **Arts Faculty** (1955), sporting features inspired by art deco. Stylized vertically fluted pilasters simulate classical pillars on either side of the entryway. The doorway is highlighted by a façade of windows extending the full four storeys, supported by exposed aluminum framing with "lamps of learning" (resembling Aladdin's lamp) on either side. Look at the metalwork detailing of the window for another stylized cross.

Continue to the corner of Waller and Laurier East. To your left (northwest) you can see the austere limestone wall of the old jail, where Patrick Whelan was hanged February 11, 1869, for the assassination of Thomas D'Arcy McGee. Whelan's was the last public hanging in Canada, and as recently as 2002 relatives such as Noble Whelan have been trying to clear his name. Research indicates Patrick's was possibly a "death sentence of convenience" by an English jury intent on making an example of the Irishman to discourage Fenian rebellion in Canada. As was *de rigueur* for hangings, Whelan's demise drew thousands of spectators who came by horse-drawn sleigh, snowshoe and foot from even remote rural locations to watch him die.

Completed in Spring 2003, the multi-storied Laurier Tower — a luxury apartment building — anchors the southwest corner of Waller and the transitway. The presence of such a tall "skyscraper" apartment adds a new element of city living at this corner which is not in keeping with the student population and heritage architecture here.

Now look at the southeast corner of Laurier East and Waller, home to the **Arts Building, 70 Laurier**. Opened on May 8, 1997, its corner tower is topped with a pointed finial, thrusting through a sphere. Look closely at the Art's complex façade: the projecting bay windows are further defined by "Y" shapes of metal, echoing the roof, which is constructed of the same material. At the base of each "Y" is a ball; such decorative devices add a definite rhythm and continuity to the design. Finally, note this "Y" shape repeated in the stonework at street level. (Note: Go inside the main entry of this building if you want to visit the little-known Ottawa gem, the Museum of Classical Antiquities. Particularly in summer, its hours of opening are "spotty.")

Directly to your right (northeast) is the splendid rear view of the classical, European-looking **Tabaret Hall, 75 Laurier**. Turn right on Laurier East and walk on the north side to the grassy park in front of Tabaret Hall. From the park you can best see the towering Ionic columns supporting the massive central dome of the building. A plaque just inside the Laurier entrance describes the 1903 destruction of the original building by fire. Tabaret Hall was designed by New York architect Count A. O. von Herbulis in 1904–05 in the Beaux-Arts Classical style, which captures the notion of the university as a temple of learning.

Return to Laurier. At the corner of Laurier and Cumberland streets is **591 Laurier, Sacré Coeur Church**. Built in 1981, it replaced the Neo-Gothic limestone church that burned down on November 24, 1978. Today's Sacré Coeur is open at noon for mass and is well worth seeing inside. The open interior space is warmed by natural and artificial

Rear view of Tabaret Hall. November 1991. K. Fletcher.

151 Laurier. November 1991. K. Fletcher.

lighting, and the sanctuary and sacristy have an air of approachability uncommon in older churches. The ceiling volumes are filled with a criss-cross of metal trusses, which relieve the austerity of the textured limestone walls. Honey-coloured oak pews are angled, seeming to invite the congregation to take full part in the service.

Opposite the church is **151 Laurier, St. Joseph's Rectory**. It is reminiscent of the California Mission style with its smooth cream stucco surface. However, some details are inconsistent with California Mission, including its oriel rounded bay windows. Nonetheless, it provides a refreshingly different architectural motif to this hectic corner.

Continue east along Laurier until you reach King Edward. Turn left (north).

Martin Terrace. Porthole windows, two "half-timbered" gables and two differently capped turrets add whimsy to King Edward. October 1991. K. Fletcher.

Number **519–525 King Edward, Martin Terrace**, is named after Daniel Martin, a grocer who developed this property with his wife, Isabella. These four townhouses, designed by German architect Adam Harvey in 1903, are among Ottawa's best-loved heritage sites. In his design, Harvey catered to the Victorian taste for asymmetrical groupings of dissimilar parts. The wrought-iron fence defining the property edge provides continuity and relief to Harvey's juxtaposition of rounded and peaked turrets, porthole, and peaked dormer windows in the mansard roof. Coly Meredith commented that fences such as these kept early residents' wandering livestock at bay: "Nearly everyone tried to grow their own vegetables and many kept a cow but frequently the cow got lost or some stray cow or horse would get in and eat and trample the garden."[18]

Adjacent to Martin Terrace are numbers **515–517 King Edward** (1895) and, built three years later, numbers **503–509, Linden Terrace**. Many residents of the area were senior civil servants who urgently required housing in the boom years following Confederation.

At Wilbrod, turn left to view **210 Wilbrod, St. Paul's Evangelical Lutheran Church**, designed in the Gothic Revival style in 1888 by Adam Harvey. This structure replaced a simple wooden church, so this indicates the German Lutheran community was expanding in Sandy Hill area at this time. Note its stone buttresses (supports) and the pointed arched windows typical of the Gothic style. W. E. Noffke (Harvey's apprentice) designed the bell tower in 1948, while a member of the congregation.

Now look at **209 Wilbrod**, W. E. Noffke's first home, which he designed in 1904 for himself and his wife, Ida.

Return to King Edward and continue north to Daly, where you will find the second Anglican parish of Ottawa, the **Church of St. Alban's the Martyr** (1867–77), the first church in Canada to offer its congregation free seats. It was built to accommodate part of the congregation of the first Anglican church of Ottawa, Christ Church Cathedral, which was bursting at the seams (see Parliament walk). After Thomas Fuller's design had been approved, and after excavation had commenced, workers discovered an unwelcome pit of unstable sand, a natural intrusion in the clay subsoil.

Fuller's design could not be built and he withdrew it, recommending that a student of his, architect King Arnoldi, complete the church. Arnoldi was hired and retained much of Fuller's plans, except for the tall spire which could not be supported by the unstable foundation. Although St. Alban's opened in 1867 it took ten more years to complete. Many political figures joined the congregation, including Sir John A. Macdonald, Sir Charles Tupper, Sir Alexander Campbell, and Viscount Monck, the first Governor General of Canada. Sir John walked to the church from nearby Stadacona Hall, as did Campbell from his residence at Varin Row on Daly.

This church and St. Bartholomew's (see New Edinburgh walk)

share medieval, early English Gothic stylistic details. However, perhaps because of its gentler, treed setting, "St. Bart's" is less austere than this church, perched here on the busy street. St. Alban's has a steep gabled main roof with two cross gables, and features prominent buttress supports. Note the slim open belfry resembling an arrowhead which has a tall wrought-iron pinnacle. It is visually connected to St. Alban's easternmost end gable by iron cresting. Look for the trefoil, quatrefoil, and cinquefoil motifs in the ornate window tracery.

Before crossing King Edward look at **149 Daly**, the **Besserer House**, on the northeast corner of King Edward. This 1844 residence was the home of Théodore Besserer, the brother of Sandy Hill's original landowner, Louis. It is strategically located on the ridge of Sandy Hill, overlooking Lowertown, which Colonel By described in 1831 as being "a large swamp." The height undoubtedly afforded Besserer and his wife some relief from the smell of Sandy Hill drains and the dust of its summer roads.

The house is a Georgian design of cut limestone. You can still see the square base of the original widow's walk atop the roof — what a splendid view it must have had! The classical balance of the façade is curiously skewed on the second storey by a fourth horizontal window

149 Daly with 157–159 Daly to the rear. November 1991.
K. Fletcher.

set between the upper left windows. Otherwise, symmetry is maintained by the two end chimneys and half-circle dormer windows inset into the roof.

Cross King Edward to walk east on Daly to see a variety of intriguing residences. Number 154 Daly was the residence of Dr. Bedford Jones, Rector at St. Alban's across the street, from 1868–1874. Number **157–159 Daly** is a whimsical potpourri of effects, including a grey tin roof with matching painted brick and circular turret. Georgian-inspired **161 Daly** was built in 1872 by the first Anglican bishop of Ottawa, John Travers Lewis. Its striking corner quoins and horizontal stringcourses of smooth cut stone contrast dramatically with the rough-cut limestone façade. Number 169 Daly is a rambling Queen Anne of red brick with the typical highly decorative shingling beneath the gable that was so popular at the time. Number **185 Daly, McGee's Inn**, was owned by John J. McGee, half brother to the famous, ill-fated, orator Thomas D'Arcy McGee.

Number **192 Daly** sports a plaque identifying it as having been built in 1893 for John Roberts Allan, "a prosperous Ottawa businessman." The house's exuberance is characteristic of the Queen Anne style. It features a rounded porch, terra cotta capitals, delicate iron cresting atop the porch and projecting bay window, and turned wooden detailing beneath sharply gabled eaves. In the late 1930s the Japanese ambassador Mr. Tokugawa was renting the premises. It became the Japanese Legation until Pearl Harbour was attacked on December 7, 1941. In her published memoirs, Lilian Desbarats of Sandy Hill reported that after war was declared the RCMP patrolled 192 Daly on a twenty-four-hour basis.

Numbers **199–205 Daly** are investment townhouses built around 1870 for William McFarlane. During the 1860s and 1870s brick became a popular building material. The regular features of the building such as evenly spaced windows and dormers are artistically offset by the contrasting yellow brick corner quoins and window mouldings. Note the wooden bracket supports beneath its overhanging eaves. Other investment properties on this block include **208–214 Daly** and **202–204**, which have gabled roofs with dormers and raised firewalls.

Number **274 Daly** was built around 1865 and in 1867 became the residence of Sir Charles Tupper, one of the fathers of Confederation. By 1874 it was home to Sir Richard W. Scott, once secretary of state, senator, mayor of Ottawa, and, earlier, one of the principal lobbyists promoting Ottawa as capital. His daughter Lilian married neighbour George Desbarats.

199–205 Daly. Beautifully restored units feature contrasting mouldings above each window. October 1991. K. Fletcher.

Number **309–311 Daly, Winterholme**, now called the **Chapel Court Apartments**, was built for George Desbarats, Canada's first Queen's Printer. The property originally belonged to Richard Scott, who advised Desbarats that building a home in Sandy Hill would be just the thing — and that, coincidentally, *he* owned the perfect spot. The rambling limestone home, complete with conservatory, was erected in 1868. It used to front upon Besserer with a gracious, treed circular drive leading to its front door.

Ottawa politics of the day conspired against the printer. Desbarat's press was at the corner of Sparks where Thomas D'Arcy McGee was assassinated. Because Desbarats erected a plaque to McGee's memory on his building, Fenians threatened to destroy his business. The building was then gutted by fire. Desbarats decided he'd had enough of Ottawa. He sold his beautiful house to Sir Sanford Fleming and returned to Montreal. Lilian Desbarats recalled the conservatory, where tropicals such as orange trees perfumed the air with their blossoms. Later on, Sir Sanford demolished the plant-filled space and turned it into a vast room that became a convalescent home for soldiers who were injured in World War I.

When the home was divided into apartments in 1925, the dramatic Besserer entry was removed. During the alterations, a large bay window that Prime Minister Mackenzie King admired was purchased by him and dismantled. He removed it to Kingsmere in Gatineau Park, where it is part of his well-known collection of "ruins." Forever gone is the lovely rose garden, Sir Sandford Fleming's pride and joy.

Before turning right on Chapel, walk a few steps farther east on Daly to view number **315 Daly**, built around 1861 for Duncan Graham, custom's collector. Later it became the residence of Toussaint Trudeau, Deputy Minister at the Department of Public Works. A stone house, it originally cost $4,000 and boasted an observatory and a verandah. The original symmetry of the house is broken by the eastern extension done by Cecil Burgess (drawings dated May, 1949). The joinery in the masonry and also in the eaves and roofline are only just visible now due to a vigorous vine growing up the façade. At its rear is a brick addition, similar to that of Philomène Terrace, added at the turn of the century. The home is now a housing co-op.

Look back down Chapel, noting the number of Queen Anne style homes gracing either side of the street.

Now backtrack to turn left (south) on Chapel, viewing in passing **229 Chapel**, the **Plummer**, or **Frederick Toller House**, yet another large Victorian Gothic brick home built in 1875 for J. H. Plummer, manager of the Bank of Commerce.

Architects Horsey and Sheard designed Toller House. *The Ottawa Citizen* of December 6, 1875 reported on its exquisite interior: "The hall floor is constructed of walnut and ash strips. The parlor, dining room and library are spacious and lofty. The upper flats are utilized for bedrooms, dressing and bathrooms, and are supplied with hot and cold water. The whole building is heated with hot air. It cost about $9,000."

The Toller House was purchased in 1877 by Télesphore Fournier, politician, journalist, lawyer, member of the Supreme Court, who was both minister of revenue and of justice in mid 1870. In 1882 the house was purchased by Lieutenant-Colonel Frederick Toller who served as comptroller of the Dominion currency for twenty-nine years. The house passed to another politician, Louis Philippe Brodeur, until 1931, when Les Soeurs Blanche D'Afrique, a French order of nuns, took it over. They ran a school and residence here for many years. Then developer Eric Cohen proposed using it as a shelter for homeless women, but in 1991 Sandy Hill residents successfully opposed the plan, obtaining the support of the Ontario Municipal Board (OMB).

346 Somerset East, the Francis Sullivan home. October 1991.
K. Fletcher.

Presently the much refurbished home is in the good hands of the **Embassy of the Republic of Croatia**.

Continue south along Chapel and down the hill to Somerset Street East. Turn left (east) and watch for 346 Somerset East, the **Francis Sullivan House**. Designed in 1914, the house shows the influence of Frank Lloyd Wright's Prairie School in its shallow roof and projecting eaves, and the horizontal stringcourses. Horizontality is further enhanced by the "frames" that surround and emphasize the actual windows and frames themselves. Because these offset frames are painted a darker shade than the house façade they serve as striking architectural features. Sullivan was having playful fun here, it seems, because the window panes are actually vertical, mimicking not only Wright but also the designs of Glasgow architect Charles Rennie Mackintosh.

In 2002 the current owners were renovating the home, putting in a "Sullivanesque" rear porch to add extra space onto the 900 square foot original living space. Fortunately, they have retained the vertical grillwork that provides privacy to the front entryway, and have also kept what they believe to be the original windows on the second floor. The ground floor windows may not be original. Apparently some of the original interior features remain, such as a nook in the front room.

At the corner of Somerset and Range streets, you could return to your car immediately ahead of you, in Strathcona Park.

However, if you wish to view a few more architectural gems, turn right (south) onto Range.

68 Range. October 1991. K. Fletcher.

Find **68 Range**, on your right. The horizontal planes and smooth surfaces of this modest modernist house are similar to its companion at 265 Goulburn (not on this tour, but nearby in Sandy Hill). Here a stepped-back plan adds extra interest. The curves of the doorway canopy are repeated in the front plant containers and the steps leading to the side entrance.

Continue north along Range. Number **85 Range**, the **Sandringham Apartment building**, is on your left, on the site of the old Strathcona Hospital. This was torn down in the early 1950s, when the East Lawn pavilion of the Civic Hospital opened on Carling Avenue.

The Sandringham was designed by architect Peter Dickinson, who came to Canada from Britain in 1950. It is one of the twin modernist blocks he originally intended for the site. Its monolithic structure is relieved by his signature flaring entrance canopy, and also by the contrast of glass, brick, and open space created by the recessed balconies.

Sandringham Apartments. October 1991. K. Fletcher.

Continue on Range Road. On your left, find **245 Range**, the **Meredith House**, perched atop a hill with a splendid view of the Rideau River. It is a charming, simple white cottage designed by Coly Meredith in 1920 for he and his wife, Aldie. Of it he wrote: "In January 1920 Aldie and I skied over to the end of Range Road ... At that time there was nothing but an open field from the Rideau River to Blackburn Avenue and from Templeton to Mann Avenue with the exception of the Nurses' Residence by the Hospital, there were no roads except on the city maps, and sewers and water were put in later. We decided to take the lot ... and build a small house. ... As the South end extended over the Hillside little excavation was required, this is the reason that part of the basement is built in masonry, the rest of the foundation was built later."[19]

Today the house retains its charming Normandy country cottage appeal, with its massive chimney, dramatic roofline of low-slung flaring eaves, and its smooth plastered walls.

Before walking down the end of Range as it curves west to form Mann Avenue, just look right, down Mann. Ahead of you is a school, followed by a housing complex of 1960s and 1990s postmodern CMHC and City of Ottawa homes, public housing that provides high-density living. These cluster beside the Queensway. The old Mann Avenue arena further along used to be a brickyard.

Now return to your car. You can backtrack ... but why bother? If you descend the paved pathway on your left (at the corner of Range and Mann) you come to the Rideau River. Veer sharply left (north) to follow a bicycle and walking path that hugs the embankment. All too soon you'll emerge from this sylvan environment into the open Strathcona Park ... and discover your car at the Somerset Street East extension.

245 Range, a cottage overlooking the Rideau. October 1991.
K. Fletcher.

Rockcliffe

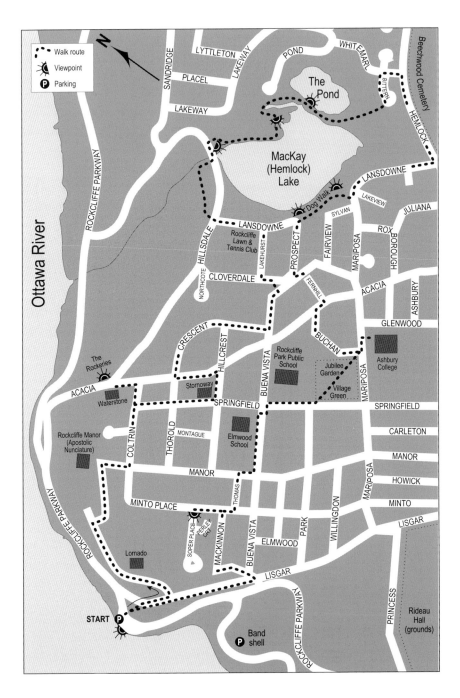

Map legend:
- Walk route
- Viewpoint
- P Parking

N

Ottawa River

ROCKCLIFFE PARKWAY

SANDRIDGE
LYTTLETON
PLACEL
LAKEWAY
LAKEWAY
POND
WHITEMARL
Beechwood Cemetery
BITTERN
The Pond
HEMLOCK

MacKay (Hemlock) Lake

LANSDOWNE
LAKEVIEW
Dog Walk
SYLVAN
JULIANA

HILLSDALE
LANSDOWNE
Rockcliffe Lawn & Tennis Club
LAKEHURST
PROSPECT
FAIRVIEW
MARIPOSA
ROX BOROUGH
ASHBURY

NORTHCOTE
CLOVERDALE
FERNHILL
ACACIA
GLENWOOD

The Rockeries
CRESCENT
HILLCREST
BUENA VISTA
Rockcliffe Park Public School
BUCHAN
Jubilee Garden
Village Green
Ashbury College
MARIPOSA

ACACIA
Waterstone
Stornoway
SPRINGFIELD
SPRINGFIELD

Rockcliffe Manor (Apostolic Nunciature)
COLTRIN
THOROLD
MONTAGUE
Elmwood School
CARLETON
MANOR

MANOR
HOWICK
MARIPOSA

MINTO PLACE
THOMAS
MINTO
WILLINGDON

SOPER PLACE
PERLEY GATE
MACKINNON
BUENA VISTA
ELMWOOD
PARK
LISGAR

Lornado
LISGAR

ROCKCLIFFE PARKWAY

START P
Band shell
ROCKCLIFFE PARKWAY
PRINCESS
Rideau Hall (grounds)

In 1885, when Lowertown was bustling with activity and after the City of Ottawa was beginning to annex its suburbs, the area known as Rockcliffe remained remote countryside. Ten years later, in August 1895, Thomas Coltrin Keefer's electric streetcar line was opened between Main Street, New Edinburgh, and Rockcliffe Park. Now Ottawans could easily travel to a new recreation venue which they could enjoy in their hard-earned leisure time. Labourers, domestics and shop clerks could never hope to purchase land, nor could they dream of heading to a summer cottage in the Gatineau Hills. Instead, in ever-increasing numbers, they visited Rockcliffe Park.

Rockcliffe Park streetcar. NCC 172-140.

The Park was essentially the creation of Thomas Coltrin Keefer, son-in-law to Thomas MacKay, contractor of the Rideau Canal. When MacKay died in 1855 at Rideau Hall, he left a significant estate and Keefer took over its management. In 1864 he had a map drawn to advertise the sale of "Park, Villa, and Village Lots" of the MacKay Estate.

Keefer was an astute businessman. He purchased the land fronting the river north of Lisgar Road, realizing it could become invaluable parkland — and a useful buffer between Rideau Hall and the development of Rockcliffe Village. He sold what is now Rockcliffe Park to the city for $34,000 on July 27, 1897. In 1904 the city arranged a fifteen-year lease with the OIC for its maintenance. Today the NCC manages it.

Keefer's 1864 map shows the "Rideau Hall Domain" and several other features of Rockcliffe Village. A deposit of white marl east of Hemlock Lake (now known as MacKay Lake) that Thomas Clark later used for his 1872 brickwork is shown. Also depicted is "Beaver Meadow," today's Beechwood shopping district. The map shows two residences in Rockcliffe: MacKay's Elmdale farm, now the site of Elmwood Girls' School, and Birkenfels, a stone dwelling. Roads such as Buena Vista were yet unnamed: it appears on the map as an access route past the farm (Elmwood) to the fishing haven of Hemlock Lake.

During his tenure as Governor General at Rideau Hall from 1867–68, Lord Monck could not abide the dust, mud, and potholes of Sussex Drive connecting Rideau Hall to his East Block office. Despite access to the most luxurious conveyances of the day, he deplored the long drive along Sussex. Instead, he insisted upon having at his personal disposal a navy ship, which was docked at Governor's Bay.

If New Edinburgh's Government House was considered too far away, Rockcliffe was even more remote. Even by 1925, early resident Asconi J. Major and his family decided to sell Stornoway, because commuting to their Lowertown business was too onerous. Population figures for the development of the village are revealing. The Rockcliffe of 1890 had only twelve households, in 1900 there were thirty, and by 1914 sixty, mostly clustered around Lisgar Road. By 1926, 150 fifty-foot lots had been laid out between Mariposa and Maple Lane, west of Ashbury, but only twenty had sold. East of Hemlock Lake was a sandy, poorly drained area.

All through these years, the park remained a popular recreation area, summer and winter. Governor General Lord Lorne installed an astonishing toboggan run, lit by a railway engine headlight that started at Rideau Hall, crossed the present Rockcliffe Parkway and cut down the steep cliffs onto the ice of Governor's Bay.

At the turn of the last century skiing became the rage. Lord Frederick Hamilton introduced the sport to Ottawa: "In January 1887, I brought my Russian skis to Ottawa, the very first pair that had ever been seen in the New World. I coasted down hills on them amidst universal jeers; everyone declared they were quite unsuitable to the Canadian conditions."[20]

The toboggan run. Rideau Hall visible at rear. NCC 172.

By 1910 the Ottawa Ski Club had erected "Suicide Hill" in Rockcliffe Park, a ski jump 128 feet high that so captured the imagination of Ottawans that thousands lined the jump on Saturdays — and even Sundays — to watch the spectacle. Lady Kingsmill, wife of Admiral Kingsmill, whose residence we view later (8 Crescent), sold coffee and sandwiches to the enthusiastic crowds watching the likes of club president Joe Morin sailing through the air on skis.

Tobogganing, snowshoeing, skiing, skating and sleighing — all these winter pastimes encouraged residents and visitors alike to enjoy the beautiful scenery of Rockcliffe Park. But who were some of the first residents of Rockcliffe Park?

Residents who came to live in the village included the Short family from England. Visible on Keefer's map of 1864, Elmdale farm was well situated to provide produce, hay, and cattle for New Edinburgh's and Rockcliffe's growing populations. Thomas Short rented the farm for many years. As a lad, Tom's son Sam held various jobs, one as Lord Dufferin's page. After being dismissed from his viceregal functions, he became a cowboy, watching upwards of 600 cows that pastured in Rockcliffe's woods and meadows. The fee for grazing was $1.00 per month per cow; Sam received a small percentage of the take.

By the year 1889, Sam had purchased one-and-a-half acres at Buena Vista and Springfield Roads, built a home, and developed one of the capital's most lovely gardens. He now worked at the Ottawa Post Office, and managed to get there even in the winter despite the distance of more than a country mile. "When there was not even a sleigh mark, young Short donned his snowshoes and broke trail to St. Patrick's bridge. Traversing Sussex Street he noticed the horse-drawn cabin sleighs of the street railway bouncing through drifts and dipping over the waves of snow ridges into the hollows or cahoots formed by Ottawa's first street transportation system. Then in the spring break-up he got to the city by laying stones and jumping from one to the other to cross the creek running from Lindenlea. When the Shorts bought a new piano it took 10 days to get delivery of it from Ottawa, and then the last mile was by stone-boat, the half-ton truck of that day."[21]

The turn of the century saw the extension of Rockcliffe Park. "The Coming National Park at Rockcliffe" was big news in the Ottawa papers, including *The Evening Journal* of January 24, 1903, which announced the OIC's intention to "make a monster pleasure ground for the capital. Nearly half a million dollars to be spent in work of beautifying the district beyond the City's present park."

When development of Sandy Hill's Strathcona Park precluded that neighbourhood's usefulness as the Dominion Rifle Range, the Rifle Association moved to a northern extension of Rockcliffe Park. So began this area's involvement with the Canadian military. Today the area once used by the 43rd Duke of Connaught's Rifles is the RCMP stables.

Enclosed on all sides by parklands, the Village of Rockcliffe was insulated from haphazard development. Thomas Coltrin Keefer, who died in 1915, successfully laid the groundwork for the planned, gradual growth of the MacKay Estate. Large lot sizes, broad streets, and the area's natural features, which include high limestone cliffs overlooking the Ottawa River and wooded hillsides surrounding Hemlock Lake, all conspired to produce an environment of great beauty.

Once known as Rockcliffe Village, the community retained its independent status, surviving two attempts at annexation. The first, in 1977, came when the Mayo Report recommended the village become part of Vanier. A year later, the City of Ottawa proposed annexation. Residents rallied and the Villagers won their battle for independent status. In 1992–93, villagers were again outraged by Graeme Kirby's study proposing a regional government which would absorb Rockcliffe Village. When the City of Ottawa's borders expanded in January 2001, Rockcliffe was amalgamated into the greater metropolitan area. Hopefully, the new neighbourhood will retain its village ambience, but, technically, "Rockcliffe Village" is no more.

Rockcliffe Park. n.d. NCC 061-3.

Gracious estates, sweeping lawns, and treed lots characterize Rockcliffe. But the absence of sidewalks lends a human scale and intimacy to any stroll around the village. Cars and bicycles, dogs and pedestrians share the road. Village by-laws of the 1920s restricted all building to single family dwellings. There are no intrusive apartment buildings, no corner stores, and no restaurants to sully the carefully preserved landscape of quiet mansions. In fact, the only break in the landscape of designer homes are the three schools nestled at the centre of the village: Ashbury College, Elmwood, and Rockcliffe Park Public School and the village police precinct. The schools surround what is known as the Village Square. Adjacent to Elmwood is the police station.

Many of the grand old homes are too large for today's families. Gardeners and domestic staff are beyond most people's means, even in well-heeled Rockcliffe. As a result, most of the large estates are now embassy properties. Although this has some drawbacks for the community, the benefits outweigh most of them, for diplomatic missions enjoy substantially more funding than do private persons, enabling the grand mansions to be looked after more or less as they were originally intended. One has only to consider such once-beautiful homes as Sir Sandford Fleming's 1868 Winterholme — now irretrievably altered into the multi-unit, forlorn Chapel Court Apartments in Sandy Hill — to realize how quickly a building can lose its soul. Although the same is not true in Rockcliffe, patrolling security guards, "hidden" cameras and the crushing congestion of embassy traffic during a midday soirée are undeniably disturbing.

Because the wealthy were attracted to the area, Rockcliffe is a repository of fashionable architectural trends. Here you find the legacy of Thomas Coltrin Keefer in the work of his architect grandson Allan Keefer, who designed many period style houses as well as Ashbury College. Omnipresent Ottawa architect W. E. Noffke's work is here too, as are the more avant-garde designs of award-winning Hart Massey. Today immense and often sadly ostentatious infill and the severing of the few remaining large estates such as Birkenfels are destroying the pastoral character of the village. Yet the splendid natural setting of Rockcliffe Park remains.

Village residents fought long and hard to establish the 1970s conservation zone to preserve the precious habitats of MacKay Lake (Hemlock Lake) and the Pond, where residents and their children still go to swim. It remains to be seen if infill developments such as Bittern Court on the Pond, and sprawling homes such as 700 Hillside, beside the lake, will obliterate this achievement.

WALK TIPS

𝆓 6 km; 3 hours

The walk starts at the lookout over the Ottawa River. There are a few parking spaces here. Although it is blocked off in winter, alternate parking spaces are available at the old band shell, situated to the west of this lookout. There are also washroom facilities here that are usually open in summer. There are no restaurants, corner stores, or gas stations in Rockcliffe itself.

Rockcliffe teems with embassy residences, so security is prominent. There are no sidewalks to amble; remember to watch for cars as you walk. Please respect private property, particularly around MacKay Lake, the Pond, and along "the Dog Walk," where gardens cascade down the sloped embankment to the water's edge. The docks are private grounds.

THE WALK

Park your car at the Rockcliffe lookout, built over the Ottawa River in 1923 by the Federal District Commission. The view north, of Pointe Gatineau, is of the homes hugging the waterfront and of the spires of St. François de Sales church.

The lookout is located east of what used to be the Ottawa Electric Railway Company's band shell and amusement park. At one time, Ottawans who took the tram to escape the city for an afternoon were entertained there by brass bands. Today, the park still offers a sylvan respite from downtown, and the NCC rents the old band shell for private parties. Below you is the spot where Seguin's ferry landed honeymooners from "the other side" to revel in strains of such favourites as "Daisy, Daisy, Give Me Your Answer Do."

With the Ottawa River at your back, turn left and walk a few paces to Lisgar Road (see map: there is no road sign here). Opposite, you will notice a smaller version of Rockcliffe Park's lookout. This Japanese pagoda-like shelter marks one of the old private entries to the electric streetcar line used by the people of Rockcliffe Village who lived on top of the craggy outcrop of rock before you. There is some debate as to how Rockcliffe got its name, but the elevation from the river to the top of the cliffs above you is the probable derivation.

Turn right along Lisgar, towards the pine knoll. After about thirty metres you will note a road heading sharply left, looping in a hairpin turn to the top of the hill. This is the roadway that ascends the cliff beside the US ambassador's residence.

This house is **500 Lisgar Road, Lornado**, the former home of Warren Y. Soper, owner of the Ottawa Electric Railway Company with partner Thomas Ahearn. Lornado is situated on land that was once part of the original Birkenfels estate. Birkenfels itself is the stone home built by Thomas MacKay. The Birkenfels property was severed, and Soper purchased it from the MacKay estate in 1890. In 1908, Soper built this stone "cottage," which he called Lornado, after the heroine of the romantic novel *Lorna Doone*. Soper rented Birkenfels to military families and used Lornado as his home. After his wife died in 1931, the Lornado portion of the estate was sold to the US Embassy and became the residence to successive US ambassadors.

Lornado, home of the US Ambassador. n.d. NCC 230.

Lornado is a solid-looking mansion, regally placed above the cliffs on its expansive lawns — hardly what anyone today would term a cottage. As you climb the hill, its stone wall rises above you on your right like a medieval castle's battlements. It even has small vertical openings reminiscent of a castle's slots for archers. Lornado, which has a widow's walk atop its flattened roof, is the first of many Rockcliffe houses that boasts a magnificent view of the Ottawa River valley.

Proceed up the driveway until you reach Manor Avenue. The road turns sharply right at **46 Manor, Coltrin Lodge**, designed by Allan Keefer when he was about eighteen years old. This is the first of the prolific architect's designs that we will see on this walk. Keefer designed the house for his older sister, who lived here until 1943 when she sold it to W. D. Mathers, assistant undersecretary of state for external affairs. Mathers greatly altered the original home.

On the left as the road curves east lies **740 Manor, Marchmont**, the Indonesian ambassador's residence.

Farther along, find **725 Manor**, a residence designed by architect Barry Hobin, built in 1992–93. Here in Rockcliffe, this style's clean design is a refreshing interpretation of Frank Lloyd Wright's Prairie

725 Manor. 2002. K. Fletcher.

Style motif. Horizontal bands of windows that wrap around upper storey corners must afford spectacular views of the private gardens of Rockcliffe Manor, the Ottawa River, and the Gatineau Hills. Note the detailing on the door, reminiscent of Glasgow architect Charles Rennie Mackintosh's designs.

Continue to **724 Manor, Rockcliffe Manor House**, the **Apostolic Nunciature**, where the Pope's Vatican Envoy to Canada lives. This historic house is Rockcliffe's answer to Rideau Hall. The original Regency style stone cottage with surrounding verandahs was built by Duncan Reynier MacNab. MacNab died before completing the cottage, which featured imposing chimneys and gables. Also included in the initial design was a Georgian entry with French doors, and a covered verandah once surrounded the home on three sides. Today the house is hardly a Regency cottage, but rather a splendid home in the style of eighteenth-century French manor houses. It is currently assessed at over $10 million.

This house has been home to several prominent Ottawans. MacNab's death and the leasing in 1865 of Rideau Hall as Lord Monck's viceregal residence prompted T. C. Keefer, as manager of the MacKay Estate, to purchase Manor House for MacKay's widow, Anne. Upon her death,

Rockcliffe Manor House, now the Apostolic Nunciature,
as seen through the gateway. n.d. NCC 230-74.

Keefer moved in here with his wife, Annie (daughter of Anne and Thomas MacKay). Keefer substantially altered the home by adding Victorian gables with dormers and a beautifully curved bargeboard trim. After Keefer died in 1915, his son Charles Keefer lived here for a few years, then rented it until 1929, when it was sold to Canada's first female senator, Cairine Wilson, and her husband, Norman Wilson.

Cairine Wilson hired Boston architect J. W. Ames to completely redo the home. The sole reminder of MacNab's original house is said to be the Georgian doorway, intact but impossible for us to see as it faces the river. In 1963 the house was sold to the Apostolic delegate, which attained the status of a diplomatic mission in 1969. Today it serves as the Apostolic Nunciature.

The only view of it today is through the arched entryway of its picturesque gatehouse. To the left are gracious gardens — vestiges of the old orchard that once flourished here.

Continue down Manor. Just before Coltrin is the start of a private driveway, sweeping off to your left, which leads to the Swedish ambassador's residence. Unfortunately, the house is barely visible from the road. Nonetheless this is another design by Allan Keefer, built for his brother, Thomas.

Now turn left and walk along Coltrin — named after Thomas Coltrin Keefer. To your left is Coltrin Place, a little residential enclave.

On the north corner of Springfield at Coltrin, is the rear of Allan Keefer's last design for Rockcliffe, **725 Acacia Avenue, Waterstone**. This is the house he built in 1930 for Frederick E. Bronson. Continue along to Acacia and turn left (north) for just a few paces to appreciate the front of this splendid stone home. Above the carriageway sparkles the gold-coloured stylized chrysanthemum identifying Waterstone as the present residence of the ambassador of Japan. (Look at the iron gates at the driveway to see the symbol of Japan, the rising sun, incorporated into its design.) True to period style houses, site orientation was of critical importance. Here, as in many of his designs, Keefer scaled the residence to suit the generous lot size.

Opposite Waterstone, find one of Ottawa's secret gardens: **The Rockeries**. This garden park is beautiful in every season: in spring it is resplendent with a carpet of nodding daffodils and narcissus, in late May crabapple and lilac blossoms perfume the air, while summer and early autumn bring wave upon wave of glorious colours. Come winter, berries along with different textures and shapes of trees and shrubs create their own special effects.

The Warren Soper memorial statue in The Rockeries. Soper obtained the fountain from the Paris Salon in 1912 and his daughter presented it to the NCC in 1960. 2002. K. Fletcher.

Explore The Rockeries, which was originally the streetcar terminus for Rockcliffe Village by walking down the paved pathway leading into the landscaped grounds. After descending a few metres, turn sharply left and cross the grassy lawn. You'll be surprised by some garden sculptures that were once the fluted columns of the former Carnegie Library, which stood on the corner of Metcalfe and Laurier. One column stands in its entirety, while other sections of decorated capitals serve as garden seats scattered about a water fountain. This is the Warren Soper memorial statue depicting two cherubs clutching one another while receiving their eternal shower.

Retrace your steps to Waterstone and continue your tour, returning via Coltrin to Springfield Road. Now turn left (south) and walk past the intersection with Thorold. At the southeast corner note the rear of **585 Thorold**, the residence of the **High Commissioner of India**. The spacious garden sets the mood for this gracious grey stucco house.

Continue south on Springfield. The next rear view is of the back garden of **541 Acacia, Stornoway**, residence of the leader of the Opposition. This plain stucco structure is by Allan Keefer, built in 1913 for first owner Asconi Joseph Major, who purchased the property for $12,000 from Charles Keefer (see Lowertown walk for Major's grocery warehouse on York Street). In 1923, Ethel Perley-Robertson purchased the house and named it Stornoway after her ancestral home on the Isle of Lewis, Scotland. She hired Allan Keefer to make renovations, adding a bathroom, three bedrooms above the kitchen to accommodate staff, and living quarters above the original stable, today's garage.

During World War II, the Netherlands' Crown Princess Juliana and her children were forced to flee the advancing German army. They escaped in an armoured truck from The Hague and made a hazardous journey to England and then on to Canada. They stayed at Rideau Hall prior to renting 120 Lansdowne (seen later during this walk) and then moved to Stornoway in 1942, where they stayed for the duration of the war.

In March 1950 a private trust was set up by Liberal and Conservative senators to establish a residence for the leader of the Opposition. In 1970, the government bought Stornoway from the trust for one dollar and turned responsibility for its upkeep to the Department of Public Works. The NCC tends the gardens. Maureen McTeer, who has lived at both Stornoway and 24 Sussex Drive, describes DPW's takeover of Stornoway as unfortunate. Among other renovations, the department, McTeer says, is responsible for the removal of Allan Keefer's trademark porte-cochère at the north end of the house in 1978.

The driveway to **540 Acacia**, residence of the Korean ambassador, is guarded by Foo dogs, thought to ward off evil spirits.

Now turn left (east) on Hillcrest and left again (north) on Acacia. At Crescent, turn right to curve southeast around this street built specifically for brothers Wilson and Harry Southam, founders of the Southam newspaper empire, who both built homes on this street.

Number **11 Crescent, Lindenelm**, the Spanish ambassador's residence, was designed in 1911 by Allan Keefer in a Tudor Revival style for Wilson Mills Southam. The house features a brick ground floor and a stuccoed, half-timbered second storey. Note the original slate roof of the house and its numerous gables and dormers.

Frederick Todd, the well-known landscape architect and author of the Ottawa Improvement Commission's 1903 Master Plan for the capital, designed the gardens and recommended the positioning of the house upon its site, overlooking the Ottawa River from the craggy bluffs. Because Lindenelm was designed by both Todd and Keefer, it deserves its special designation under the Ontario Heritage Act.

11 Crescent, Lindenelm. 2002. K. Fletcher.

Number **9 Crescent, Casa Loma**, the Austrian ambassador's residence, was Keefer's 1913 design for Harry Southam. A 1940 fire devastated the original home, but architect A. J. Hazelgrove redesigned Casa Loma, staying true to Keefer's plan. Built in the Elizabethan style the house features a slate roof, and parapet gables that stand clear from the steeply pitched roof. Keefer cleverly designed the Southam brothers' houses to maximize their views over the cliffs to the Ottawa River. As well, their angled frontage onto Crescent Road takes full advantage of the curving street, once their exclusive driveway.

Adjoining number 9 Crescent is **8 Crescent**, the former Admiral Kingsmill House. It presents a stone façade to the street and is marked by solid symmetrical features. This was once the residence of Lady Kingsmill, whom the Lord's Day Alliance of Toronto once tried to have arrested for selling coffee on the Sabbath to Suicide Hill ski-jump spectators.

For a completely different architectural flavour, look across the road at **7 Crescent**, the William Teron House. Teron was a major developer of the Ottawa area, perhaps best known for his design of the suburban community of "old" Kanata. There, Teron experimented with an organic approach to house design. His Kanata creations are a combination of cedar, brick, horizontal planes and split levels that

7 Crescent nestled into its wooded gardens. 2002. K. Fletcher.

take great advantage of natural light and aspect. Number 7 Crescent, built as his residence in 1970, is designed as three contiguous hexagonals clad in cedar, nestled into pines that screen the view from the street.

Continue along the curving sweep of Crescent. While walking, note that the houses on the inside of the street are more modern — and modest — than those overlooking the Ottawa River.

Number **3 Crescent**, the residence of the Ambassador of Turkey, exhibits the symmetry of a Georgian Colonial Revival house. Regularly spaced windows and dormers and raised side-gables with flanking chimneys give a rhythmical, predictable look to this façade. Note how the brick pilasters create the impression of the centre pavilion characteristic of the Georgian style.

Number **2 Crescent** is a contemporary interpretation of an end-gabled "farmhouse" complete with airy looking verandah. It surely must command a splendid view of the Ottawa River and Gatineau Hills to the north.

Turn left (east) to descend on Buena Vista, so named because of its beautiful view of MacKay Lake, the little oasis of Rockcliffe. Buena Vista is one of several streets with a Spanish name (another is Mariposa: "butterfly") that is another legacy of Rockcliffe developer Thomas Coltrin Keefer, who visited Mexico at the turn of the century.

3 Crescent's classical colonial appeal. 2002. K. Fletcher.

412 Lansdowne. January 1992. E. Fletcher.

Pass **459 Buena Vista** on your left (north) and watch for the staircase descending to Cloverdale. Take the stairs and then bear left across Cloverdale and walk down Lakehurst to Lansdowne Road South. You are walking past the **Rockcliffe Lawn and Tennis Club**, once the private tennis courts of the Southams.

In front of you is **412 Lansdowne, Byng House**, the Israeli ambassador's residence. J. W. Ames of Boston — the architect who redesigned Rockcliffe Manor House for Senator Cairine Wilson — designed this house in the style of a French country manor for Colonel H. Willis-O'Connor, who was aide-de-camp and friend to many Governors General: Byng, Willingdon, Bessborough, Tweedsmuir, and Athlone. The turret with staggered vertical windows gives the house its special charm. Inside, the turret accommodates a staircase. Of note are the vertical bars masking the windows and doors, a disfiguring security precaution that detracts from the home's otherwise cozy, welcoming ambiance.

Turn left (north) on Lansdowne. On your left are the two tennis courts that were once the private domain of the Southam brothers. When they were built in 1926 the only house on Lansdowne was **456, Miss Wright's House**. A red brick, single family residence, it is similar to houses in the Glebe. This modest home has cut-out maple leaves on its shutters. The shingled third storey is set within the steeply gabled roof, which features dormer windows at either side. Note the carport's cupola with its duck-in-flight weathervane so appropriate to a residence overlooking MacKay Lake.

Next door is **494 Lansdowne**, the Swiss ambassador's residence, which also hugs the lakefront. Built in 1927 by the Kemp-Edwards lumbering family, in 1948 the house underwent alterations designed by W. E. Noffke.

Lansdowne South ends at Hillsdale. Straight ahead of you are the parklands maintained by the NCC. Cross Hillsdale and enter the grassy area via a little footpath amid the trees. When you emerge onto the grass, veer right and descend the gentle slope to the small stone bridge on Hillsdale at the outflow of MacKay Lake. It was built by the Ottawa Improvement Commission in 1905 and restored by the Village of Rockcliffe Park in 1996. To the east of this watercourse were the grounds of the Dominion Rifle Range. These then became part of the National Park accessed by the extension of the Ottawa Electric Railway, which transported Ottawans to The Rockeries opposite Waterstone.

If you walked left to follow MacKay Lake's watercourse to its confluence with the Ottawa River, you would arrive at the old site of Julius Caesar Blasdell's 1849 steam-driven sawmill, the first in the area.

But for today's walk, re-cross Hillsdale and enter the **Caldwell-Carter Conservation Area** (open 7:00 a.m. to 8:30 p.m.) encircling MacKay Lake. To do this, walk through the metal gateway and down the trail following the north side of the lake. If you've brought your binoculars you can do some serious bird watching here, and if you tread softly in summertime, you may spy a painted turtle basking on a log. In fall or early spring, when the trees are not in full leaf, there are clear views of the lake's northern bank. Watch too for the sudden sighting of a great blue heron, or listen for the rustling skirmish of a chipmunk among autumn's leaves. This is a lakeside worth preserving for its tranquil beauty and what little is left of its natural habitat.

As you walk beside the lake, you see the many additions to the lakeshore built in the late 1980s. Number **700 Hillsdale**, to your left, is architect Wolfgang Mohaupt's modern montage of cedar and limestone ashlar, at once both angular and sprawling on top of the sloping bank. Next find **710 Hillsdale**, Barry Hobin's traditional English country house of cut stone. Nestled on the edge of the bird sanctuary, its splendid view is somewhat cut off by number 700, which was built later. Even in Rockcliffe, "infill" can be irritating.

Keep the lake on your right, following the trail as it wends through these mixed woods. There are several pathways here that provide access points to the main trail. Soon you'll find a major fork in the path, and here you'll notice a second shallow body of water to your left. Walk left to **the Pond**, where there's a tiny public swimming access. (**Note:** There are no changing facilities or washrooms here, just a park bench: this is truly a "secret" community swimming spot.)

Note the terraced condominium complex across the water, first of Leonard Koffman's 1986–87 **MacKay Lake Estates**, and then, to their right, Barry Hobin's 1988–89 **Bittern Court**, whose staggered brick façade cascades down the Pond's western embankment. Their high-density population imposes pressures on the wetlands habitat of the park.

This is the area marked "Extensive deposit of White Marl" on Keefer's 1864 map of Rockcliffe. Thomas Clark operated brickworks here that supplied both red and white bricks to the entire region. His Rockcliffe white marl brick was popular: the 1877 town hall at Luskville, west of Aylmer in Western Quebec, features corner quoins from here (though they have been painted white in recent times). The Pond itself was not shown on Keefer's map, as it did not exist until 1908, when sand from the site was excavated for construction of the Château Laurier. Water flowed in — and the Pond was created.

Retrace your steps the few metres back to the main pathway, which is on your left. Now the Pond is on your left, MacKay Lake on your right. Watch for the sign dedicated to the people who constructed this path. Shortly you ascend steps to the street called Bittern Court. Turn left here and then right onto Whitemarl and right again onto Hemlock Street.

Hemlock is the north-eastern boundary of **Beechwood Cemetery**, burial ground of many well-known Rockcliffe and Ottawa residents. Established in 1873, it is home to well over 60,000 graves, including those of the MacKays, Keefers, and such Ottawa notables as poets Archibald Lampman and Duncan Campbell Scott, who are buried adjacent to each other, befitting their close friendship. Exploring Beechwood Cemetery is a walk unto itself and so is not included here.

Continue southwest on Hemlock until you come to the first street, Lansdowne South. On the corner, find the walled, spacious grounds of **120 Lansdowne**, formerly "**Noot gedacht,**" the residence of the deputy high commissioner of the United Kingdom. That home was originally built in 1938 by John Roper for Col. Shirley E. Woods, historian and inventor of the down-filled vest. Woods rented the premises between 1940 and 1942 to Crown Princess Juliana, before she moved with her family to Stornoway (because 120 was too small). She called the house "Noot gedacht" (Dutch for never thought) because she had never thought that she would have to flee her homeland.[22]

But "never thought" now has a new meaning, for the original Woods' home was demolished so that new owner Antoine Paquette and wife Kerry Peahl could build a mansion to their specifications. It was designed by architect Barry Hobin and has been evaluated at over $7.5 million — the second most valuable home in Rockcliffe. (We will see the most valuable residence later — the Marlen Cowpland home.) In autumn of 2002, stonemasons working on the entryway told me that Paquette had spent "eight million and counting." Certainly this immense estate home suits its grand setting very well indeed. Although the new mansion is huge, it is extremely well sited on its gracious setting overlooking the lake and woodland. *The Ottawa Citizen* reported on November 21, 2002 that Mr. Paquette left for California. In the autumn of 2003 the mansion was sold for a multi-million-dollar price.

Turn right on Lansdowne and walk to **115 Lansdowne**, once the **Diefenbaker residence**, on your left. This 1949 house is an unassuming clapboard, colonial-style home, quite without the dominating presence of many Rockcliffe houses. It is the only house that former Prime Minister Diefenbaker owned.

Number **187 Lansdowne**, the residence of the Ambassador of Iraq, is notable for its imposing security features. A cedar hedge scarcely hides a sturdy steel and concrete fence. Cameras peer down at walkers gazing up. Its fortress qualities are emphasized by its location on the rise of land overlooking MacKay Lake.

Continue down Lansdowne until you reach the sharp turn to the left, at Mariposa. Straight ahead of you is a shingled Queen Anne mansion resembling a rambling Cape Cod home. Here, veer right and then turn immediately left, along the footpath called the **Dog Walk** that leads quietly behind Sylvan Way. MacKay Lake is directly to your right, so here you pass by private accesses to docks and boats belonging to the property owners of the residences to your left.

The second house on the path, **250 Sylvan**, **The Ledges**, was built in 1934 by architect A. J. Hazelgrove for well-known Ottawa businessman Lawrence Freiman. Its layered planes and hipped roof are particularly well suited to the terraced slopes, which give the house its name. A later sunroom addition with cantilevered corner arches adds interest to the original structure.

The third house is **245 Sylvan**, the **Rowley Home**, was built for Graham Rowley, eminent Canadian Arctic explorer and geologist. Its 1909 date makes it an early home in Rockcliffe. Rowley would have looked down on both MacKay Lake and the Southam's twin tennis courts. Rounded fieldstones from the excavation were used in its façade. From this lakeside perspective, the heavy-looking black roof appears gambrel-shaped: however, if seen from its front façade on Sylvan, it shows a mansard style roof. These features, along with its stuccoed, round-cornered tower, give it an eclectic look.

The path ends at the corner of Prospect. Stop to look at **400 Lansdowne**, the **Hart Massey House**. This design won the coveted Massey Medal in 1959 and is important for several reasons. Because of its modernist, avant-garde design that is perhaps only echoed here in Rockcliffe by Teron's 1970 cedar home on Crescent. Turning their backs on vernacular and revivalist designs, which looked to the past for inspiration, modernists such as Hart Massey experimented with new structural technologies, stripping buildings of unnecessary

245 Sylvan, the Rowley Home. 2002. K. Fletcher.

400 Lansdowne, Hart Massey's "cubist creation," as seen from MacKay Lake walk. The accented steel supports mimic the vertical lines of the surrounding trees. 2002. K. Fletcher.

accoutrements. The result was an entire movement inspired by the Bauhaus and International Style groups in Europe. Here architect Hart Massey experimented with basic rectangles, or cubes, projecting from the hillside.

Despite its studied horizontal massing, the house is organic, integrating into its wooded site extremely well. This is due to such elements as the home's steel supports, which are entirely visible, being painted black for emphasis. They very successfully echo the verticals of the surrounding tree trunks — an effect that is dramatically enhanced by a fresh winter snowfall. The steel supports have another intriguing design feature: within the modular steel frame, the cubes were designed so that they could be added to or interchanged.

The resulting effect is of an intriguing modernist home that exhibits definite artistic qualities. You might find that Massey's house recalls Mondrian's cubist paintings, which featured dramatic vertical and horizontal black lines.

Now climb up Prospect, with the lake at your back. Cross Cloverdale and immediately watch out for the steps leading up the hillside to Fernhill.

Note **393 Fernhill**, on your right as you emerge from the steps onto the street. This is an English country "cottage," built between the wars and designed by W. E. Noffke after the fashion of English architects Edwin Lutyens and C. F. A. Voysey. Both were influential architects in the Arts and Crafts Movement. This home's steep asymmetrical main gable with its flaring buttresses is mirrored by a smaller gable housing a sunroom to the right of the main arched doorway. Two flanking chimneys with sloped offsets further balance the house. The design is charming, situated as it is atop Fernhill overlooking MacKay Lake.

Continue on Fernhill to Acacia. Cross it and note its width. Acacia is one of the main arteries of Rockcliffe, with houses set well back from the road. After a few paces to your right, turn left (west) on Buchan. Number **270 Buchan** is another colonial house with a pronounced horizontal composition. Its first storey is limestone, the second is clapboard, and the third horizontal layer is its steeply pitched roof with dormers. Shutters accentuate the house's New England colonial look.

At the corner of Buchan and Mariposa, you can see the grounds of **Ashbury College**. Cross Mariposa and walk a few paces east (left). The main building was designed by Allan Keefer in an utilitarian red brick Elizabethan period style. Keefer had attended Ashbury in 1891 at its former location on Argyle Avenue, the present site of the Windsor Arms apartments, opposite the Canadian Museum of Nature. The new site in Rockcliffe was purchased from the Rockcliffe Property Company for $12,000. In 1910 the school opened at its new location.

The grounds of the school were once a rocky field. It was cleared by Ashbury's handyman, Fred Oliver, who built the rock walls surrounding the school from the fieldstone. It was Oliver who dug, lifted, and hauled every stone to its place along Springfield, Mariposa, and Glenwood.

Turn west (right) to cross Mariposa, and then cross diagonally through the **Jubilee Garden**, the centre of the village. As you approach Springfield Road, you walk through the **Village Green** where you will once again find the ornate capitals of Corinthian columns from the demolished Carnegie Library. This central park was planned under the direction of Humphrey Carver as a community Canadian Centennial project in 1967. Rockcliffe residents planted trees and erected lampposts to create a "people place" out of a former tangle of rocks and bush. Note the trees that resemble Acacias, which gave the name to the street. According to Roman Popadiouk, arborist at Ontario's Ministry of Natural Resources, these trees are actually black locust.

393 Fernhill, English country cottage style home. 2002.
K. Fletcher.

Stroll about this pretty park filled with park benches that are memorials to village residents, before continuing your walk on Springfield Road. Turn right on it to walk alongside **Rockcliffe Public School** and the **Police Station**.

Princess Juliana's children attended this school during the war years when the family resided in Rockcliffe. The Princess chose to send her children to a public rather than a private school, and so her children enjoyed a regular, rather than an exclusively privileged and protected, life while in Rockcliffe. On April 22, 1952, as Queen Juliana, she returned to Rockcliffe to lay the cornerstone of the gymnasium and community hall at the public school. The stone is still visible although somewhat overgrown. As a lasting gift of thanks to Canada for providing her family a refuge in wartime, she donated thousands of tulip bulbs that were used to grace the parkland around Dow's Lake and the Queen Elizabeth Driveway.

Now turn left on Buena Vista and proceed north. On your right is the third village school, **261 Buena Vista, Elmwood**. Situated on the former MacKay farm of the same name, the old rambling farmhouse was occupied for years by Charles Keefer, son of T. C. and father of

Elmwood's half-timbered façade and red roof add colour to Buena Vista. 2002. K. Fletcher.

architect Allan. The school's playing fields preserve the lovely openness at the heart of Rockcliffe.

Elmwood was founded by Mrs. Hamlet S. Philpott, the wife of one of Ashbury College's teachers, in 1915 as the Rockcliffe Preparatory School serving both boys and girls. In 1923 it became a private girls' school. That year saw the addition of a dormitory wing and an assembly hall. In 1925 the original stone farmhouse was demolished. Today, boys join the girls for their early schooling at Elmwood from junior kindergarten to grade 3. Afterwards, it's a girls-only environment here until graduation prior to university entrance.

Turn right on Manor Avenue and cross to the far side of the street. Watch carefully for David Thomas Laneway leading off to the left (if you reach Hillcrest you've gone too far). Walk down the narrow lane and emerge onto Minto Place. Turn right on Minto Place and go a few steps until you reach Soper Place. Pause and look to your left.

The pocket of land described by Soper Place used to be the site of Thomas MacKay's stone Victorian Gothic "cottage," **Birkenfels**. The story of this last part of the original MacKay Estate is a sad reflection of Rockcliffe's infill and density pressures. Birkenfels property owners Mike and Tim Perley-Robertson subdivided this once fine old house with its estate grounds into eighteen lots. Rumour has it that the estate was divided such that the limestone house straddled *two* lots, and was thus considered too expensive for anyone to purchase and restore. Birkenfels, Rockcliffe's oldest house, was torn down in the summer of 1991, despite the outcry of heritage-minded residents. Because the house is gone and the estate destroyed after being divided, the name "Birkenfels" retains no meaning.

In March of 1993, when this book was first published, only three lots on Soper Place had houses. At time of writing, giant mansions crowd the street.

Enter this tiny cul-de-sac. Immediately to your left is **272 Soper Place**, an immense home erected in 1992–93. Its quasi-Georgian details include the symmetrical arrangement of windows and an imposing central doorway pavilion. Brilliant white corner quoins are sharply at odds with the red brick façade. This oversized house dominates its lot, achieving a startlingly ungainly effect at the entrance to Birkenfels grounds.

On the right, notice the twin gables of the original Birkenfels' carriage house and stables, now **299 Soper Place**, transformed in 1992 by architect Richard Limmert into a spectacular collage of forms and materials for businessman Michael Potter. A limestone wall extension to the northwest of the home cleverly shields the gardens from public scrutiny. It also masks the rear glassed extension of the home, which accommodates a sunken living room with a cozy fireplace. The original Birkenfels' house stood on the far side of the wall. To the east at the rear is a separate building housing a swimming pool, connected to the main house by an outside walkway.

Beyond these transformed Birkenfels' stables find another Barry Hobin creation, **247 Soper Place** completed in 1991. It also possesses design elements reminiscent of both Wright and Noffke as evidenced most particularly in its window treatment, horizontal composition, and mix of sheer stucco with rough-cut stone walls.

247 Soper Place. January 1993. K. Fletcher.

234 Soper Place, Cowpland residence. 2002. K. Fletcher.

But the most famous home in Birkenfels is the unimaginably ostentatious bronze-coloured glass residence at **number 234 Soper**, built by multimillionaires Marlen and Michael Cowpland. In 2003 this private residence was assessed at over $10 million — the highest evaluaton in Rockcliffe to date. Forever flamboyant, the couple here created a startlingly office-like edifice of boldly reflecting glass — an "in-your-face" statement for this small enclave if there ever was one. The Cowplands can survey their neighbours indiscriminately, but no one can glimpse inside these mirrored windows, which peculiarly distort the reflections of passersby and adjacent residences. Such efforts at distancing seem most peculiar in this otherwise pastoral residential setting.

At the rear of the home and to the right, find the garden gateway, through which you can spy an immense fountain of joyous-looking figures. The splashing of the water, at least, is refreshing, as is the glimpse of colourful flowers.

Now exit. As you do, you pass by Perley Court. Here find **280 Perley Court**, a gabled cut stone home after the English Arts and Crafts style.

Return to Minto Place, turn right, and proceed to MacKinnon where you'll turn right again. On the corner find **95 MacKinnon**, once home to Thomas Coltrin Keefer and his wife, Annie MacKinnon (daughter of Thomas MacKay). This picturesque clapboard cottage and its garden are lovingly maintained and form an ironically understated, modest juxtaposition to the Cowpland place. This home features a steep gable with dentil trim and peaked window mouldings, both common details of Victorian vernacular cottages.

By 1903 the couple had relocated to the Manor House, and Keefer sold the cottage to William Gerard, a former New Edinburgh resident. Gerard was millwright and superintendent with the Maclaren mills in New Edinburgh. He brought his wife and nine children to this little cottage (see New Edinburgh walk).

As you walk down MacKinnon, you will see Gerard's legacy to Rockcliffe. In 1912, after his wife died, he built **79 MacKinnon**, and in successive years built two more homes both for his sons: in 1915, number **63** and, in 1923, number **49 MacKinnon**. Like the corner cottage and Gerard's three brick homes, all these houses lack the grandeur and prominent situations of many of the houses in Rockcliffe. They are particularly at odds with the immense mansions you just discovered at Soper Place. Like the red brick house you saw earlier at 456 Lansdowne, these houses on MacKinnon have much more in common with their counterparts in the Glebe (see Glebe walk).

MacKinnon ends abruptly, joining Birkenfels Road. Turn left here and then almost immediately right onto Buena Vista, which in turn ends at Lisgar. At the corner is **412 Lisgar**. There is no unifying focal point to this home, which sprawls over its sloping site in a confusing collection of competing textures.

Compare 412 with the subtle, organic design of **420 Lisgar**, the Danish ambassador's residence. While the former imposes itself upon passersby, number 420 is a masterpiece of environmental integration. It is neatly tucked into the slope. Its cedar grillwork averts the fortress-like aspect of the ground-floor concrete retaining wall. The cedar staining of the vertical woodwork on the main and second floors fronting Lisgar is set off by vermilion window trim. Its horizontal planes and successful integration into the hillside may seem to be strongly evocative of Frank Lloyd Wright's style. However, post-and-beam construction with broad eaves is also common to Scandinavian architecture.

Complete this walk around Rockcliffe by ambling through the gentle wooded slopes of the park, first heading to your right on Lisgar and then continuing on the Rockcliffe Parkway to return to your car at the Lookout. If you parked at the band shell, cross the Rockcliffe Parkway and walk through the pine knoll down to the parking lot.

420 Lisgar. The organic lines of the Danish Embassy help it blend into its hillside location. January 1992. E. Fletcher.

Ottawa River Parkway

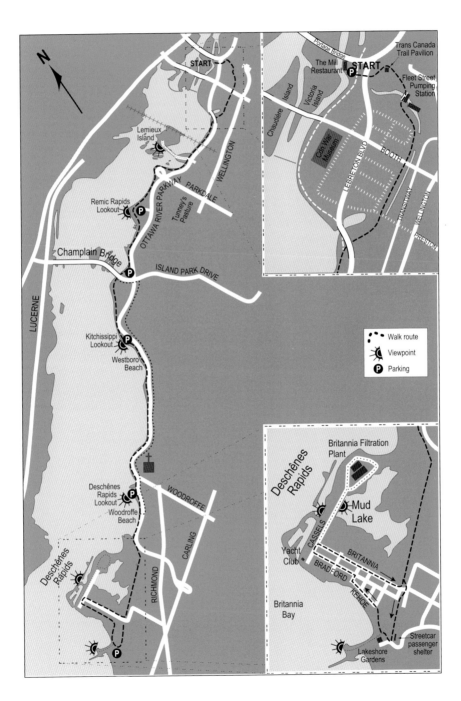

START

Portage Bridge

The Mill Restaurant

START

Trans Canada Trail Pavilion

Fleet Street Pumping Station

Chaudière Island

Victoria Island

Coin War Museum

LEBRETON BLVD

BOOTH

TRANSITWAY

WELLINGTON

PRESTON

Lemieux Island

WELLINGTON

OTTAWA RIVER PARKWAY

PARKDALE

PARKWAY

Remic Rapids Lookout

Tunney's Pasture

Champlain Bridge

ISLAND PARK DRIVE

LUCERNE

Kitchissippi Lookout

Westboro Beach

Walk route

Viewpoint

Parking

Deschênes Rapids Lookout

WOODROFFE

Woodroffe Beach

CARLING

RICHMOND

Deschênes Rapids

Britannia Filtration Plant

Deschênes Rapids

Mud Lake

CASSELS

Yacht Club

BRITANNIA

BRADFORD

KEHOE

Britannia Bay

Lakeshore Gardens

Streetcar passenger shelter

Residents of Ottawa might be forgiven for taking water for granted. That's because the Ottawa, Gatineau and Rideau rivers define the capital's physical topography. The waterways surrounding us have provided food, trade and transportation highways, and strategic defence routes — not to mention potable water — for over 4,000 years.

From ancient Paleo-Indian trade routes, *coureur-du-bois* explorations of the hinterland in the 1600s, through to development of the Chaudière and other falls in the 1800s, the Ottawa River has had a particularly significant impact on the capital's development. As European settlements spread, sawmills and gristmills were erected along its shores, stretching to the west and east (see New Edinburgh walk). And after all, a watercolour painting of the view upriver from Barracks (now Parliament) Hill was possibly the final enticement Queen Victoria needed when choosing Ottawa as the capital of her Dominion in 1857.

First Nations' people first paddled the river system from the Great Lakes to the St. Lawrence, transporting goods such as copper and tobacco along the ancient trading route. In 1610 Étienne Brûlé became the first European to paddle from Montreal to the Rideau. One year later, Nicolas de Vigneau — who Samuel de Champlain called "the boldest liar" he had ever met — claimed he had travelled to Allumette Island where he had seen a large body of salt water. In so saying, de Vigneau convinced Champlain he'd found the passage to the Far East. How excited Champlain must have been: he had seen the Pacific Ocean from Panama in 1599, and was intent on finding a route to China for the King of France. The explorer was also aware of Englishman Henry Hudson's recent discovery of Hudson Bay, a northern sea which might link to the Pacific. Accordingly, Champlain hired native guides and, outfitted with two birch bark canoes and with de Vigneau on board, the party disembarked from Montreal. As the party approached Allumette Island, de Vigneau grew increasingly agitated, until his deception was discovered.

Champlain's journal of 1613 documents this along with other intriguing insights. He notes passing the Gatineau River, and describes the Rideau Falls where Algonquin and Hurons would hide behind its cascade. And a particularly interesting entry describes the *tabagie* (tobacco ceremony) routinely made at the Chaudière portage:

After having carried their canoes below the falls, they get together in one place, where one of them, with a wooden plate, takes up a collection, and each of them puts into this plate a piece of tobacco ... the plate is put into the middle of the band, and all dance around it, singing in their fashion. Then one of the chiefs makes a speech, showing that for a long time they have been accustomed to making this offering, and that by this means they are guaranteed against their enemies; otherwise, misfortune would befall them. That done, the speaker takes the plate and goes and throws the tobacco into the middle of the cauldron, and they raise a great cry altogether.[23]

Evidently the offering worked for Champlain's group, for they paddled on uneventfully.

No wonder the Chaudière's boiling waters prompted offerings to the Manitou. Called *Asticou* in Algonquin, the French aptly translated it to *Chaudière*, or kettle, successfully conveying the image of boiling waters. Upstream lie the Remic, Little Chaudière, and finally the Deschênes (oak) rapids at Britannia, marking the end of this tour. Of course, the Ottawa continues west, and other treacherous waters lie ahead. For example, the Chats Rapids that link Quyon, Quebec, and Fitzroy Harbour, Ontario, lie just inside the National Capital Region, being on the outskirts of the City of Ottawa (whose western boundary is Fitzroy). Beyond these are falls (now the Chenaux Dam) at Portage du Fort and others at Rapides des Joachims, in the Pontiac region of West Quebec.

In the early days of our history, portages were required, forcing people to pause in their weary journeys upstream. Portages made good sites for entrepreneurs to establish trading posts, stores, and stopping places, where travellers would spend money on supplies, food, and shelter. Later, as settlements grew, mills were needed to grind grain, saw timber, and spin wool.

Forty-year-old Philemon Wright arrived from Woburn Massachusetts (near Boston) via Montreal to land at the Chaudière Falls area in March 1800. Although he had explored this region in 1797, '98, and '99, this year marked the year of settlement. Twenty-seven family members and other settlers accompanied him, along with two teams of oxen, and two sleighs loaded with tools and equipment needed for clearing and planting the land.

A flurry of work commenced not just to plant crops but also to erect homes before the cold weather. By winter of 1800 Wright's community had harvested an astonishing thousand bushels of potatoes and had sown seventy acres of wheat. In 1801 they constructed a barn and had surveyed what became the entire township of Hull, some 82,000 acres. And, to grind their grain and saw their timber, they built a saw- and gristmill, powered by the Chaudière.

Wright made his fortune, however, when Napoleon blockaded the Baltic Sea in 1806. In that year, Napoleon's Prussian Campaign was on, and he had won total control of Prussia's ports. As a result of this, Napoleon indirectly created the economic niche and momentum for the Ottawa Valley lumber industry. The blockade effectively barred Britain from the rich timber stands of the Baltic, forcing the nation to look elsewhere for timbers for its Navy. Wright considered the vast tracts of white and red pine surrounding his community, and determined to make his fortune. In the winter of 1806 he had pine cut, squared, and piled in staging grounds below the Chaudière. The following spring Wright made history by floating the first rafts of squared timber to Montreal, thereby birthing the Ottawa Valley lumber industry.

But what of the Ontario side of the river? Its development was slower, undoubtedly because of daunting topographical features such as the cliffs of what is now Parliament Hill, the impenetrable cedar bush crowding Lowertown, and the swamps and beaver meadows of Uppertown.

In 1809 Maryland settler Jehiel Collins built a store on the south side of the falls, but he soon sold to Caleb Bellows from Vermont and the little site became known as Bellow's Landing. It was subsequently renamed Richmonds Landing (see Parliament Hill walk).

Then along came Captain John LeBreton. He was granted land on the south side of the river for his loyalty to the Crown after serving in the War of 1812. He called the property Britannia, a name that lingers to this day. But LeBreton is better remembered for the land immediately south of the Chaudière, LeBreton Flats.

In December 1820 this property was being auctioned in Brockville: both LeBreton and another gentleman, District Registrar Levius P. Sherwood of Brockville bid upon it, and together purchased it for under £500. The two men had their land surveyed, proposing the name "the Town of Sherwood" for the little community. The town never developed.

Later, when then Governor of Lower Canada, Lord Dalhousie, and Colonel By were searching for a site for the Rideau Canal, LeBreton proposed his land. But arguments between LeBreton and Lord Dalhousie over what the Governor considered to be land speculation, plus questions of clear title, led to the current canal site beneath the Château Laurier being selected, thus thwarting Captain LeBreton's entrepreneurial aspirations. Colonel By started building the Rideau Canal in 1826 and it was completed within six years.

The Chaudière remained largely unexploited until after the Rideau Canal was completed in 1832. Bytown was prospering and finally conditions were economically feasible for the realization of the falls' potential. The trigger was America's insatiable demand for sawn timber; the US building boom was on, and the Ottawa Valley became its supplier. Thus began the American invasion of the capital, which saw Captain Levi Young arrive in 1851 to build a sawmill on the falls. O. H. Ingram and A. H. Baldwin came next, and it was Baldwin who sent the first shipment of sawn lumber to the American construction market.

Still another American, Ezra Butler Eddy, arrived at the Chaudière from Vermont in 1851. Although not monetarily rich, he possessed great wealth of vision. Along with his wife, he started making safety matches. These sold briskly, so they branched out into clothespins and other wooden items. By 1866 Eddy had purchased Victoria Island from the Wrights, and constructed a match factory. Seven years later he was a millionaire.

"Mother Firth's Tavern" located on LeBreton Flats, at the corner of Booth and Oregon streets (now part of Canadian War Museum site) as drawn by Colonel By in 1830. Née Miss Dalmahoy, she married Yorkshire man Isaac Firth, who joined her in operating the inn/tavern. City of Ottawa Archives, CA 11912.

Another man indelibly associated with the Chaudière Falls is John Rudolphus Booth, a Canadian icon born in 1827 near Waterloo, Quebec. Booth arrived in Bytown in 1852 when the population was approximately 8,000. Although he came with what legend dictates was $9.00 in his pocket, within ten years his company was producing thirty million feet of pine. Upon his death in Ottawa in 1925 he was one of the wealthiest industrialists in the world, with extensive markets in the United States and Britain.

Tailrace emanating from Pooley's Bridge, near Fleet Street Pumping Station with piles of sawn lumber in rear, n.d.
City of Ottawa Archives, CA 19026.

As Bytown and then Ottawa's population expanded, the old system of conveying water to households proved inadequate both in terms of potability and volume. Lowertown workers collected river water and hauled it through the city streets in puncheons (large barrels) on horse-drawn wagons. But the water smelled and was suspiciously brown. By 1859 the municipal politicians determined a waterworks was imperative not just for drinking, but also for fire prevention. City engineer Thomas Coltrin Keefer proposed a $300,000 project. However, it was postponed for years while municipal and federal governments wrangled over the site, whether or not it was truly required, and, of course, who would foot the bill. This divided city residents, too: the

Lowertown folks who delivered the water opposed the new-fangled system because they didn't want to lose their jobs. Uppertown residents, however, lobbied for a safer delivery system, if not a cleaner product.

Carleton County's devastating fire in August 1870 swept the Ottawa Valley, creating the famous Burnt Lands to the west of Ottawa. A year later, a horrific fire destroyed much of Chicago. The conflagrations terrified Ottawans, and once again the waterworks issue bubbled up.

Fleet Street Pumping Station as originally designed/built (prior to second-storey addition), showing the mansard roof and ornate iron cresting, plus stylized garden and fountain. 1898. City of Ottawa Archives, CA 1588.

Concurrent with the waterworks project, a city sewer was being planned. Finally, in 1874 both systems were implemented. Despite the intervening years, Keefer was named chief engineer for what became the Fleet Street Pumping Station. Completed in 1875, it still stands at the foot of the Pooley Bridge. It served the populace well, until 1911 and 1912 when typhoid struck. Because intake pipes drew water from the river, and because the water was ineffectively treated, many people fell sick — and some died. The 1911 epidemic saw 987 cases and 83 deaths, whereas in 1912 the disease claimed 81 lives out of its 1,378 cases.[24]

Ottawans continued to agitate over water safety and in 1915 the city's second pumping station was built on Lemieux Island. Because of the concern over typhoid, water intake pipes were extended into the middle of the Ottawa River. To avoid potentially defective underwater joinery, water was delivered to the mainland via above-ground pipes that still span the river crossing beside the island bridge. Previously the intake pipes collected water from Lazy Bay, the backwater immediately east of Lemieux Island.

Lemieux Island pumping station was built in 1915, while the water purification plant was erected in 1932. Further upstream, the Britannia filtration and pumping facility was built in the early 1960s.

The impact of water on Ottawa wouldn't be comprehensive without mentioning its recreational aspects. The tailrace of Keefer's 1874 Fleet Street station is a favourite kayaking course today. And both the Lemieux and Britannia plants are havens for birdwatchers, cyclists, and walkers who appreciate their natural settings.

Britannia Schoolhouse with children 1904–05.
City of Ottawa Archives, CA 15340.

Britannia is far more than the site of a filtration plant. The area first attracted settlers in the late 1800s, when Captain LeBreton erected a mill here on the shores of Lac Deschênes, opposite rival Aylmer. To thwart the competitive development of Hull-Aylmer (now all part of Gatineau), in 1835 residents on the south recommended building a macadamized (paved) road to connect their community to Ottawa. But because his land would be split in two if a road was built, LeBreton never supported the project ... and without his support the concept died. Notwithstanding their competitor's efforts on the south shore, by 1820 Aylmer residents already had a turnpike road from Hull's Chaudière Falls to Aylmer, called the Britannia Road. By 1830 this original portage road linked communities as far away as Eardley to Hull (Gatineau).

Britannia residents didn't give up: they envisioned Plan B, a "portage railway" designed to transport goods and passengers around the portages between them and Ottawa. In 1849, forty private investors met, including Hamnett P. Hill, who owned a large estate in Carleton County. The portage railway never materialized in Britannia. However, after Ottawa became the capital, and while citizens searched for retreats from summer's heat, dust, and odours, Britannia gradually became a desirable resort destination. Properties were purchased and cottage style homes built. By 1869 the Brockville and Ottawa Railway opened a branch line extending from Carleton Place to Britannia and then Ottawa. Ten years later, Belden's *Historical Atlas* noted, "The C.C.R. have a flag-station in the Township, known as Britannia, but there is no village there."[25]

Better late than never. Ottawans quickly responded to convenience: catching a train to the city every morning and returning to Britannia come evening proved appealing. Recreational activities on the water became increasingly attractive to the cottagers, so by 1891 residents had formed the Britannia Aquatic Club, today's Britannia Yacht Club. Also around this time, camping beside the river was becoming a popular summer pastime.

Between 1899–1902 William Soper and Thomas Ahearn's Ottawa Electric Railway Company developed the Britannia streetcar line. Ever the astute businessman, Ahearn agreed to spend $30,000 on a clubhouse built at the tip of the Britannia pier. Ahearn understood that a pleasant park, pier, and clubhouse would be a big draw for passengers eager to spend their new leisure time in "the country air." Not only would it provide an attractive day's destination for the streetcar crowds, but he could also launch his then state-of-the-art motorboat from the boathouse, too.

Members of the Scott and Bishop families camping at Britannia, 1896. NAC PA-126534.

Postcard of Britannia Pier depicts old dance hall/boat house, plus canoes, sailboats and Ottawa River steamboat, n.d. City of Ottawa Archives, CA 18975.

The pier immediately drew enthusiastic crowds who enjoyed taking the air from its boardwalk. In 1906, in his book *The Hub and the Spokes*, American raconteur Anson A. Gard compared Britannia to Coney Island. The clubhouse served as a popular dance hall. Meanwhile the Upper Ottawa Improvement committee capitalized on the new market by offering scenic day trips to Quyon on steamers such as the *Albert* and the *G.B. Greene*. Trips were offered three times a week to the Chats Falls (at Quyon/Fitzroy Harbour) and on Thursday nights young people particularly enjoyed the moonlight cruises, complete with live bands playing dance tunes.

Finally, everything seemed to be going swimmingly for Britannia.

But the forces of nature, WW I, and technology intervened. In the winters of 1915 and 1923 river ice severely damaged the sailboat slips and pier. Fire destroyed Ahearn's clubhouse on August 29, 1918. By 1920 cars had replaced the streetcar as conveyances of choice. Also in 1920, dwindling membership in the Britannia Yacht Club prompted someone to suggest that women be accepted as members. The deeply disturbing motion was unceremoniously quashed!

The car particularly affected membership in the Britannia Yacht Club: young people preferred exploring the region in their own vehicles rather than attending club meets and sailing the Ottawa. Membership dwindled until by the 1930s, the club property was sold for arrears in taxes. All was not lost, however, because a member purchased and reopened it. And after club member Frank Amyot won the gold medal for single blade paddling in the 1936 Berlin Olympics, he prompted a revival of recreational boating that continues with today's kayakers and canoeists who enjoy playing in the Ottawa and its tributaries.

But the history isn't complete without noting the building of the Ottawa River Parkway, part of Jacques Gréber's Master Plan for Ottawa (published 1950). From LeBreton Flats west to Britannia, homes, businesses, and industries were purchased or expropriated by the Federal District Commission to create the driveway, bicycle, and walking paths residents so love. This western parkway project displaced 2,000 or so people from 658 homes. Time heals, so we say, and perhaps this is true. These days, LeBreton Flats is the site of the new Canadian War Museum (opening in 2005) and pretty parklands. As you explore, the Ottawa River flows past you, to the north, mirrored by the original late 1800s aqueducts designed to divert that river's waters to the Fleet Street Pumping Station. History never stands still.

Dancing in Britannia was a popular pastime here at Lakeside
Gardens. This building was originally located at Victoria Park and
Holland, n.d. City of Ottawa Archives, CA 18289.

NEIGHBOURHOOD STYLES

This walk highlights a network of aqueducts, filtration plants, and
pumping stations integral to the heritage and contemporary functioning
of Ottawa. Included in this walk, we'll look at the Pooley Bridge and
the industrial Italianate style of the Fleet Street Pumping Station.
Both make intriguing stylistic contrasts with the Lemieux Island plant
which sports art deco and Moderne elements, largely in brick and
concrete. Built two decades later, Britannia's filtration plant, continues
the industrial vein.

As you walk (or cycle), the Ottawa River is your constant companion,
along with its own waterfowl residents to keep you company. Watch
for viewing platforms and interpretive signs, glimpses of blue heron
and water lilies, and inukshuks-stylized human-shaped cairns built by
people who enjoy splashing about in the shallows.

The walk (or bike ride) culminates at Britannia Village and Lakeside
Gardens Park, where the rocky breakwater enables you to wander onto

the water to get breathtaking images upriver, across to Aylmer, and downriver to the spires of Parliament.

Policeman in front of S. Poulin's shop, Rochester Street (south of LeBreton Flats area), n.d. City of Ottawa Archives, CA 1216.

WALK TIPS

🚶 **12 km *one way*;**
4 leisurely hours by bicycle; a half-day on foot.

You can accomplish this delightful but long outing in many ways: in winter, strap on skis or snowshoes; in good weather, consider biking the route (the Parkway is closed to vehicles on Sunday mornings), or travelling by scooter, in-line-skates or on foot. At the time of writing, this route is completely wheelchair accessible because all pathways are paved (the interiors of the plants, however, may not be wheelchair friendly, so inquire). The Ottawa River Parkway has many picnic tables, park benches, and grassy areas to enjoy.

As well, in summer there is swimming at Britannia Beach and nature walks in Britannia's Mud Lake Conservation Area (bikes are banned there). Pack accordingly: birders or heritage buffs who want to peer at views of Aylmer across the river in Quebec should bring their binoculars.

Special caution: the river is deceptive. It appears calm around the scattering of tiny islands near Lemieux Island but strong undercurrents exist. In the summer of 2002, three youngsters decided to beat the heat by taking a dip here. One drowned, another was only just saved. Please: do not swim *anywhere* other than designated beaches.

Also some paths are shared bike and walking paths. Others are for walkers only, so bicyclists are asked (by signs) not to proceed on these.

Finally, dogs are becoming increasingly unwelcome. At the time of writing, the NCC has just imposed penalties for letting your dog run free in any but a few designated parks. Beware, and always, always leash your dog, and stoop & scoop.

THE WALK

Special note before you start: *At the time this edition went to press, the new LeBreton Boulevard section of the Ottawa River Parkway was under construction. The start to this walk, therefore, may not flow precisely as written. The NCC planners helpfully met with me to discuss their future plans for this area — the map at the beginning of the chapter reflects these plans. Be aware that although road work may necessitate minor changes in the route, the NCC intends to keep this important urban pathway well-marked.*

Start your walk at **The Mill** restaurant, formerly the 1842 **Thompson-Perkins Mill** (555 Ottawa River Parkway). A former grist and sawmill, it's the oldest building of the industrial complex spanning the Chaudière, one that was fortunate to survive the 1900 conflagration that destroyed most of Hull and significant portions of Ottawa. It is now owned by the National Capital Commission, which renovated it in 1968–71. Its classical style features seven second-storey and six first-floor windows, now enhanced by blue shutters. Walk to the right of the building, where a patio area off the kitchen overlooks a channel of the Ottawa.

Directly opposite is Victoria Island where you'll spy a timber chute, once used to channel logs past the falls. You are looking at the site of **Bellow's Landing**, later **Richmond Landing**. This is where Jehiel

Collins built his store in 1809 to capture the business of rivermen and settlers who would stop and portage their goods around the Chaudière. Renamed Richmond Landing, this island was the first home to British soldiers in 1818 who were among a group of pioneering settlers who pitched their tents here. They immediately started work building the Richmond Road that linked the settlement which would become Bytown to what became the military settlement of Richmond and Perth, where the Crown had granted them land to erect their homes. To your immediate right is the 1973 Portage Bridge connecting Ottawa to Gatineau (Hull), Philemon Wright's original settlement.

Now turn around and walk south, across the parking lot through the underpass of the Ottawa River Parkway. Immediately turn right to ascend the shared bicycle and walking path.

Stop briefly to appreciate the industrial complex spanning the Chaudière. The closest body of water to you now is the **bypass channel** for timber built in 1847. It was considered great sport to swoosh down this channel on a raft; tourists as well as notables such as the Prince of Wales (in 1860) enjoyed this precursor of today's river rafting. The first timber slide was erected here in 1826 by Colonel By. It was Lord Dalhousie who ordered him to do this, possibly to thwart Captain

Old timber slide, Bronson Co., Chaudière District — man on right, Bronson foreman W. J. Nichol, Victoria Island, circa 1890.
NAC PA-148844.

LeBreton's access to the waterfront. As a result, LeBreton couldn't build a mill here on the flats — nor did he and his partner Sherwood ever build Sherwood town here.

Beyond the city of Gatineau you'll see the wooded hills of **Gatineau Park**. When paddling past in 1613, Champlain recorded the view of this ridge of mountains. Over three hundred years later, engineers at the city of Ottawa waterworks contemplated piping water from the park's lakes, a notion that proved too costly.

Turn around and walk downhill, keeping right. To your left (east) you can see the spires of Parliament Hill echoed by Christ Church Cathedral's steeple. After passing some pine and cedar trees, step inside the **Trans-Canada Trail Pavilion** dedicated June 29, 1998.

Built to connect Canadian communities from sea to sea to sea, over 16,000 kilometres the Trans-Canada Trail is the longest recreational trail in the world. Plaques list the names of Canadians who donated time, effort and money to the construction of the trail.

This trail and the Ottawa River are critical "highways" that link Canadian communities and foster understanding among our peoples. Historically, the Ottawa was the highway to the hinterland, used by explorers like Étienne Brûlé, le Verendrye, Champlain, Mackenzie, and Thompson. Today, the Trans-Canada Trail creates a similar link for today's recreational explorers.

On your right is the vast expanse of land known as **LeBreton Flats**. This was once a thriving neighbourhood of residences, small shops, and industries, as well as the **Broad Street Station** (demolished) where streetcars commenced their trip to Britannia. The streetcars ran along Broad Street, and then traversed Scott, Preston, Somerset, and Holland streets, before connecting to the Ottawa Electric Railway streetcar right of way on Byron.[26] The Broad Street Station closed in 1930, overtaken by Union Station opposite the Château Laurier.

In the early 1960s the NCC purchased thirteen acres here and started to demolish the community, creating a vast open space whose use was hotly debated for thirty years. Some people wanted it to be developed into a park where they could run their dogs and enjoy a breath of country within the city. But the developers and city planners had other ideas; over time uses such as an aquarium and a zoo were entertained here, and while the planners planned and held public consultations, the Flats welcomed such visitors as Le Cirque de Soleil. This company raised its multi-peaked tents and caused residents of the National Capital Region and beyond to ooh and ahh at their imaginative performances.

Eventually a raison d'être for the Flats was found and as you gaze west today, you'll see the site of the **Canadian War Museum** (a collaboration between the Toronto firm of Moriyama & Teshima, and Griffiths, Rankin, and Cook of Ottawa). At the time of this writing in November 2003, construction was well underway. The total cost of the Canadian War Museum is projected to be $105.75 million. It should open in 2005, the 60th anniversary of the end of World War II.

The plans for the museum, an unusual interpretation of this spectacular and historic site, are exciting. The roof of the building will be sod, a feature that reminds us of war in the trenches as well as the first pioneer homes. Since architects have incorporated walking paths on top of it, upon completion of the museum, you will be able to make a detour and view the industrial complex of the Chaudière and the Ottawa River from it.

Development of the site was an expensive proposition: the NCC spent $99 million to remediate it, relocate the Ottawa River Parkway (see map) and bring services to the site. Because the soil was contaminated with industrial waste left by the industries once thronging the flats, the NCC spent between $30 and $50 million on decontamination and clean-up.

Excavation of an old foundation on the north side of Fleet Street in LeBreton Flats in August 2002, just before the area was relandscaped by the NCC. E. Fletcher.

During this process, some of LeBreton Flats' old building foundations were dug up and teams of archaeologists scurried down to investigate the ruins prior to them all being bulldozed and buried — presumably permanently this time around. Isaac Firth's tavern was excavated, as were the foundations of some buildings directly opposite the Fleet Street Pumping Station. Alas, no foundations were considered worthy of stabilization and interpretive signs, so the entire LeBreton Flats industrial and residential complex is now nothing but a memory.

For the present, continue downhill, staying right while the path bisects a small woods in a gully. On your right, watch for a gurgling stream, the **tailrace** of the Fleet Street Pumping Station, which you're approaching. This watercourse is a favourite "secret" kayaking spot where enthusiastic paddlers practice their strokes.

Turn right, crossing stone arched **Pooley's Bridge** (1872), which is the oldest bridge in the capital's downtown area. It was designed by George Hugo Perry and built by Alexander Sparks, and replaced the original log structure designed by one of Colonel John By's Royal Engineers, Lieutenant Henry Pooley, in 1829.

A few paces beyond and to your left is the **Fleet Street Pumping Station**, at 10 Fleet Street. Built of rusticated limestone in 1874–75, it

Fleet Street Pumping Station and Pooley's Bridge, c. 1901 after second storey was added. Note the LeBreton Flats buildings at rear, demolished by the NCC commencing 1960s. City of Ottawa Archives, CA 6013.

City workers and diver (note air hoses) searching Ottawa River for source of contamination for 1911 typhoid outbreak, near Lemieux Island. City of Ottawa Archives, CA 2258.

Hintonburg Pumping Station adjacent to Lemieux Island Bridge, c. 1932. City of Ottawa Archives, CA 6065.

still functions as an integral part of Ottawa's water delivery system. Walk just past the building to view the 750 metre long aqueduct transporting water from the Ottawa River to intake pipes on the west side of the station. Keefer's creative design used water to power the reciprocating pumps that deliver as much as three million gallons of water a day to citizens.

In 1888 three more pumps were added and by 1899 the city's needs had expanded such that a second storey was added. At this time the original mansard roof was replaced by the stringcourse and Italianate style second-floor windows you see now. The early 1900s saw more improvements and the first electric pumps were installed here in 1916.

Continue west veering left to walk alongside the **LeBreton Flats Aqueduct**, itself a marvel of engineering six metres wide and four metres deep. You'll then cross Booth Street, named for lumber baron J. R. Booth. While walking, pause at lookouts over the channel Keefer designed, constructed in 1872–75 and restored in 1999.

Your path soon curves right, and as it does you can see the white office building whose name, "**City Centre**," is announced to all and sundry by gigantic red letters on its roof. Although many could be forgiven thinking the Parliament Hill is Ottawa's "centre," this building marks the site where railway yards used to exist. Livestock, grain and other goods were shipped to this location from Western Canada. Today, its name appears incongruous — but nonetheless it's a well-known landmark.

Now walk through another Parkway underpass where your first unobstructed view of the Ottawa River rewards you. Proceed west and note the grand **Prince of Wales railway bridge** spanning the Ottawa ahead of you, to **Lemieux Island** and Quebec. It was built in 1880 by the province of Quebec for the Quebec, Ottawa and Occidental Railway, which became part of the CPR. Then find the second steel bridge, which supports two gleaming metal pipes transporting water to the city.

Watch for the right-hand turn to the **Lemieux Island Water Purification Plant** (1932). After turning right here find the remains of the **Hintonburg Pumping Station** (c. 1895), before walking over the **Lemieux Island truss bridge** (built by the city in 1915, the piers were repaired in 1962 and rebuilt in 1989).

When on-island, veer right to stroll past a small pond with fountains to the river's southernmost channel. The little woods and grassy area here is a little-used park frequented by dog walkers and birdwatchers. You can ascend the very steep embankment to stand on the railway

bridge you saw earlier, to get an unrivalled view of Ottawa and Gatineau —
but watch out for poison ivy here.

Return the way you came and at the fountain turn right to look at
the purification plant's complex of buildings (1928-32). The **Services
Building** (1 River Street) presents its Art Deco façade first, on your
left as you proceed. (Here you can book a tour of the plant, the only
way to view the fascinating interiors of these buildings that still provide
the capital's water supply.) The attached structure with its symmetrical
red-brick façade, features a classical, pedimented portico (doorway)
further ornamented by a discrete Romanesque-style "arch" made of
brick, with two panels of green marble flanking it. Note the ironwork
pattern in the window, a detail repeated in the tall tower of the
building behind.

The tragedy in Walkerton, Ontario, in 2000 where several
townspeople died due to water contaminated by E-coli bacteria was a
contemporary wake-up call to Canadians. But back in the 1913-32
period, Ottawans were equally concerned about how to purify water,
particularly after the typhoid epidemics of 1912 and 1913. Between
1872 and 1913, Ottawa water was untreated; from 1913 to 1932, a
"temporary" solution of treating water with chlorine and ammonia
prevailed. In December 1928, Ottawa spent $1.3 million on a rapid
sand water purification system that was installed here.

This complex of buildings includes the **Main Pumping Station**,
the **Chemical Building**, and **Purification Building**. The latter, on
your right opposite the Service Building, is a long structure with
Queenstown limestone base and fluted stone pilasters. If you can book
a tour do so, for its interior is absolutely spectacular, with highly
polished walls of Hauteville marble and Travertine floors. Light sconces
are Art Deco, and upstairs in the well-lit viewing gallery there is a
dramatic spandrel over a doorway ornamented by a bronze clock, a
gauge that measures water flow, along with other instruments.

This complex of industrial buildings didn't have to be designed
with such stunning and detailed beauty in mind. But they were...
Certainly for its time, the Lemieux plant was a much-heralded addition
to Ottawa, because everyone wanted clean water after the typhoid
epidemics. And, this was a state-of-the-art plant. But as architect
Michael Neelin observed, it is heartening to know that so much
attention was paid to the interiors — not simply the exteriors — of
the complex. After all, although the public can freely wander the
grounds, to view the insides we must register for a tour. Neelin

commented that mills and their industrial machinery in Upper Canada Village often possessed decorative and thus extremely humanizing touches such as a floral or other design. Such attempts to make an object — or a building — beautiful to look at while employees toil are much appreciated.

Return to the parkway path and continue walking west leaving the island behind. Next find the **Remic Rapids**, where the river becomes extremely shallow. This is a favourite spot to hang out, dabble in the ankle-deep water while building inukshuks (stone sculptures styled after Inuit cairns). Ducks, Canada geese and other birds will amuse you by their endless quacking and requests for food.

Inukshuk overlooking Remic Rapids with ducks. 2002. E. Fletcher.

To the south of the parkway, opposite the rapids is **Tunney's Pasture**, the sprawling complex of government offices constructed during the Cold War years. Formerly the pasture land of Irish settler Anthony Tunney who arrived in Confederation year, the federal government decided to decentralize its downtown offices due to fears of nuclear attack. (At the same time and for the same reasons, the Carp Diefenbunker was constructed as an underground refuge for the prime minister and his strategic advisors.)

Continue your stroll, approaching the **Champlain Bridge**, erected thanks to foresight of Thomas Ahearn. (This was the same gentleman who was president of the Ottawa Electric Company and who, along

Ottawa Electric Company workers preparing the right-of-way
from Holland Avenue to Britannia Bay, 1899.
City of Ottawa Archives, CA 18256.

with partner Warren Soper, operated streetcars to Britannia from
LeBreton Flats). At the time of the bridge's construction, Ahearn was
chairman of the Federal District Commission (1927-32) and it was
due to his generosity that the bridge could be built. When the FDC
ran out of money for the project, Ahearn stepped in, financing its
construction to the tune of many hundreds of thousands of dollars —
at a better rate than the government itself could procure.

The original bridge featured an open deck design that had "twenty-
five 70 foot spans and four 125 foot spans."[27]

Its base is partially supported by three islands: Riopelle, Cunningham
and, the most northerly, and the largest, Bate. The rapids on the north
side of Bate Island, called "the Wall," are particularly choppy, and a
favourite hangout of kayakers. In summer 2002 the NCC completed a
four-year project to expand the bridge from two lanes to three at a
cost of $32 million.

Continue past the bridge to the next stopping point, **Kitchissippi
Lookout** (*Kitchissippi* means "grand river," which gives us the derivation
of an early appellation of the Ottawa River) and **Westboro Beach**, a
popular swimming spot.

The lookout is a favourite spot for residents to stroll, sit on a park
bench, have a picnic or otherwise enjoy the breeze and view on a

North span of Champlain Bridge. 2002. E. Fletcher.

sultry summer's day. The ruins of Skead's Mill and a historic plaque commemorating the 1884 British expedition up the Nile to rescue General Charles Gordon, who was besieged at Khartoum are here. The contingent of men was headed by Viscount Wolseley who had led the 1870 expedition to the Red River. Wolseley insisted that Canadian rivermen be hired for the task for he knew them to be a hardy bunch, wise to the mercurial challenges of rapids. Accordingly, he amassed a group of 400 men, the majority of whom lived in the Ottawa Valley.

Further west, and on the south side of the parkway, watch for the pointed steeple of the **First Unitarian Church** (2101 Algonquin). Built in 1967 and designed by the architectural team of Craig and Kohler, its dramatic, sharply pointed spire is constructed of four single beams. Its graceful design befits the equally beautiful sweep of parkway and greenspace.

About two kilometres beyond the church, and past the Woodroffe exit off the parkway you come to **Deschênes Rapids Lookout** and, next, **Woodroffe Beach**, which is close to the former site of yet another early sawmill, **Johnston's Mills**, named for Joseph Johnston.

As the Parkway curves away from the river continue along the pathway. Soon you lose sight of the river and a woods appears also on your right. This is the **Mud Lake Conservation Area**. If you're biking, take note you cannot bicycle along its nature paths. Mud Lake is a nature lover's paradise, a superb bird watching area particularly in spring migration when warblers, scarlet tanagers and Baltimore orioles flit about. Painted turtles bask on logs while woodland paths introduce you to chipmunks, squirrels and the like.

Biking along the pathway with First Unitarian Church steeple in
background. 2002. K. Fletcher.

Britannia streetcar stop; the turnaround and shelter are visible today
in Lakeside Gardens Park, n.d. City of Ottawa Archives, CA 18259.

Continue west, passing the complex of apartment buildings and open playground to your left. Note the slight rise of land also on your left: this is the raised embankment created for the **streetcars** that transported revellers to and from the Britannia pier and dance hall.

Cross Britannia Road and instead of turning right to explore Britannia Village, continue to **Lakeside Gardens**, and Britannia's beach and rock breakwater. Ahead is the old **streetcar passenger shelter**, where passengers disembarked and strolled to the pier. Today the shelter still serves the public as a covered picnic area. The park here commemorates the old streetcar system, for the turnaround for the cars can still be seen.

Walk to the river and view the magnificent sweep of **Britannia Bay**. There's a windsurfing and a swimming beach, while a **rock breakwater** recalls the memory of the former pier. Imagine it extending into the Ottawa at the turn of the last century, with the two-storey boathouse-cum-dance hall. When standing at the end of the breakwater, orient yourself by looking north to Quebec. Directly across from you is Gatineau (formerly Aylmer) and the ruins of a mill.

View along beach toward pier at Britannia, circa 1900.
NAC PA-106244.

As you start your return eastwards by walking through Lakeside Gardens you will come to the **Ron Kolbus Lakeside Centre**, built in 1957-58 and still operated by the City of Ottawa. In summer it is home to a patio restaurant where you can have a break. Washrooms, changing rooms and showers are open during the summer season. The Centre was named in memory of a City of Ottawa councillor who represented Britannia ward. He died April 7, 2001 in a freak accident, where he slipped on the ice after a charity hockey game for the Boys and Girls Club.

Jamieson's Mill in Britannia, 1870s.
City of Ottawa Archives, CA 17002.

Leaving the Centre behind, find the red-painted anchor of the **G.B. Greene**, a steamer that plied the waters here, which was built upstream in Quyon. Continue walking east, keeping the river on your left. Stroll through the park's treed sanctuary past a children's playground, then veer diagonally left. Find the exit onto Kehoe Street and enter **Britannia Village**. Walk north on Kehoe, right on Jamieson, and left again on Bradford. In 1873, this peninsula was owned by an astute businessman, John McAmmond Jr., who paid $5,450 for 54 acres.[28] His parcel contained two mill sites, including Jamieson's Mill. McAmmond, incidentally, also owned a farm at City View, now part of the Central Experimental Farm (see The Farm walk). An astute entrepreneur, McAmmond surveyed the acreage into 65 lots along Britannia, Bradford and Cassels (a map dated 1873 shows the site of Jamieson's Mill, plus an allowance for a second railway line that would service the mills, presumably). McAmmond's vision marks the first development of the village into a residential area.

Continuing the walk, pause at the southwest corner of Bradford and Rowatt. Although now long gone, this corner was home to **Château Von Charles**. Operated by widow Frederica Von Charles in 1891, it was renowned as a place of distinction, where guests dined elegantly. Frederica was born in Paris on December 18, 1851, educated in London, and after her husband died she immigrated to Ottawa in 1888 with her daughter Catharine. After hearing of booming Britannia, she decided to operate this hotel and cater to elite clientele. The Château burned in 1901.

Brigantine *The Black Jack* docked at Britannia Yacht Club. 2002.
E. Fletcher.

That hotel soon saw a competitor at the corner, the **Balmoral**. Both served the burgeoning tourist industry which by 1890 was considerable. In July 1893 visitors were staying at some 60 cottages, travelling here along the bumpy, dusty Richmond Road by horse and carriage, bicycle, or by train (there was a station at Britannia in 1869).[29]

Stay north and find 84 Bradford, **Arbour House** built in 1893 as one of the first year-round homes in Britannia. Formerly the residence of Dr. E. Stone Wiggins, amateur meteorologist and his wife, Susie Anna Wiggins, a writer. Note this home's quaint corner tower, shingled gables and typically irregular Queen Anne plan, and also the unique window surrounds that lend the clapboard home a colonial aspect. Contrast its massing with diminutive **83 Bradford**, across from it, which resembles a cabin.

Continue, and find 66 Bradford, **Rowatt House** (c. 1875). It was constructed by John Rowatt and subsequently used by his son William who was the CPR agent in Britannia, living year-round here at this attractive home.

At Cassels, look ahead to the **Britannia Yacht Club (2777 Cassels Street)** whose construction first commenced in 1896. Although its grounds are private to members, if you call ahead you may be permitted entry to enjoy spectacular views of Britannia Bay. Here you'll also notice the jaunty sound of sailboats, bobbing on the water. And, note the channel carved in the tip of the peninsula, which is closed to provide protection for the moored boats during winter and high water in spring. This channel was originally cut as a bypass to the Deschenes Rapids. Also watch for the brigantine called *The Black Jack*. Owner Thomas Fuller used the hull of an old logging boat which was recycled into a steamer named the *G. B. Pattee*, which plied the waters here.

Turn right on Cassels and if you want, continue to its end, to view the complex of the **Britannia Filtration Plant** at 2731 Cassels (1956-61). Tours are available. On your right, you pass entries to the Mud Lake Conservation Area and if you venture here in May through September, watch for turtles crossing the road.

Backtrack and turn left on the Britannia Road, once called Main Street. Find **48 Britannia, Harmer House** (c. 1863) built in the vernacular style as a workingman's home. But it was home to three significant "firsts" in the village, being its first post office, general store and, in 1887, the first telephone office.

Cross Rowatt Street and find **127 Britannia, William Murphy House**, a red brick residence whose simplicity lends it great beauty.

Corner of Rowatt and Main (now Britannia) roads, Britannia Village. Note plank sidewalk and home at rear with outhouse at rear right behind plank fence. (n.d.) City of Ottawa Archives, CA 2363.

154 Britannia, Robinson House. 2002. E. Fletcher.

Bull's eye windows, brick "eyebrow" surrounds on its other windows, plus a stringcourse encircling it are its modest adornments. Murphy, who owned a carting company, sold ice that he cut from the river for a nickel a block.[30]

Next is **154 Britannia, Robinson House** (c. 1895), a gracious Queen Anne style residence with a new (as of 2002) cedar shingle roof. A picket fence surrounds the generous corner lot with its spectacular blossoms come summertime, sheltered by mature trees.

Built by Charles Robinson, a carpenter, the home is surely a showcase for his professional capabilities. Here Robinson incorporated a seven sided, second-storey porch, a variety of window shapes, double projecting end-gables, and a bay window. All transpire to give it an airy Cape Cod feel.

Number **175 Britannia, Trescoe**, was built in 1908 by Edward and Albert Murphy for their sister Emma. It's a shingled home with a half-moon second storey, enclosed porch which lends it a summery, cottage-style. However, Emma and her brothers were year-round residents here.

175 Britannia Road, Trescoe. 2002. E. Fletcher.

The ground-floor porch off the angled main entryway also adds interest, showing off the design-build skills of the Murphy brothers.

Next door is 175B, formerly **St. Stephen's Anglican Church** (1892), now a residence. It was built by Charles Robinson. The church created a welcome focus for Anglicans who for years had simply gathered at people's homes — often on verandahs — where ministers conducted services. Nowadays, St. Stephen's is a private home. Its change of purpose symbolizes a fitting last stop on this tour, for Britannia has survived many shifting senses of purpose since Captain John LeBreton first built his log cabin, merchant shop and sawmill on Lac Deschênes around the year 1818 or so.

Walk south to rejoin the paved shared bike/walking path and turn left. Return to The Mill Restaurant.

Streetcar and patrons boarding Britannia streetcar, c. 1900.
City of Ottawa Archives, CA 1574.

Central Experimental Farm

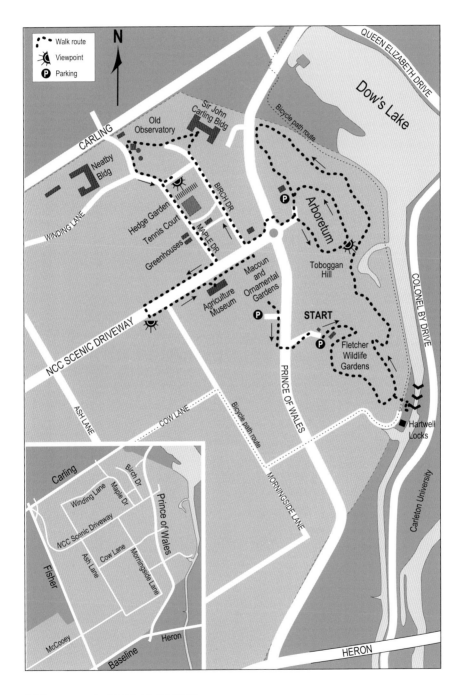

Walk route
Viewpoint
Parking

N

QUEEN ELIZABETH DRIVE

Dow's Lake

Sir John
Carling Bldg
Old
Observatory

CARLING

Bicycle path route

Neatby
Bldg

BIRCH DR

WINDING LANE

Hedge Garden
Tennis Court

MAPLE DR

Greenhouses

Arboretum

Toboggan
Hill

Macoun
and
Ornamental
Gardens

Agriculture
Museum

START

NCC SCENIC DRIVEWAY

Fletcher
Wildlife
Gardens

COLONEL BY DRIVE

ASH LANE

COW LANE

Bicycle path route

PRINCE OF WALES

MORNINGSIDE LANE

Hartwell
Locks

Carleton University

Carling

Birch Dr

Winding Lane

Maple Dr

NCC Scenic Driveway

Prince of Wales

Ash Lane

Cow Lane

Morningside Lane

Fisher

McCooey

Baseline

Heron

HERON

Ottawa is the only city in the world boasting an experimental farm in its midst. And residents of the capital cherish it dearly, finding its precious cultural landscape of "country within the city" spiritually restorative. In all seasons Ottawans of all ages can be spied enjoying the open space. In wintertime children's shouts colour the air in the Arboretum as they hurtle down what might be the capital's most beloved tobogganing hill. Come June, plant breeder Isabella Preston (in 1920 the first female hybridist to be hired in Canada) would be delighted to see people admiring the scented blossoms of lilacs and crabapples regally flanking Prince of Wales Drive. Summer brings its own heady joys, as visitors can plunge into the shady world of the Hosta Garden, or view boats passing through Hartwell's Locks. Finally, autumn's harvest brings reminders of our rural roots: the farm's Agricultural Museum presents programs that connect us to the past while promoting the new technologies and breeds that keep Canada abreast of change.

But of course, the over 400 hectares of crops, grazing cattle, and agricultural machinery and buildings didn't exist here when Queen Victoria chose the capital. Nor did the Arboretum or recently created Fletcher Wildlife Garden.

The story of the Central Experimental Farm (CEF) starts with the land … First Nations' people were here before Europeans, particularly at nearby Hog's Back Falls, where the waterfall and rapids forced early passersby to portage. Who knows when the first Europeans set foot on this land? Braddish Billings and his Merrickville bride Lamira Dow paddled up the Rideau to settle in their log cabin in 1813. And in 1826 Colonel John By's surveying party, led by his Clerk of the Works John MacTaggart, staggered through the swamps of what we now call Dow's Lake while siting the route for the Rideau Canal. MacTaggart was an excellent storyteller, and his descriptions of the expedition to Dow's Lake in the winter of 1826 are enough to make us all shiver. He describes how the trip took four days, during which the party fell through the ice innumerable times as they clambered through the snowy cedar bog. At night the men slept together, literally, sharing one another's body warmth beside an all-too-dim fire. It does not sound like fun winter camping. Nonetheless, MacTaggart and his crew succeeded and the Rideau Canal cuts through this and many another uninviting bog.

The mosquito-infested, swampy landscape was altered dramatically by the canal builders who built two locks at Hartwell's Lock station (located directly southeast of the Arboretum, below the Fletcher Wildlife Garden). Trees were felled, their timbers in demand for structures such as cookhouses, dwellings, and sheds to shelter the stonemasons while they laboured. And according to a watercolour painted by John Burrows circa 1845, the landscape to the northeast was almost completely denuded of trees by then. Two large earthen dams to the north and southeast contained Dow's Great Swamp, into which the Rideau River overflowed each spring. Skeletons of drowned trees stood amid the lake, trees that would be felled and cleared sixty or more years later by CEF staff.

But what of the rise of land above Hartwell's Locks where the farm would be created?

The first building appears to have been Finlay's Tavern and house, located beside a fork in a rough road that extended to Hartwell's Locks and Hog's Back Falls, just east of the traffic circle inside the Arboretum grounds.

So began what appears to have been a series of questionable titles to the land which would cause difficulties for creation of the farm in the 1880s.

In the 1850s the Shea farm was located where the current farm's Birch Avenue extends, east of the Saunders building. Evidently there

Collapse of one of Nepean's first log schools (SS No. 14) which was located south of traffic circle leading into Arboretum on Prince of Wales Drive. Reverend John May, Carleton County School Inspector assesses the damage in his top hat and frock coat. 1880. City of Ottawa Archives, CA 17001.

were several children in this and other rough homesteads, because two years later a school appears on maps, located east of Prince of Wales's Drive, opposite today's ornamental gardens. As the canal builders moved downstream, and as settlers searched for homesteads, surely the building thrown up in haste by Colonel By's crews must have made welcome shelter for squatters.

Also in the 1850s, the Garland and Kennedy family farms appeared. The former was located 500 metres south of the current traffic circle; the latter was halfway between Garland's farm and the locks.[31]

Eventually there were eight farms located in what became the CEF, belonging variously to Donald Kennedy, John Lewis, Richard Taylor (these three were the largest operations), Patrick and Alexander Kennedy, Thomas Stackpole, John Shea, John McAbe, and John McAmmond.

Sometime between then and the mid 1860s, Thomas Clark purchased Garland's farm and built what became a well-known residence that was prominently featured in Belden's *Historical Atlas*, 1879. Known as Canal Bank Farm, the atlas depicts a well-laid-out farm with a tidy, symmetrical home complete with central gable. It also notes Clark raised prizewinning livestock and horses.

After Ottawa was selected as the capital in 1857, land speculation became fierce. Everyone knew the city would expand; it was simply a matter of time. Lumber baron and canny businessman J. R. Booth got into the act, according to rumours still circulating among CEF staff. Booth purchased land here concurrent with the parliamentary debate over the location of the experimental farm.

By the late 1870s and early 1880s, something else was happening in Canada that would create appropriate conditions for the creation of the CEF. The British Government urgently wanted to populate the west with loyal settlers who would build homes and farms, grow crops to feed the nation, and thus secure the west from those pesky Americans.

But as homesteaders penetrated the western provinces, they encountered entirely different growing conditions than were known in the Atlantic Provinces, Quebec, and Ontario — not to mention Britain and Europe. Not only were the soils different, but so were the growing seasons. And because pioneering families depended upon growing their own crops to sustain them during the first years of homesteading, knowledge about what to grow when, became increasingly urgent.

The Department of Agriculture for Canada had been created on May 22, 1868 and one of the first Bills passed in Parliament on its behalf was the 1899 "Act Respecting Contagious Diseases of Animals."

But what about conducting research on crops? What about research on soils? Settlers throughout the Dominion urgently needed information born from scientific research and development. In 1883, then Minister of Agriculture J. H. Pope appointed James Fletcher to the position of Dominion Entomologist as a result of the infestation of insects in seeds Canada had sent to the Philadelphia agricultural exhibition of 1883.

And on January 30, 1884 the government created a Select Committee of the House of Commons whose mandate was to research how to improve agriculture in Canada. The committee's chairman was Quebec MP G. A. Gigault and under his direction a survey was mailed to 1,500 Canadians. Five questions were asked, the first of which was whether they were in favour of the government creating an experimental farm. Of the 350 replies, 278 voted for it, and the rest is history: the raison d'être for the Farm was born.[32]

The Committee did not stop at recommending the creation of an experimental farm; they also recommended a centralized bureau, appointment of an entomologist, a statistical department, and the publication of handbooks and pamphlets to help farmers throughout Canada. Scientists trained in the fields of botany, entomology, horticulture, and soils would be hired for ongoing research on everything

Barn, 1890s. Central Experimental Farm collection.

from plant and animal diseases to analyzing and recommending breeds of cattle, horses, pigs, and poultry.

Key to the Committee's concept was the creation not only of a centralized bureau, but also a string of experimental stations throughout Canada. These would be strategically located in diverse geographical areas, so that farmers would be supported by reliable information emanating from government research stations that approximated conditions (climate, soil) on their own farms.

Context is everything, and the federal government knew that experimental farms were meeting the needs of other country's agricultural challenges. The first experimental farm in the world had been created in Rothamsted, England in 1843. By the 1880s, Russia, Germany, France, and America had jumped on the bandwagon. Precedence had been more than set, and on November 2, 1885 William Saunders, a professor at London's Northwestern University was asked to develop the Committee's recommendations. On February 20, 1886 Saunders formally recommended the creation of the central bureau and satellite stations to John Carling, the new Minister of Agriculture.

Parliament debated the location and need for a central farm plus five research stations, but no members spoke against it. Many questions were directed at Pope and Saunders, however, and it's interesting to note that the cost of fencing the farms was a significant issue. But by far, most questions centred on the locations of the five farms. Because of proximity and similar growing conditions, Saunders proposed Quebec and Ontario share a centrally located farm in Ottawa, and that the four others should be located in one of the three maritime provinces (Newfoundland didn't join Confederation until 1949), Northwest Territories (created in 1868 from lands owned by the Hudson's Bay Company), and British Columbia. "Probably the most significant proposal, however, was that Canada should produce a spring wheat that would ripen before the fall frosts in Manitoba and the North-West Territories. In addition, this spring wheat should be of superior baking quality."[33]

Incidentally, this came about when William Saunders' son Charles developed Marquis wheat at the CEF, which he sent out to prairie farmers for testing in the summer of 1909. "Marquis proved to be such a superior variety that by 1920, 90 percent of the 6.9 million ha seeded to hard, red, spring wheat on the Canadian prairies was Marquis."[34]

The Experimental Farm Station Act became law June 2, 1886 under the government of Sir John A. Macdonald. Today's Farm now would take root and grow under the auspices of its first Director, Dr. William Saunders.

Saunders selected the four other sites: Nappan, Nova Scotia; Brandon, Manitoba; Indian Head, Northwest Territories; and Agassiz, British Columbia. He chose this site for the Central Experimental Farm, citing its geographical position with respect to Quebec and Ontario — plus its proximity to the seat of government, and its convenient access to road, rail and water transportation (Carling Avenue was then known as the road to Merivale, plus the canal and rail were close by). Naturally there were agricultural reasons, too. Its height of land permitted good drainage to the Ottawa and Rideau Rivers; moreover the site's soil varied from sandy loam to clay. Saunders recognized researchers here would find conditions similar to those that challenged farmers they were intended to help across both provinces … and throughout the nation.

As director, Saunders travelled the Dominion extensively by train, visiting the satellite research stations. He appointed superintendents for the other four sites, who regularly visited the central bureau so they could be effective members of the team. The team was comprised not only of government employees: active participation from farmers was key, and in 1895 Saunders enlisted the help of more than 31,000 farmers who sent samples of seed they had been growing for testing at the Farm.[35]

Team-building efforts prospered: farmers contributed information and samples of their crops, keeping the researchers in step with what was actually happening "in the fields" whether it be in the farmland of the Northwest Territories or the Okanagan Valley. And let's not forget the needs of the general public, either: like today, many people maintained ornamental as well as vegetable gardens. They were just as interested as farmers in controlling noxious weeds and insect pests.

Of course, Saunders couldn't possibly do all the work at the Farm. In 1886 he appointed W. W. Hilborn as agriculturist; in 1887 James Fletcher came on board as entomologist and botanist, as well as Frank T. Shutt in capacity of chemist. Note the titles: although Shutt possessed a university degree, most were "serious amateurs." Fletcher, for instance, was an accountant at the House of Commons library. However, it wouldn't be fair to consider them anything other than professionals.

For instance, as Chief, Entomology and Botany Division, Fletcher wrote detailed annual publications until his death in 1908 on such topics as tent caterpillars and codling moths — still pernicious pests.

His particular interest was the economics of entomology, in other words, how insect damage seriously decreased yield and hence, the prosperity of farmers. In 1879 he helped found the Ottawa Field Naturalist Club, and wrote many papers for their annual journal. Today's Fletcher Wildlife Garden is named in his memory. And it was Fletcher who was the first member of the Farm to be on the Board of Directors of the Central Canada Exhibition at Lansdowne Park (see Glebe walk).

Macoun residence. Home was demolished to create the sunken gardens in 1934. Central Experimental Farm collection.

Another name long-associated both with the Farm and Field Naturalist's Club is horticulturist W. T. Macoun who took the position of Chief, Horticulture Division in 1898. His memory is recalled at the Farm not only at the sunken garden that takes his name, but also in the many perennials he planted that we can still enjoy today. Although he, too, was an "amateur professional," Acadia University gave Macoun an honorary doctorate of science degree.

William Saunders residence, circa 1900.
Central Experimental Farm collection.

As the Farm grew, so did the numbers of buildings dotting its acreage. At first, Saunders and the other chiefs lived on-site in residences befitting their positions. All welcomed not only government officials to their homes, but also international dignitaries and scientists: it was important that the houses reflect positions of stature. Similarly, because the Farm was a showcase, and one situated in close proximity to the capital, its design took on symbolic meaning.

Today's Farm is more than "just" a research station. It's more than a beloved local hangout where everyone from dog walkers to skiers can find spiritual renewal in the countryside within the city.

It is what heritage types call a significant "cultural landscape" that is worthy of protection. Evidently the government of Canada agreed for on February 4, 1998 then Secretary of State Andy Mitchell announced the designation of Agriculture and Agri-Food Canada's Central Experimental Farm in Ottawa as a National Historic Site.

How do we define a cultural landscape? Simply put, it is a space that defines us as Canadians. But how does the Farm accomplish this? Today's CEF reflects the nineteenth century philosophy of agriculture in a picturesque setting. The word "picturesque" is key, because it describes a nineteenth century approach to garden design where beautiful vistas and meandering, romantic drives were equally as important as plantings of as-exotic-as-possible trees, shrubs, hedges, and flowers.

In conjunction with the picturesque, the CEF still plays a key role in Canadian agriculture and food protection. For instance, located on-site is the Eastern Cereal and Oilseed Research Council (ECORC). It is responsible for the sustainable production of crops such as corn, wheat, barley, oats, and soybeans through the development of new varieties as well as new land resource management systems. Today, Saunders' approach to teamwork continues, for ECORC employs seventy or so scientists in multidisciplinary teams to develop improved varieties of winter wheat, soybeans, etc. that can withstand Canadian changing climatic conditions, transportation, and storage demands. As well, there are now nineteen satellite research stations across Canada. Also on-site at the Farm are Canada's national collections of insects and arachnids, fungi and plants.

The Agriculture Museum is part of the Canada Science and Technology Museum Corporations, while Agriculture and Agri-Food Canada maintain the Arboretum and Ornamental Gardens.

Meanwhile, life on the Farm continues, though its location is now deep in the heart of the sprawling new (2001) mega-city of Ottawa. Visitors no longer arrive by horse and buggy or on Thomas Ahearn's streetcar. Now we arrive on foot, by bike, snowshoe, or skis, by car or city bus. More change will occur: in late November 2003, Agriculture Minister Lyle Vanclief announced plans to overhaul the CEF over the next twenty-five years. The Sir John Carling building may be demolished, and new buildings erected to enhance the Farm's stature as a research facility.

STYLE

Picturesque design was *de rigueur* for public parks and gardens at the end of the nineteenth century. The mid 1800s saw tremendous exploration throughout the world, and the Industrial Revolution and the growth of international trade meant that new plants were available to everyone from ordinary gardeners through to botanists. Everyone wanted to try growing the latest exotic flora — hopefully within a carefully designed setting that would showcase the grower's eclectic tastes and status. And public gardens had been popular for centuries — botanic gardens such as Kew Gardens (founded 1759), and Sans-Souci in Germany (1825) drew crowds of spectators who, just like us, enjoyed taking the air in a pretty setting.

Looking south to America, by the 1880s landscape designer Frederick Law Olmstead (considered the father of landscape architecture) had already gained an international reputation for his democratic designs for parks. He promoted parks as being essential to advance the public's health and well being, and he strongly believed that neighbourhood parks should be dotted throughout any city to increase the public's access to and enjoyment of fresh air. Inasmuch as the CEF wasn't to be only a park, many of Olmstead's design principles were applied, because it was important to create a central bureau that would be a showcase for the capital, welcoming to both the public and international scientists alike.

In 1859 he designed New York City's Central Park; and in the 1870s he was hired by the City of Montreal to design Mount Royal Park.

In keeping with picturesque design, the Arboretum's winding lanes take good advantage of the hilly topography of the site. Two lookouts overlook the generous sweep of the toboggan hill and canal to the southeast, while the northeast view shows view of the far-off downtown core, with Dow's Lake and the canal in the foreground. Immediately east of Prince of Wales Drive is a row of ornamental crabapples, all hybrids developed by Isabella Preston.

To the west of this and south of the NCC Driveway, which bisects this sector, the Farm takes on a more formal rectilinear design which is further segmented into three design elements. First, directly west are the ornamental gardens, and sunken gardens. Creating a spectacular effect in June when in blossom, Isabella Preston's lilac trees make a delightful "avenue" of flowers lining both sides of the roadway. Further west is the second sector of the west farm: its horticultural and other buildings plus the complex of barns comprising the Canada Agriculture Museum. To the south is the grand expanse of fields where crop varieties are tested. The apartment buildings, office towers, and homes of the city fringe this rural landscape of barns, outbuildings, and agricultural machinery.

The third design component of this western sector is the functional research buildings which are all identified by number. The Friends of the Farm are keen on replacing, or at minimum supplementing, names for the buildings, which would both further humanize the site as well as maintain the memory of key farm workers and scientists. Only two

Arboretum, 1961. Central Experimental Farm collection.

buildings here survive as examples of residences (numbers 54 and 60). They are important to the cultural landscape, and exemplify a shingled Queen Anne style of architecture, an extremely popular design for residences throughout North America in the late 1800s. Architectural pattern books of the day, in which blueprints for homes were published much as today, promoted shingle style as the darling of the decade. Unfortunately, Saunders' grand residence was demolished so we cannot take in how picturesquely it fit into the grounds here. It was replaced by what is known as the Saunders' Building in 1935.

By the 1940s, such decorative designs as the romantic-looking shingle style were no longer in vogue. Instead, the undecorated, no-nonsense brick and stone formalist designs were chosen, most probably as they conveyed a seriousness befitting the research being conducted on-site. Moreover, the times had shifted: no longer did workers live on-site. As the city encroached, workers lived nearby and travelled to work by public or private transit. Finally, residences and romantic-looking, rambling Queen Anne buildings didn't offer requisite lab and office space.

However, dotted about the almost 500 ha property are a few remnants of the early pioneer farms. The barn on the Fletcher Wildlife Garden (south of the Arboretum) was owned by Thomas Clark and then J. R. Booth (building 82). A second Booth barn is located north

Test plots, n.d. Central Experimental Farm collection.

of Cow Lane; both structures have board-and-batten exteriors typical of their day, and the solitary Booth barn also has a silo.

The functionality of farm buildings was part and parcel of the experimental aspect of the CEF. Accordingly, between 1915 and 1924 roughly twenty circulars on the design of buildings and equipment were published and distributed by the then Dominion Experimental Farm. Agriculture is a complex science. It's not easy for those of us who aren't farmers to realize how important the design of a poultry house is to the health of the animal — and hence, the building's effect upon egg or meat production capabilities.

WALK TIPS

🏃 **Various kilometerages and times (see below).**

Park your car at the Fletcher Wildlife Garden (watch for the turnoff south of the roundabout). If it is full, you can also park in the large public parking lot immediately south of the ornamental gardens, then cross Prince of Wales Drive very carefully and walk up the Fletcher Wildlife Garden lane. Pause at the un-numbered log cabin to start the walk. (Most buildings on-site are identified by a number, which I indicate as #72, for example.)

Because this walk is extensive, you could consider breaking it into two or four segments: 1) Fletcher Wildlife Garden and Hartwell's Locks; 2) Arboretum; 3) Ornamental and Macoun Sunken Gardens; and 4) the Farm proper. (How extensive? The arboretum is 25.5 ha; Canada Agriculture Museum, 2.0 ha; Fletcher Wildlife Garden, 7.5 ha; Lawns and Buildings, 33.3 ha; Ornamental Gardens, 3.2 ha; and Roads & Pathways, 27.9 ha.)

There are many birds in the gardens and the Arboretum. Take binoculars and a daypack with water, snacks, camera and sunscreen. The Farm is exposed, so sunhats and sunscreen are advisable here. **Note:** The Farm is an excellent bicycle, ski or snowshoe destination. Also, children are welcome everywhere and often there are exhibits and happenings at the museum directly geared to them. There is an admission to the museum, but all other access is free. Vehicular access to the Arboretum is blocked between sunset and sunrise.

Aerial view showing Arboretum Lookout and Friends of the CEF Building. October 1963. NAC PA-132624.

Fletcher Wildlife Garden was named in memory of James Fletcher, the farm's first Chief Entomologist and Botanist, and the first Arboretum Curator. Because he was one of the founders of the Ottawa Field Naturalist's Club (1879), it's fitting that its volunteers maintain the wildlife preserve. Whereas the Garden's location is on property once belonging to the Kennedy farm, the Arboretum is on the original Garland property, according to maps drawn by David Bouse.[36]

Our 1.5 km loop starts at the un-numbered small **log building** to the left of the driveway. It used to be the clubhouse adjacent to the farm's tennis courts (still located north of #49, the Saunders' Building). Turn around to spot the rock with a plaque on it, identifying the start of our walk through the meadows. The walk is named for Bill Holland, a long-standing member of a club that spearheaded the creation of the Fletcher Wildlife Gardens. As you stroll alongside the garden's featured habitats (amphibian pond, hedgerow, woodlot, butterfly meadow, old field, and ash woodlot) you will note a variety of native and non-native species. Keep all your senses alert: in summer look for monarch butterflies; in fall watch for Vs of geese on their southerly migration; come winter, search for paw prints which give you a clue of who passed by before you; and in spring listen for the chorus of spring peepers.

Clubhouse, once at the tennis courts, now at Fletcher Wildlife Garden. 1941. NAC PA-132932.

Keep to the main trail and, if you can, pick up a trail guide pamphlet published by the club; our walk follows their route. First head downhill to the pond, watching for the hedgerow that almost immediately appears on your right. Immediately past it, turn right towards the **Clark-Booth Barn** (#82), with its simple L-shape and board-and-batten façade. Built approximately 130 years ago as part of the **Garland Farm**, it is one of the oldest agricultural buildings in Ottawa. It was purchased by Booth in 1886. Now continue, curving to your left through the butterfly meadow.

You soon arrive in an old field to the south of the wildlife garden. A major trail heads south (right). Take it, and find yourself walking alongside trees that were evidently part of the CEF itself, planted over one hundred years ago. Find another trail at the back of the old meadow, heading abruptly downhill to **Hartwell's Locks**.

Begun in 1827, these two locks are noteworthy because they recall many Ottawa figures and heritage constructions. First, Colonel John By designed them. Thomas McKay (see New Edinburgh walk) was the masonry contractor who interpreted his designs. Philemon Wright (founder of Hull, now Gatineau) erected the earthen embankment directly south of the canal, which extends northeast to become the dam retaining the waters of **Dow's Lake**. Colonel By Drive runs on top of this dam, following the canal north to the Entrance Bay Locks

View of Hartwell's Locks and Canal extending to Dow's Lake. 2002.
E. Fletcher.

(see Parliament Hill and Canal walks). Formerly, the embankment circumscribed "Dow's Great Swamp," the dark stretch of boggy cedar woods that MacTaggart explored in December 1826, while surveying the canal. (The north side of Dow's Lake is the site of a second major dam, the St. Louis Dam, whose embankment was broken in two places during the Great Fire of 1870 which threatened the city of Ottawa. Dow's Lake waters rushed up Preston Street and the lowland directly north of the reservoir, thus preventing the fire from advancing further on the city.) The **lockmaster's house**, built in the 1830s or 40s, is located here.

During World War I soldiers marched past the lockmaster's house on the canal road and used an adjacent field for target practice.

Retrace your steps up the hill and back into the Wildlife Gardens (alternately, walk northeast along the canal on the paved pathway). At the top of the hill you're once again in the old meadow. Cross through it (on the path) and plunge into the woods, noting the sudden drop in temperature on a hot summer's day. Mature white ash mix here with pine and spruce; verges of different habitats like the ones on this walk (called ecotones) provide great habitat diversity, so keep your binoculars at the ready to spot woodpeckers, warblers, and hawks in the heart of the city.

Proceed through the woods, emerging onto a broad path. Head right and you'll descend into the **Arboretum** and briefly rejoin the trail alongside the canal. Although one fork of the bicycle path hugs the waterway, with the canal at your back turn left to stroll up a gentle rise. At the next junction in the trail, pause to find the first old-timer of the Arboretum: a hybrid black poplar planted here in 1911 (beyond it is the small island in the inlet).

The 26 ha Arboretum contains several thousand trees and shrubs, some of which date back to Saunders' day. As the Experimental Farm gained international attention, botanical gardens in Russia, Japan, Germany, England, and Jamaica — along with American states such as California and Minnesota — donated specimens. Some trees date from 1889.

Continue straight ahead, passing two pathways heading left (west). On your right is a little inlet which, come summertime, is full of dabbling ducks. On your left is the gentle hillside so popular for tobogganing come winter. Beyond it is the wall marking a lookout over the Arboretum. As you walk, you'll discover labels identifying the specimens. Often the labels show the Latin and common names, and if there's a country of origin to help you identify non-native species. A date might also be shown — this is the planting date. As well, other labels mark "donor trees," planted in the memory of someone. The donor tree program is a popular project managed by the Friends of the Central Experimental Farm.

As you round the northeastern base of the lookout hillside, look to your left and you'll find a bur oak planted when the Arboretum opened in 1889. Beyond it, veer left. Ahead of you to the right are several other pathways leading variously to the canal, a swampy area, and Dow's Lake. For now, ascend the gentle rise and pause at the three rows of evergreens on your right. These originally formed part of an extensive windbreak completely surrounding the farm; this is the only remnant remaining. The first row is Ponderosa pine, the middle is Norway spruce, the third is Scots Pine. In the wild these would be much healthier and bigger, but here at the Farm they suffer from human impact. The lawns are mown, needles raked, people wander over their root systems and touch their trunks. According to Brian Douglas, foreman of the Arboretum, these factors all add up, stressing the trees, which miss their natural environment consisting of a humus-rich earth and sheltered understorey.

William and Agnes Saunders planting a tree, n.d. Central Experimental Farm collection.

Continuing uphill, walk round the loop. To your right, off the Arboretum grounds and beside Dow's Lake you can see the **H.M.C.S. Carleton** property, formerly one of J. R. Booth's lumberyards. Now walk south on the loop paralleling Prince of Wales Drive, with the Arboretum's cluster of buildings ahead of you, on your left. Look for two old specimens before reaching these buildings, both on your right. First is a smooth-leafed elm planted in 1896 and, further back (it is okay to walk on the grass), a Colorado spruce (1899), north of building #189. Continue walking on the path. Now you approach the roundabout drive encircling an "island" of trees and shrubs.

On your right are a cluster of buildings (#72 is the home to **Friends of the Central Experimental Farm** an organization dedicated to the preservation of the Farm, whose volunteers actively assist the full-time gardeners here. Feel free to head inside to look for pamphlets or to obtain membership information. Public washrooms are located on the west side of building #72.)

Behind the parking lot find a pyramidal Norway spruce planted in 1897 — don't confuse it with the larger, draping Norway spruce to its left!

Return to the circular drive and walk right in counter-clockwise direction around the island. This is approximately where **Finlay's Tavern** was located. Immediately opposite building #74, on your left, find an Austrian pine planted in 1889. Continue along the drive, and pause at the lookout over the toboggan hill, one of Ottawa's favourite views. From here you can see the **Carleton University Campus** which moved here from the Glebe in 1959. (See Glebe walk.) Hart Massey and Balharrie, Helmer and Morin were the local architectural firms involved in the design of the original campus and quadrangle. Arthur Erickson and John Bland, from the Montreal and Toronto schools of architecture respectively, served as consultants to the project. In 1974 the Ottawa firm Murray and Murray designed the tall arts tower situated near Hartwell's Locks. Several other firms were employed over the years adding to the campus buildings.

Behind this lookout find a grouping of junipers, among which you can find the needle juniper planted in 1897. Brian Douglas, CEF Arboretum foreman (2002) notes, "it is definitely out of its hardiness zone and has survived –39°C." Continue walking; on your right find the Hosta garden's pretty gateway, leading into the woods. Immediately opposite find two black walnuts inside the "island." Planted in 1889, they are "famous" since their photos are in the first and second editions of *Trees of Canada*. Further on is the second lookout: judge for yourself whether these wending trails form a critical component of the Arboretum's picturesque design.

Return to the cluster of Arboretum buildings, looking for a large white poplar planted in 1890 appearing on your right, opposite building #72.

As noted previously, this is a logical conclusion to one segment of this walk. If you wish to return to your car, simply walk down the Arboretum's grassy lawn immediately east of the Drive. Otherwise, continue this long walk.

Proceed to the traffic circle at Prince of Wales Drive and cross with extreme caution. (It may be prudent to cross further down, to your left or right, so as not to confuse drivers, since the traffic circle is a relatively unfamiliar concept to Canadian drivers.)

Arboretum Lookout over duck pond with Canal in distance, 1961.
Central Experimental Farm collection.

Continue exploring the Central Experimental Farm by walking down the broad, tree-lined Driveway. In 1900 the **Ottawa Electric Railway's** streetcar tracks culminated here at a turnaround located near building #75 (near the Macoun Sunken Gardens). These are the tracks that connected to the Broad Street Station once located in the community at LeBreton Flats (see Ottawa River Parkway walk).

Turn right on Birch Drive. On your left find the oldest ginkgo tree on the farm, planted in 1897. This primitive species is a true evergreen, being one of the unusual deciduous variety (the other evergreen in Canada that loses its leaves is the tamarack).

On your right you can't miss heritage **building #60**, built in 1900 as a residence for senior staff of the Farm. Between the years 1919 and 1939 George Ben Rothwell, Chief of the Animal Husbandry Division, lived here, and so the Friends of the Farm suggest it be known as the **Rothwell Building**. In 1954, a few years after his death, it became the office of the animal husbandry division, but now it is home to the **Canadian Agri-Food Research Council**. Built in the shingled Queen Anne style, it was repainted in its original heritage colours during 2000. The wooden clapboard façade is highly decorated with shingles under the gable ends, which, when combined with the asymmetrical massing lends a whimsical if not studied romantic aspect to the residence. It well suits the planned picturesque design of its setting.

Just to show how much our cultural landscape has altered, cast your mind back to the 1920s and '30s. George Rothwell's daughter, Margaret Smith, lived here then and she recalls looking out the northern window, then her bedroom, and seeing the Parliament Buildings from it, "when the leaves were off the trees."[37]

At the end of the semicircular drive leading to building #60, find three trees. Planted in 1897, two are immense silver maples with deeply indented leaves. The third is a magnolia tree located a bit farther down Birch Avenue, at the southeast corner of the **Saunders Building (#49)** that you're now approaching on your left.

Built in 1935, it was erected on the site of William Saunders' shingled Queen Anne style residence. Turn left to walk in front of this solidly symmetrical composition, with its collegiate-style architecture. A Tudor-inspired portal with an oriel window overhead, asserts that this is a structure of importance. On the grassy lawn in front of the building find the red oak planted in 1911 by the Duke of Connaught: the only known commemorative tree on the Farm.

Continuing north on Birch, keep a lookout for the tall Douglas fir, which is over one hundred years old, located near the turnoff to the parking lot.

Next find the **Sir John Carling Building** defining the northeast section of the Farm on a rise of land that once was a popular toboggan hill for the children of Farm staff. Building #132, it is now headquarters of Agriculture and Agri-Food Canada. It commemorates the name of the Minister of Agriculture responsible for establishing the Farm in

1886 under the government of Sir John A. Macdonald. Enter it to explore architect Hart Massey's formalist style building (1963–67), where you'll discover a huge sixties-style wall mural decorating the well-lit interior. Although you must get a visitor's pass, the public can use the building's library (though not borrow books).

Once outside again, turn right (northwest) across the grassy lawn. On your right, you pass another heritage residence, building #2, the **Dominion Observatory house** (1909), before you reach the **Dominion Observatory (#1)**, one of the capital's cherished heritage buildings. It was designed by Chief Dominion Architect David Ewart, who also built the Mint, War Museum, and Revenue (a.k.a. the Connaught) buildings thronging Sussex (see Sussex walk) along with the Museum of Nature at the foot of Metcalfe Street (see Canal walk).

The Dominion Observatory was erected between 1899 and 1900. Richly ornate, many carvings adorn its red sandstone, including the highly decorative Canadian coat of arms above the Romanesque-arched doorway. Look up to see a saucy looking unicorn and bold lion gazing back at you. It's almost unbelievable to believe these days, but the building was located here because the ambient light of the city beyond didn't obstruct the astronomers' vision. But times changed rapidly and observatory's thirty-eight centimetre reflecting telescope was moved to the Museum of Science and Technology (at 1867 St. Laurent Boulevard).

Photo Equatorial Building with sundial-shaped garden in foreground and Sir John Carling Building behind. 2002. E. Fletcher.

Two other associated buildings that can be found on either side of the Observatory also housed telescopes. When facing the Observatory, to your right is the **Photo Equatorial Building (#9)**, built in 1912. A telescope in it took wide-field photographs of constellations and larger fields of view. The 1905 **Azimuth Building (#8)** to the left, also housed a telescope for accurate surveying measurements, which are based on the astronomical observation of latitude and longitude.

In the centre of the structures find the flowerbed in the design of a sundial, which nicely symbolizes the way all three buildings were used in the measurement of time.

Still facing the old observatory, head left and look for the bronze plaque on the southwest façade, denoting Canada's Prime Meridian: 5 hours, 2 minutes and 51.940 seconds west of Greenwich in England. At an international conference in 1884, delegates from twenty-seven countries adopted Canadian Sir Sanford Fleming's proposal for Standard Time. The globe was divided into twenty-four standard meridians of longitude, where 0 was located at the Royal Observatory in Greenwich.

Fleming came to Canada at age seventeen, on a ship called the *Brilliant* which left Glasgow's docks on April 24, 1845. He accomplished many achievements in his lifetime. He surveyed the CPR line (the first Canadian railway to cross the nation), and he designed the first

Bronze plaque on Dominion Observatory denoting the Prime Meridian of Canada. 2002. K. Fletcher.

Canadian postage stamp issued in 1831, which depicted the beaver. (It was a three-penny stamp.) But the plaque here is dedicated to his memory because of his efforts to have the current international system of time zones adopted. Fleming lived in Ottawa for some time and his home on Daly Avenue, Winterholme, still stands albeit urgently in need of restoration (see Sandy Hill walk).

Now pass the Azimuth building and, with your back to Carling Avenue, walk south on Maple Drive. At the corner of **Winding Lane** look west (right) to see the **K. W. Neatby Building**, the **Eastern Cereal and Oilseed Research Centre** (#20). From here you can see that its no-nonsense red brick appearance is fitting home to agricultural offices and laboratories. Distance allows you to spy the "chimneys" crowding the rooftop, giving the solid structure some welcome "comic" relief from its otherwise functional look. The chimneys are actually vents from the labs inside.

Also at the corner of Winding Lane, find **building #26**, the **Canadian 4-H Foundation and Council**. The bee atop the weathervane is your clue that this used to house the offices of Charles Gooderham, Dominion Apiarist from 1921–1949. Friends of the Farm hope this building will be renamed in his honour, for he worked as tirelessly as his bees to promote honey production in Canada. He travelled the country speaking on the topic, and wrote technical pamphlets explaining how to control diseases in bees, and detailing how the insects assist crop pollination. Gooderham's influence was immense: he "actively promoted the expansion of Canadian honey production from a mere 5 million pounds (2.3 million kg.) in 1921, to nine times that quantity in 1964."[38]

Outside building #26 there used to be another home, the residence of John Fixter who was not just the first farm foreman, but the CEF's first apiarist. So it was fitting that Fixter's residence would be located here, beside this brick building with the bee weathervane. The Fixter home actually predated the creation of the farm, being a stagecoach stopping place along the old Merivale road (Carling).[39]

Lenore Newman, child of another resident here, commented, "On the inside it was very pretty. It had the original wood, sort of a cherry wood colour, and it had a red brick fireplace. We had rosy red rugs. Mother had it decorated to bring out the wood colour. It wasn't an elegant house, but it had a lot of charm to it."[40]

The converted stagecoach stop served as residence to Fixter, Newman, and then to Dr. Cyril Goulden who served as Farm director

Main greenhouse, formerly located in Major's Hill Park. 2002.
K. Fletcher.

Macoun garden, c. 1934.
Central Experimental Farm collection.

between 1955–59 (by which time the stately home of the first Farm director, William Saunders, had already been demolished, replaced by **building #49**, seen earlier). The old Fixter–Newman–Goulden home was left vacant one winter and when its pipes burst it was torn down. Before continuing the walk, look for two Norway spruce planted a few metres apart in 1897 to line the driveway of the home.

Proceed south on Maple Lane and watch for Birch Drive. Turn left and pause to examine the oldest hedge collection on the farm. You'll find some surprising examples of trees that have been continuously pruned for over one hundred years. The hedge collection demonstrates how successful certain species are for functional use as windbreaks and shelter for wildlife as well as ornamental decoration around a home. Identification labels (new in spring 2003) will help you find two hedges planted in 1897: the European larch and American beech. Then look for the thread leaf cypress (1916) and the short, square-shaped Korean boxwood (1945). Note how different the shapes of these contiguous trees are — an age-old technique that adds interest to a garden landscape.

Return to Maple and continue south. On your left beyond the hedges are the tennis courts. The original courts were actually located in the Arboretum and were grass, not paved courts. These were built sometime in the 1920s by the Experimental Farm Athletic Association (1923), formed because the director thought Farm workers would be healthier with more exercise. The log cabin (now at Fletcher Wildlife Garden) originally stood here. As you walk alongside the courts, you'll see the greenhouses opposite; they stand on what was actually the Association's first project: an outdoor skating rink.

The **main greenhouses** (#50) are home to the farm's **tropical gardens**. Note the highly decorated entranceway to the middle glass house, and the building's curvilinear shape. Greenhouses have been used since Roman times, and became highly popularized in the Victorian era, when growing "exotics" such as pineapples or oranges from far-away lands was a status symbol. Enter to explore the humid world within (times of opening are listed on the sign outside). The central, most ornate greenhouse graced Major's Hill Park until then-Minister of Agriculture, Dr. Richard Motherwell (1926–1930) had it moved here. The other greenhouses were built 1926–60.

Continuing south, find **building #54**, a highly decorated, shingled Queen Anne style former residence, that now serves as the **Canadian Centre for Swine Improvement** — rather a far cry from an elegant-sounding home. However, for thirty-six years it was home to Malcolm

Bancroft Davis who started out as assistant horticulturist to Dr. W. T. Macoun, then became the Farm's Chief and Dominion Horticulturist (1933–1955). As a horticultural researcher, Davis worked on fruit breeding and on developing the frozen food industry, as well as upon dehydrating and packaging vegetables. He also hired landscape architect Warren Oliver to design the Macoun Sunken Gardens in 1934.

Walk up the semicircular laneway to appreciate this former residence's decorative shingle work beneath the gables, and mount the stairs to stand on the porch and admire the view. Imagine how the home must have looked in years past, when it and the Rothwell house (**building #60**) were grand homes set in a landscaped, deliberately picturesque setting. When you stand on the porch, you will notice that the Rothwell house is still visible across the expansive lawn.

Walk west on the Driveway until you can get a view of the crop research fields. The Eastern Cereal and Oilseed Research Centre continues to use over 300 ha for research, and you can spy well-laid-out fields of crops such as soybean and corn. (If you're interested in seeing these up close, you can extend your walk by strolling through the "country fields" along Ash Lane.)

With the house behind you, cross the Driveway and head right to explore the **Canada Agriculture Museum** and related barns. The main barn (#88) sits on the site of the original built in 1887, which burned in 1913. Erected in 1914 as a dairy barn, this picturesque structure reflects some of the changes in barn design popularized at the turn of

Canada Agriculture Museum. 2002. K. Fletcher.

Behind the main barn and early sprayer, n.d. Central Experimental
Farm collection.

the twentieth century. For instance, the plank frames replace the
former timber frame structure. Moreover, the roof rests upon a raised
knee wall, a feature which allows more space for storage and ventilation,
and greater head room so that workers can move about. The addition
of dormer windows permits more light into this second storey, too. Finally,
just to emphasize its picturesque symmetry, the central cupola flanked

Stacking hay, n.d. Central Experimental Farm collection.

by two vents is a pretty touch. The museum and its outbuildings are well worth visiting, and can easily absorb an hour or so of your time.

The open space behind the barn once housed a second barn for beef cattle. But a fire destroyed both it and the herdsman's residence in 1996. Fifty-seven oxen, sheep and horses perished, but a Limousin heifer that suffered second- and third-degree burns to fifty percent of her body survived, becoming a symbol of the Farm.

While exploring these farm buildings, keep in mind the layout of the complex. Animals place their own special demands on architecture, particularly when they are the size of Clydesdale horses or Holstein cows. Farmers don't want their animals to slip and fall on slippery surfaces, for example, and cleaning barns and yard areas of manure poses challenges too. As well, as large-scale farming became *de rigueur,* it placed its own constraints upon economies of scale. Ventilation, always critical not only for animal health and disease prevention, but also for fire retardation while hay or feed is being stored, is also critical.

Far off in the distance, south of Cow Lane, you might be able to spy the old **Booth Barn** with its silo, built appropriately enough on the protected south side of the barn. Recently restored, the barn has a board-and-batten façade stained a heritage shade of ox-blood red.

For now, walk east (towards the Arboretum), past the Canada Agriculture Museum. As you walk, note **building #55**, the Horticulture Building, built variously in 1930, '37 and '43. Its central gable and fake half-Tudor second-storey façade lend it a romantic look and, hence, the building adds to the Farm's picturesque look. Note the detailing beneath the double window in the projecting gable-end which lightens the look of the arched central doorway. Behind it, find another storage building (#56). This barn-like building features two picturesque cupola vents atop the roof, plus generous windows that allow light into the interior space. Note too the pitch of the roof punctuated by the second-storey gables.

Continue east, on the south side of the Driveway. You pass by the **Fruit and Vegetable Dispute Resolution Corporation (#75)**. With a name like this, it's all too easy to imagine dusty, bespectacled bureaucrats arguing over whether a tomato is a fruit or a vegetable. Disregarding how amusing the building's name might sound, take a moment to note the attached greenhouses at the rear. To the immediate east and facing onto the Driveway, find the **Fletcher Memorial** dedicated to the Farm's first Chief Entomologist, Dr. James Fletcher, and erected by the Ottawa Field Naturalist's Club.

On your right find what is arguably the prettiest part of the Farm: the **ornamental gardens**. As you explore, keep your eyes tuned to the buildings to their immediate west. For example, building #76, the Cereal Barn, was built in 1900. Note the roof's end-gable: this is a Dutch hip roof, whose design shares Japanese design elements.

But back to the gardens! Find the pathway to the **Macoun Sunken Gardens**, dedicated to W. T. Macoun, Chief of the Horticultural Division. Enter its quiet oasis to discover the flowering perennials Macoun planted when this was the site of his official residence. His home was torn down and this garden, designed by Warren Oliver in 1934, is located in what was essentially the basement of that home. Notice the rocks comprising the layout: most were taken from the farm quarry, located where the Neatby building stands overlooking Carling Avenue. However, Oliver had to procure more to complete the project, so he drove a horse-drawn wagon to Tunney's Pasture to haul the remainder from a quarry there. The gardens were officially opened on the Farm's fiftieth anniversary in 1936.

The central feature of the gardens is the rectilinear pond, complete with two frog fountains spouting water. Macoun's perennial border is on the upper north side, while at the eastern entryway there is a sundial dedicated to his memory.

Continue exploring the delights of the **ornamental gardens'** 3.2 ha via the southern exit. On your left find the immense plane tree grown from a seed given to the farm from Kew Gardens in 1896. Pat Macoun, Will Macoun's daughter, remembers swinging from its branches as a small child growing up here in the former residence. We can thank Warren Oliver for having the foresight to preserve this tree as well as Macoun's perennial border.

The Ornamental Gardens now presents you with a series of flower beds, arbours, shady benches, and a vast array of ornamental trees and shrubs described with winding paths, stepping stones and fountains. Grassy lawns provide pleasing continuity to the eye ... and a luxurious carpet on which to sit and enjoy a well-deserved break. Explore freely, heading generally in a southerly direction. Most plants are identified. Of special note are the iris beds with over one hundred varietals.

Continuing southwards, you'll find the Explorer Rose section, and also the Isabella Preston lilacs. Preston emigrated to Guelph, Ontario from Lancaster, England in 1912, where she studied at the Ontario Agricultural College — today's University of Guelph. Four years later her work in hybridizing lilies made her renowned as Canada's first woman hybridist, an achievement that caught the interest of W. T. Macoun at the Central Experimental Farm. By 1920 she was working here, where she developed almost two hundred hybrids. Among these she "created" twenty roses, several lilacs and iris varieties, and fifteen crabapple trees which still blossom in June.

In fact, during June, hybrids that Preston developed line either side of Prince of Wales Drive. To the west, her lilacs create a heady fragrance, while to the east, her rosybloom crabapples create appealing waves of pink blossoms. A fitting memory to this devoted individual. When naming her hybrids, Miss Preston sometimes chose Shakespearean names (for her lilac crosses, although she named one Macoun), Amerindian names (Iroquois, Huron), and Canadian lakes (for the rosybloom crabapples). Other plants immortalized names of staff children or workers.

As you walk through the ornamental gardens, you are approaching your car at the Fletcher Wildlife Garden. Cross Prince of Wales Drive very carefully. While walking south, look left and see if you can spot the immense, perhaps most gracious tree in the Arboretum. A hybrid oak (cross between a bur and a white oak), this specimen was planted in 1908.

McCormick/Deering tractor and three-furrow plow, circa 1930.
NAC PA-130414.

Glossary

Arcade: . . . . an arched passageway, usually along a wall.

Ashlar: . . . . rough-cut stone "bricks."

Atrium: . . . . an enclosed space within or between a multi-storey building, often now roofed with glass.

Bargeboard: . . . . decorative boards along the edge of gable or roof, also called gingerbread.

Board and batten: . . a vertical cladding of planks with protective trim nailed over the joints.

Boss: . . . . a raised ornament or knob.

Buttress: . . . . integral wall supports, built at right angles to the wall.

Capitals: . . . . the very top of a column or pillar, often decorated.

Chamfer: . . . . a bevel or groove.

Cinquefoil: . . . . clover-like design with five "leaves."

Clapboard: . . . . a cladding of horizontal overlapping planks.

Colonnette: . . . . a small, non-structural column.

Coping: . . . . the sloped top of a wall.

Corbel: . . . . a stone or timber projecting from a wall to support a weight or for decoration.

Corinthian: . . . . a style of column with ornate capitals.

Cornice: . . . . the projecting moulding at the top of a building or wall.

Crenellation: . . . . . . the classic castle wall-top with alternating spaces and walls, also called a battlement.

Crocket: . . . . ornament, usually shaped as foliage, that projects from a pinnacle, gable, spire, etc.

Cupola: . . . . a small round dome atop a roof.

Curtain wall: . . . . . . exterior non-load-bearing wall.

Dentil trim: . . . . small, tooth-like decorative moulding, usually under a cornice.

Doric: . . . . a style of column with plain capitals.

Dormer: . . . . a projecting window in a sloping roof.

Entablature: . . . . the horizontal beam that spans two or more columns.

Façade: . . . . the front wall of any building, or the faces of several buildings along a street.

Fenestration: . . . . . . the arrangement of windows in any building.

Finial: . . . . the topmost ornament on gable, pediment, etc.

Flashing: . . . . metal strip over a roof joint that prevents water seepage.

Gable: . . . . triangular upper part of a wall under a ridged roof.

Gambrel: . . . . a roof consisting of a lower steeply sloping part and an upper, ridged and gabled part.

Gargoyle: . . . . carved grotesque in the form of a water spout projecting from a gutter.

Gingerbread: . . . . . . *see* Bargeboard.

Grotesque: . . . . fanciful ornament, usually a caricature of an animal or human.

Hipped roof: . . . . . . one that slopes from a central ridge on the ends as well as the sides.

Ionic: . . . . a style of column with a capital of two ornamental scrolls.

Lancet window: . . . narrow window with pointed head.

Lintel: . . . . horizontal timber or stone over doorway or window opening.

Mansard: . . . . a roof with two slopes on each side, the upper almost flat, and the lower slope very steep and usually pierced with dormers.

Massing: . . . . the "shape" or "footprint" of a building, as created by its over all composition. Projections, recessions, vertical and horizontal elements that all affect the structure's over shape ... or massing.

Mouldings: . . . . material such as stone or brick used as a surround, or trim, framing a window or door.

Mullion: . . . . a vertical bar dividing a window.

Oriel window: . . . . . a bay window that projects from an upper storey and is supported by corbels.

Palladian: . . . . neoclassical style characterized by a central arch flanked by rectangular openings.

Parapet: . . . . a low wall or railing around a roof.

Pediment: . . . . triangular section above an opening, especially above the portico in classical Greek buildings.

Pier:	the upright, solid wall between windows, pillars supporting an arch or projecting canopy over an entryway.
Pilaster:	an ornamental, non-load-bearing pillar.
Pinnacle:	small, ornamental turret or tower.
Porte-cochère:	a covered entry extending over the width of a path or driveway.
Portico:	a porch fashioned as a roof supported by columns.
Quatrefoil:	clover-like design with four "leaves."
Quoin:	stones or bricks, often decorative, forming the corner of a building.
Rustication:	deep-set masonry joins, sometimes used to exaggerate the base of ground-floor walls.
Sill:	horizontal timber or stone that foots a door or window opening.
Skeleton frame construction:	a freestanding, load-bearing frame of iron or steel upon which floors, exterior, and interior walls are hung.
Spandrel:	structural horizontal sections of a wall between windows and vertical piers, or the section of a wall described inside a pediment or arch.
Stringcourse:	a raised horizontal band of bricks or stones.
Terra cotta:	fired, unglazed red pottery.
Tracery:	decorative stone or woodwork separating the glass at the head of a window.
Transom:	a horizontal bar dividing a window, or horizontal window above a door or another window.
Trefoil:	clover-like design with three "leaves."
Trompe-l'oeil:	an illusion, or literally, a "trick of the eye" as in the use of iron cresting on top of the Parliament Buildings. The cresting reaches skywards, creating the illusion of a tall, gothic spire.
Voussoir:	the wedge-shaped stones that form an arch.

Endnotes

1. Leaning, John and Lyette Fortin. *Our Architectural Ancestry*. Haig & Haig, Ottawa, p. 73.

2. Macbeth, Madge. *Over My Shoulder*. Ryerson Press, Toronto, February 1953.

3. Bourinot, Arthur, editor. "Letter to Dr. Pelham Edgar, Feb. 11, 1916" *More Letters of Duncan Campbell Scott*, Rockcliffe Park, 1960, p. 8.

4. Lett, William P. *The City of Ottawa and Its Surroundings*, A. S. Woodburn Press, Ottawa, 1884, p. 5.

5. MacTaggart, John. *Three Years in Canada*, Volume 1, page 162, 1829.

6. John By to the Ordnance Board in letter dated January 19, 1829, as found in Michael Newton's *Lower Town Ottawa, 1826–54*, Volume 1, Manuscript Report 104, p. 76.

7. Gwyn, Sandra. *The Private Capital*, McClelland & Stewart, 1984, p. 202.

8. Abbott, George F. *Abbott's Guide to Ottawa, Hull & Vicinity*, 2nd Edition, Ottawa, 1911, p. 11.

9. *The Journal*, August 13, 1888, letter to the editor entitled "Speaking Out."

10. *The Ottawa Packet and Weekly Commercial Gazette*, Dec. 22, 1849.

11. Fréchette, Annie Howells. "Life at Rideau Hall," *Harper's New Monthly Magazine*. July 1881. Volume LXII, No. CCCLXXIV.

12. Gwyn, Sandra. *The Private Capital*. p. 209.

13. Askwith, John. *Recollections of New Edinburgh*, 1923 [no page numbers]

14. *The Ottawa Citizen*, February 21, 1875.

15. *The Ottawa Citizen*, July 14, 1992.

16. Ricketts, Shannon. *W. E. Noffke, An Ottawa Architect*, City of Ottawa, 1990. p. 67.

17. Desbarats, Lilian Scott. *Recollections*, p. 48, Ottawa, 1957.

18. Meredith, Colbourne. "Short Talk Before the Woman's Canadian Historical Society of Ottawa." PAC–MG29E62 Vol. 8. p. 6.

19. Meredith, Colbourne. "My Victorian 80s and 90s," unpublished manuscript, MG29E62 Vol. 10.

20. Gwyn, Sandra. *The Private Capital*, p. 238.

21. Walker, Harry and Olive Walker. *The Carleton Saga*, p. 313.

22. Kalman, H. & J. Roaf. *Exploring Ottawa*, University of Toronto Press, 1983. p. 135.

23. Champlain, Samuel de. *the voyages and Explorations of Samuel de Champlain (1604-1616) Narrated by Himself*, Volume II; translated by Annie Nettleton Bourne, Toronto, 1911, p. 38.

24. City of Ottawa, *Departmental Reports, Corporation of Ottawa 1911*, and *Departmental Reports, Corporation of Ottawa 1912*, 1911, 1912.

25. Taylor, Eva and James Kennedy. *Ottawa's Britannia*, Britannia Historical Association, 1983, p. 36.

26. Tennant, R.D. *Capital Traction: An Outline History of the Street Railway System of Ottawa*, 11 October 1968.

27. Cook, Fred. *Appreciations: the Hon Thomas Ahearn, P.C.*, printed for private circulation only, p. 33.

28. Taylor, Eva and James Kennedy. *Ottawa's Britannia*, Britannia Historical Society, 1983, p. 38.

29. ibid, p. 46.

30. ibid, p. 57.

31. Bouse, David. *From Nature to Culture, A Study of Ottawa's Central Experimental Farm Using the Sequent Imaging Antithesis Method*, Volume B, December 1 1993, Carleton University, p. 115.

32. Anstey, Dr. Tom. *One Hundred Harvests, Research Branch Agriculture Canada 1886-1986*, Agriculture Canada, 1986; p. 5.

33. ibid, p. 8.

34. ibid, p. 212.

35. ibid, p. 15.

36. Bouse, D. pp. 87-88.

37. Smith, Helen. *Ottawa's Farm, A History of the Central Experimental Farm*, General Store, 1996, p. 140.

38. Anstey. ibid., p. 40.

39. Smith. ibid, p. 99.

40. ibid, p. 99.

Further Reading

The following books and periodicals have been indispensable aids to my understanding and appreciation of the history and architecture of the capital.

Note that the list does not include archival resources. I encourage interested readers to go to the National Archives on Wellington Street to peruse the manuscript, photographic, and architectural and mapping collections. Also, the City of Ottawa Archives with its helpful staff, books, photographs, computer records, and city by-laws is a rich mine of information. Neighbourhood community associations, Heritage Ottawa, and the archives of *The Ottawa Citizen* — as well as many journalists there — are equally fine sources of information. In particular, the National Capital Commission Library and the Ottawa Room of the Metcalfe Branch of the Ottawa Public Library offer many rare manuscripts of the city.

Lastly, of special note were newspaper correspondents such as "Amaryllis" and Annie Howells Fréchette in the late 1800s, and the more contemporary Gladys Blair and Madge MacBeth, who wrote lively columns for a variety of publications.

Anstey, Dr. Tom, *One Hundred Harvests: Research Branch Agriculture Canada 1886-1986*; Historical Series No. 27, Research Branch, Agriculture Canada 1986

Askwith, John E., "Recollections of New Edinburgh", *Burgh Breeze Bits*, 1923.

Bernstein, William, and Ruth Cawker, *Contemporary Canadian Architecture*, Fitzhenry & Whiteside, 1988.

Blumenson, John, *Ontario Architecture: A Guide to Styles and Terms*, Fitzhenry & Whiteside, 1990.

Bond, C. C. J., *City on the Ottawa*, Queen's Printer, 1971.

Bouse, David, *From Nature to Culture, A Study of Ottawa's Central Experimental Farm Using the Sequent Imaging Antithesis Method*, Volume B, Carleton University, 1 December 1993.

Brault, Lucien, *The Mile of History*, National Capital Commission.

———, *Ottawa Old & New*, Ottawa Historical Information Institute, 1946.

Canadian Institute of Planners. Capital Cities: perspectives and convergence. Plan Canada April-May-June 2000. Canadian Institute of Planners, Vol. 40, No. 3.

Carver, H., *The Cultural Landscape of Rockcliffe Park Village*, Village of Rockcliffe Park, 1985.

City of Ottawa, *Departmental Reports, Corporation of Ottawa 1911*, 1911.

City of Ottawa, *Departmental Reports, Corporation of Ottawa 1912*, 1912.

Cook, Fred, *Appreciations, Hon Thomas Ahearn, P.C.*, n.d.

Desbarats, Lilian Scott, *Recollections*, Ottawa, 1957.

Eggleston, Wilfrid, *The Queen's Choice*, National Capital Commission, Ottawa, 1961.

Farr, David, *A Church in the Glebe: St Matthew's Anglican Church, Ottawa, 1898–1988.*

Farrar, John Laird. *Trees In Canada*, Fitzhenry & Whiteside and the Canadian Forest Service, Natural Resources Canada, 1995.

Fletcher, Sir Banister. A History of Architecture, 19th Edition. Butterworth Group, London (England), 1989.

Gard, Anson A., *The Hub and the Spokes*, Emerson Press, 1904.

German, Tony, *A Character of its Own: Ashbury College 1891–1991*, Creative Bound, 1991.

Guernsay, Terry G., *Statues of Parliament Hill: An Illustrated History*, National Capital Commission, 1986.

Gwyn, Sandra, *The Private Capital*, McClelland & Stewart, 1984.

Kalman, Harold and John Roaf, *Exploring Ottawa, An Architectural Guide to the Nation's Capital*, University of Toronto Press, 1983.

Keshan, Jeff and Nicole St-Onge, Editors, *Ottawa: Making a Capital*, University of Ottawa Press, 2001.

Leaning, John and Lyette Fortin, *Our Architectural Ancestry*, Haig & Haig, Ottawa.

Leggett, Robert, *Rideau Waterway*, University of Toronto Press, 1972.

Lett, William Pitman, *Recollections of Bytown and Its Old Inhabitants*, Citizen Printing and Publishing Co., Ottawa, 1874.

Macbeth, Madge, *Over My Shoulder*, Ryerson Press, February 1953.

McTeer, Maureen, *Residences — Homes of Canada's Leaders*, Prentice-Hall Inc., 1982.

Maitland, Leslie and Louis Taylor, *Historical Sketches of Ottawa*, Broadview Press, 1990.

Maitland, Leslie, Jacqueline Hucker, & Shannon Ricketts, *A Guide to Canadian Architectural Styles*, Broadview Press, 1992.

Mika, Nick and Helma Mika, *Bytown: The Early Days of Ottawa*, Mika Publishing Co., 1982.

Newton, Michael, *Lower Town Ottawa, Volume 1: 1826–1854*, Manuscript Report 104, NCC 1979.

————, *Lower Town Ottawa, Volume 2: 1854–1900*, Manuscript Report 106, NCC 1981.

Passfield, Robert W., *Building the Rideau Canal: A Pictorial History*, Fitzhenry & Whiteside in association with Parks Canada and the Canadian Government Publishing Centre, 1982.

Phillips, R. A. J., *The East Block of the Parliament Buildings of Canada*, Ottawa, 1967.

Ricketts, Shannon, *W. E. Noffke: An Ottawa Architect*, City of Ottawa, 1990.

Rybczynski, Witold, *Home*, Penguin Books, 1986.

Smith, Helen, *Ottawa's Farm: A History of the Central Experimental Farm*, General Store Publishing House, 1996.

Smith, Julian, et al., *Byward Market Heritage Conservation District Study*, 1990.

Taylor, C. J., *Some Early Ottawa Buildings*, Historical Research Section, Canadian Inventory of Historic Buildings, 1975.

Taylor, Eva, and James Kennedy, *Ottawa's Britannia*, Britannia Historical Society, 1983.

Taylor, John H., *Ottawa, An Illustrated History*, James Lorimer & Co., 1986.

Tennant, R. D., *Capital Traction: An Outline History of the Street Railway System of Ottawa*, October 11 1968.

Wallace, W. Stewart, *The MacMillan Dictionary of Canadian Biography*, 3rd Ed., MacMillan, Toronto, 1963.

Walker, Harry, and Olive Walker, *The Carleton Saga*, Runge Press, 1968.

Acknowledgements
to the Second Edition

It is always a pleasure to thank colleagues and friends for their support.

Major thanks must first go to my husband Eric who cycled, walked, and drove along with me, while exploring and then mapping the two new chapters. As well, Eric designed new maps and updated others. Secondly, I thank my mother who has had a lifelong fascination for architecture. My late father was an architect: thus I grew up with an appreciation for art and architecture.

While considering maps, thanks go to Stephen Perkins, City of Ottawa Photogrammetrist, who ably provided Eric and me with maps of the new boundaries to our mega-city.

A good friend of mine was very helpful to me during my research of Rockcliffe. Tony Ahearn, grandson of the Federal District Commission Chairman Thomas Ahearn, offered many insights into the former village of Rockcliffe, where he grew up. He, his sister Lilias, and wife Pat, provided much information.

Regarding the two new walks, I particularly wish to thank the dedicated folks at the Central Experimental Farm as well as the Friends of the CEF. First, thanks to Dr. Tom Anstey, Archivist for the Friends and author of *One Hundred Harvests: Research Branch Agriculture Canada 1886-1986*. I've known Tom for several years, informally, so it was a delight to be squired about the Farm with him as a capable guide. As well, thanks to Bob McClelland, Science Communications Advisor, at the Farm. Brian Douglas, Head of the Arboretum, introduced me to the oldest trees in the collection and drew me a map depicting their location.

With respect to the second new excursion — the Ottawa River Parkway — thanks are due to the National Capital Commission's Director of Communications, Laurie Peters, and her assistant John Kane. Both were particularly helpful with the changes to LeBreton Flats and the Parkway that commenced in 2002 and which will be completed in 2005.

Very special thanks go to the staff of the City of Ottawa Archives. Archivist Serge Barbe not only read my first edition, he agreed to read the new walks, making kind suggestions for their improvement. Serge Blondin, Photographer at the City of Ottawa Archives assisted me by producing excellent CD-Rom heritage images of over eighty archival photographs. And last but not least, Senior Archivist David Bullock capably ensured I had the right person to talk to for the question of the moment. David also arranged for all the city of Ottawa Archive photos to be given to me on CD-Rom, which was a great advantage for both myself as author, and for my publisher. Architects Graham Murfitt and Michael Neelin answered questions and once again, Michael read my new walks, checking for architectural accuracy. Also, Carleton University's professor of architecture Ivan Cazaban assisted with terminology. The Chief Planner to the NCC, Pierre Dubé, provided insights to the growth and planning of the Capital.

Katharine Fletcher, January 2004
Quyon, Quebec

Reader's Note: Finally, while I strive for accuracy, buildings are demolished or altered, pathways do change. As well, you might have historical or other details to share with me—or, indeed, to offer corrections. I invite you to contact me with your comments on the history, trails, and maps in this new edition. Thank you for your help. Please contact me with your thoughts and comments. Katharine Fletcher, 4316 Steele Line, Quyon, Quebec J0X 2V0 email: chesley@allstream.net.

Original Acknowledgements

A mine of heritage information and a warm human being died in 1990. Michael Newton, chief historian of the National Capital Commission was with me in spirit, however, as I perused his historical files at the NCC and walked my walks. *Capital Walks* is indebted to his scrupulous attention to detail as documented in his files and notes.

Several NCC staff members gave me expert advice and access to photographic and other historical records. Among them are Denis Drever, chief photographer, and his 1992 summer assistant, Paddye Thomas. Denis gave me free access to the NCC photographic files; Paddye reproduced many of the NCC heritage photographs used in these pages. Lark Hodgins, chief of systems and practices, information holdings; Gwyneth Hughes, head of library services; and Nancy Veenstra, supervisor of central records operations cheerfully granted special access to Michael Newton's heritage files and somehow managed to answer all of my many queries.

Brian Meredith granted me permission to quote from his father's, architect Colbourne (Coly) Meredith's, unpublished memoirs.

Bruce Weedmark, architectural archivist, of the National Archives, Cartographic and Audio-visual Architectural Archives Division tirelessly answered detailed questions.

Louise Roy-Brochu, chief archivist at the City of Ottawa Archives and City archivists David Bullock and Serge Barbe paid similar attention to details. Particular thanks go to Serge, who scrupulously read my manuscript for historical accuracy.

Architectural designer and illustrator Michael Neelin also read the manuscript and walked the eight walks, checked the maps and, most importantly, acted as my architectural editor, ensuring my terms and points of reference were appropriate. Architect Barry Hobin kindly responded to my last-minute requests for specific details of many buildings.

By-Rideau Councillor Richard Cannings provided his special heritage perspective, list of contacts and personal encouragement to my project.

Stonemason Norbert Senf provided details about masonry construction and engineering. Both he and Leila Nulty-Senf offered cheerful, unflagging support of *Capital Walks* from its inception.

Dinah Forbes is that rare breed of editor who dispenses excellent advice in a discerning, sensitive manner.

Thanks to Eric Fletcher, who walked every walk with me, produced all the maps, and helped me execute the final design and layout of *Capital Walks* on our Macintosh computer.

Finally, thanks to my mother and father, who nurtured in me a lifelong respect and appreciation of the arts, architecture and the outdoors.

Thank you, one and all.

Index

Explanation to the Index: Numbers in bold represent a term found in a photo caption. When noted specifically, street addresses are included and, in the case of buildings within the Experimental Farm, by the building number and name.